23 Years in the Irish Guards

by

Philip Anthony McDonnell

Grosvenor House
Publishing Limited

All rights reserved
Copyright © Philip Anthony McDonnell, 2024

The right of Philip Anthony McDonnell to be identified as the
author of this work has been asserted in accordance with
Section 78 of the Copyright, Designs and Patents Act 1988

The book cover is copyright to Philip Anthony McDonnell

This book is published by
Grosvenor House Publishing Ltd
Link House
140 The Broadway, Tolworth, Surrey, KT6 7HT.
www.grosvenorhousepublishing.co.uk

This book is sold subject to the conditions that it shall not, by way of
trade or otherwise, be lent, resold, hired out or otherwise circulated
without the author's or publisher's prior consent in any form of
binding or cover other than that in which it is published and
without a similar condition including this condition being
imposed on the subsequent purchaser.

A CIP record for this book
is available from the British Library

ISBN 978-1-80381-816-0
eBook ISBN 978-1-80381-817-7

Poem in my Book

*Street walker & Lips. Touched, in book
A Wonderful World*
Pro Print

Born at Sixteen & Stones in book A Wonderful World 2
Central Publishing Services

My Remembrance A Wonderful World 3
Grosvenor House Publishing

Other Books by the same Author

A Wonderful World 4
Grosvenor House Publishing

A Wonderful World 5
Grosvenor House Publishing

In Darkness
Grosvenor House Publishing

Book Dedicate to my wife of
55 years Miriam McDonnell.

Chapter 1

In hindsight I look back over my life and think in all honesty if I had to live my life all over again, would I do anything differently, possibly, yes. I would have made this adventure a few years older with more knowledge of the real world, and not run with my boyhood dreams aimlessly on a boat out of Dublin to anywhere. I had not thought about the pitfalls of real life and had no answers in how to overcome like when I desperate, hungry and lonely when not having found work. I had not analysed the downside of my dream adventure for as a sixteen-year-old near seventeen I knew nothing of the big wide world and my knowing nothing I truly believed was the magic of my survival. For I went forward fearlessly in my childhood mind adventure believing the realism in my head that like the swashbuckling stories Paddy Maher told around his fireside of his life on the seven seas, I too would win in my own dream adventure.

I had no idea of the thousands of Irish labourers that because of no work and jobs in Ireland had taken the boats to find work in England, Scotland, Wales, working on the motorways, and railways that help make those early years of the sixties when the streets were truly pave with gold and the big building company like WIMPY was at the four-front of employing thousands of Irish labourer that worked their backsides of from morn till night to support their family back home and lived in the hope of been handsomely rich on returning home.

With no real education behind me and no certificate of skills past I was nothing more than an orphan farm labourer with a belief I could do better if I was free. The Irish government was my guardian until I became eighteen years old due to being a ward of the state and having no known family I would remain in their care until my eighteen birthday when I be free to do and go where I wish. Having reached an age deemed by the government to be able to work independently and thereafter make my own contribution to the state as a responsible citizen able to look after myself.

Leaving Ireland on a boat for Scotland was for me escaping as the captive St Patricks did a few centuries before. So unprepared was I for the loneliness and hardship of walking off and starting a new life in a new place of another country I knew little or nothing about. Getting off the boat at the Clyde docks on that first Scottish morning of my new life I had notice that it had the same smell and way about it as the busy dock of the North Wall of my own wet grey Dublin that I left some twelve hours ago.

Scotland for me was a strange land where I knew not a living soul and very little or nothing of its people and history, other than that it is one of our nearest neighbours that many Irish had gone to in the past to do season or full-time work. Understanding their ways and laws, and how the people live was something I yet had to learn as with all things new from now on. Being on my own was my first education of my life and as a sponge I soaked all in. I found to my horror I'm a baby in so far as never being street wise having live to date inside of four walls that now did not exist and the wolves of the street are free to attack and take advantage of my ignorance which made me more scared having no knowledge of how to protect myself. Without lodging, family, or work to fall back on I had no answer in how to survive especially no great amount of money. I was free, alone, homeless, a street bum out of my depth in a strange land and for the first time in my life truly afraid.

Scotland main industry other than farming was whiskey making, weaving, light industry and other sort of commerce I had not a clue about. By all account I was an eejit of the first order as I would learn later in my life how I started out on this stupidest adventure I undertook with no preparation in going forward in the freedom and dream of wealth and fortune I saw in my mind eye.

At just seventeen years of age I was a mere boy with no real skills I had come from an institutional background, a church upbringing, raised by nuns, and the Christian Brothers, taught only about God, and hell, nothing about money, real life, sex, how to survive in the outside world, earning a living, and learning to stand on my own two feet as a man.

Leaving care at sixteen to do farm work I practically knew nothing of anything about life skills, money, even to look after myself, I was raise by the church state that as a child prisoner I had wanted for nothing, and nothing did I have other than my name on leaving. I was so dumb that I did not know if they even spoke my language and would I understand them for even in my own island of Ireland, a small country that it is within our own counties people speak with the same tongue but their accent so different in each county that it make it hard to know what they are saying that they too can sound as if they come from a foreign land.

I knew nothing of sex, the birds and bees, no understanding of the inner feeling I was having and how to really controlled them. When I'm around young lads of my age who talk about girls and how they open to them to know if they have the same agony and growing pains that causes us boys to be so mixed up that our body action and changes happen without warning and our mindset are out of sync with our body. Feelings running so fast you cannot control the unwanted sexual intrusion that are blowing your teenage mind and unable to control. These teenage urges rage so strong about your body that you are a gibbering eejit with no understanding of why your sexual need rises and fall. Leaving you stranded in confused desperation and frustration in a no man's land hungry to discharge with no one to guide you through the difficult years of teenage ramping pain.

With no real knowledge on anything about life or heroes to imitate, with no family or a home to run back to if I failed in my quest to be successful in making my fortune or a good living as others who had gone from Ireland before have. It was that burning desire to do well that I started out with for there was no going back to anything, and it was forward at all haste be it egg on my face if I fall flat on my face. Now in my twilight years having run the race got pass the obstacle in my path and other hoops I've jumped through, I've done generally good for an orphan if I don't mind complimenting myself when I look back and recall those early days when first I made my Ireland escape to Scotland in 1964 with not a clue as to how my life then would pan out.

How did I do it those fifty-nine years on I still try to make sense of those early days starting out and my reason for leaving Ireland walking the lonely plank of the boat into the unknown. I was nothing as I knew nothing of life, how it worked, how to go about asking anyone anything, as I was afraid they might report me as a runaway, and I would be sent back home for being under age and handed over to the

Irish state board whose charge I would stay until I became eighteen.

I was not free as told by the Christian Brothers in Artane Industrial on been discharge from their care to work for a pittance as a farm labourer in Tipperary under my new guardian farmer who was happy to use and cheat me till I was eighteen.

Now I find myself thinking back over my life when a boy near his seventeen birthday and running away to God knows where on the first boat out from the North Wall in Dublin on the spur of the moment with no real plan of where I'm going and what I might do. Question ran around in my head as I try to answer these needling thoughts of how I would live. Does everyone in the world speak the same language, will I find work when I get to where the boat pulls in. So many question in my head as I set out on this boat going to Scotland and to be honest had not a clue as to where Scotland was situated on the world map or knew anything about it, language, currency, its people or industry, what it boasted and what Scotland is most proud about, or for that matter any other country. When I hardly knew anything of my own Ireland where I was born.

Leaving Ireland and seeing the world was first planted in my head by two special people in Glenart College who became two good friends the first Father Maurice Kavanagh my spiritual adviser who on many a confessional walk told me that there is a bigger world outside of Ireland and one day I should go and explore. The second the older of the Maher brothers, Paddy, who was a former merchant marine sailor and from my first days of getting to know him it was to his tales of the sea that set my boyish mind and imagination racing, and the wonders of places he saw that he brought alive in me.

While Dennis on the other hand was a very funny man tall and thin with buck teeth that I saw the resemblance of Bugs Bunny in him and he was great at home cooking, making cakes and bread, and telling fantastic jokes and a great teller of Irish ghost stories.

Glenart College was situated in a quiet place not far from the hill village of Kilcarra and about three miles on the Avoca road from Arklow town which was Wicklow County's main fishing port where you could watch the trawler fishermen leave and bring back their catch. Arklow had a first-class pottery factory and was also grace with a beautiful sandy seaside beech and dunes that brought many from Dublin city for weekend and holiday break. Father Maurice was my first real mentor as a young adult also a proper father figure who took me under his guiding wing, and in my private walk and talk with him he very often gave me special advice on what I should do.

How I must not let my life lived so far dictate or be ruined by my past experience but to look forward to what he said could be a better and great life in the adventures my life yet to be if I have the mind to win and make it happen.

His advice to me was always to look and go forward with my dreams whatever they may be and lived out your dreams, and make true the ideas you have. But most importantly never look back to what has past and just keep going forward toward the future that may surprise you.

He would always say and remind me that there is another big world out there which is bigger than the Ireland you have known or seen so far, and that one day in the not too distant future I'm sure you will go and know it, explored it, grabbed it, and when you're ready and confident to move on and face that scariest of life demon of going, doing, walking alone, and not afraid to take the leap of faith into what is for anyone leaving what they known for the first time a big and frightening decision especially harder for someone like you, he said, who in your predicament as an orphan, without education, and school certificates, without any real skills will leave you greatly disadvantage as opposed to others that have vocational skills as plumbing, electrical, and carpentry to call on, and those who have financial backing from family, a job, and contact when they choose to work abroad. Your leaving Ireland with only an institutional mind on your own is not going to be easy and not one I would advise until you have earn a good bit of money to pay your way and have a better understanding of the ways of life, and what it is you want to do.

It is probably too late in the day as I already made up my mind come hell or high water I was going to get away and make my way on my own using the advice and tips given to me by Paddy Maher and Father Maurice Kavanagh who had themselves left and venture when young out into the big wide world one to the merchant navy in England, and the other as an obedient priest when first ordained and sent to China in the early nineteen hundreds on his own first adventure of his life.

Leaving Ireland in my youth was the number one topic I remember and heard especially in pubs and social gatherings that many young men wanted to make a better life in earning a bit more money that they could send home to support their family for in most cases there was no jobs at home and many were force to leave and work away in England or somewhere else to survive. There were many upping sticks as soon as they had a job offer that a relative in England, Scotland, and Wales could accommodate until they found themselves secure in work to go and find a place themselves to live in that many Irish found labouring work a plenty.

I made up my mind that I would go and take my chance without any support machine of relative or job contact and just go with the hope that something might just turn up praying that good luck would be on my side. Like thousands of Irish before me and still are doing today the attraction of seeking work and new opportunity somewhere else was too much to ignore and for the young with no opportunity at home the attraction of plenty of jobs abroad was hard to resist.

I too had caught the bug and with no real love for the Ireland of my youth that I was reared by the church and the state hell hole I spent eight long years in called Artane Industrial School that left little for me to want and stay from leaving Ireland. Other than the few friends I had made and my godparent who did right by me in visiting and taking me out for a day to their home and the nearby Herbert Park and to Sandymount Strand were we played around with a football. Nothing else in my teenage thinking held any reason for me not going and taking a chance of a better life away across the Irish Sea to places I knew nothing much about other than hearing from overheard conversation of people who long ago had gone and had done well in America, Australia, England as the brothers mention travel in those famine years and their descendants now are the contact for many of their great grandchildren who now follow doing the same.

How far away from Ireland those country or places where I had not the foggiest as my knowledge of anything even this place called Dublin was limited to the bus trip in and out of O Connell Street.

I knew from listening to others story and their going away without any contact of family or even a friend to meet and help you out would be very hard and yet I had this burning in my heart and the strongest of beliefs that like Paddy who went on his sea adventures when young that I too must take my chance and go forward given myself the opportunity to try my own luck in finding my fame and fortune.

Leaving behind the little I knew of Ireland and going forward to find my fortune and future and to face alone whatever challenges I may encounter with a positive belief that this is my destiny, and making it work is to all intents and purposes not a foolish idea but one I truly believe in. Yes I will leave it in the hands of my dear lord and pray I've made the right decision that from now on there is no going back only forward as Father Maurice said was the only way to go.

My thoughts on my escape to Scotland as I reminisce often about me being nearly seventeen years old living in Ireland and what it did for me, and why I'm leaving. As I look back over the good and bad times I've been through that has me taking this boat to Scotland and going forward with no real idea how all will work out if at all.

I think back to the convent in Rathdrum where I was looked after by the nuns from naught to eight years old then sent to Artane to live with hundreds of other boys some I knew in Rathdrum Convent that too were sent before me, and after to this industrial school. I made many friends through the years there that at sixteen the school sent you away to work in a job similar to the work you'd be doing in your years employed in the industrial school. Because I belonged to no one had no family or other relative other than the Catholic Church and its institutional life I was sent to Tipperary to work on a farm. It did not work out and I had a serious altercation with my farm boss that meant me running away that I explain in my own words of my anger and my godparent coming to my help.

Father Maurice like my childhood saint Brother Columba that I knew for two years 1955 to 1957 in Artane Industrial

School from age eight to ten years old told me one day that now seemed far away will come, and you my boy will become a strong young man who'll stand on his own two feet and make good. Your time here with us Christian Brothers will have finished and passed and you will surely conquer, and make good in whatever the good lord has plan for you to do.

Brother Columba was my childhood saint and the first person I ever saw dead though seeing him in his coffin box he looked very pale-white and lay peacefully as if he was just fast asleep.

Brother Columba for me as a boy of eight was a very holy man and a sort of big friend to all of the boys especially the under tens a grandfather figure we all loved. Brother Columba had served God faithfully in the mission fields of China for many years before the government of Mao Tse-Tung turned all westerner/foreigner especially the religious order out of the country in which to cleanse its people's mind from years of western philosophy, theology and other ingrained western influence and lifestyle, all this happen in his making a success of his revolutionary great march of 1948 in taking back control of the China he wanted to create and re-educate his people that he fed from his little red book to learn the thoughts of their new country leader Chairman Mao.

Father Maurice Kavanagh like Brother Columba also served as a missionary in his earlier days as a young priest, a man of great wisdom and charity who had great experience of Chinese culture after many years of learning and understanding of their ancient tradition in the art of mind control his quiet patient had been his trademark which made him stand out from the other priests, and in a class of his own. His spiritual contentment and quiet meditation was another art form he had perfected in knowing God through his work and prayer and when alone with his thoughts in the seminary garden he found a serious closeness to prayers for all souls in his own spiritual gethsemane.

It was because of Father Maurice Kavanagh and my new life in Glenart College that I was able to make some sense of the real against the false love I've known in Artane and thankful too that I got away from the greedy farmer I had injured and made good my escaped from. My godmother's husband George made contact on my behalf with the nuns at Rathdrum Convent were I had been cared for from a baby until my eight birthday when the nuns passed me over to the Christian Brothers at Artane Industrial School for boys in Dublin till my sixteen birthday.

Birthdays were nothing special in my institutional life they came and went no one I knew celebrated any or really knew how old they were in the orphanage. In the industrial school you only believed from what you'd been told by the sisters and the Christian Brothers what they wanted you to know and what your age is they never told to you. This way of living for the state abandon orphans in Ireland would be the only home we would know good or bad it was our lot. The church nuns and brothers were also your stand in parent until you reached sixteen when they found you work, a new employer/guardian without you having any say if you wanted to go or not until your eighteen birthday. I only have the brother's word that on leaving Artane Industrial School I was sixteen because they told me so.

The nuns and brothers in the years of been in their care treated everything about my upbringing as confidential and never in all my years with them say how or why I ended up in their care I was never told. I knew nothing about how I came to be in their care, if I had any living family, what information they held about me, certificate I might need after I leave them, like birth, baptism, confirmation, education I achieved to show proof of where I went to school. No contact address or named Christian Brother to ask for if I found myself in need of help.

Orphan children under the state/church caring hands were mushrooms and numbers not names, kept very much in the secret dark to protect them from Irish society that view their existence as sinful children of unwed love the church class as devil spawn.

Knowing no other life you just got used to the nun's system in Rathdrum, and the same in Artane Industrial School under the Christian Brothers that made prison guards in Mount-Joy jail Dublin seemed like mere novices when it came to administering harsh and God-fearing discipline. On my sixteen birthday without any choice or warning and given no information about the why you have to leave all you'd known for the last eight years is like been thrown into a bin. You're uprooted from the school and your friends, sent to work for a stranger, a farmer, to be his slave-hand for very little money board and lodgings till your eighteen birthday.

Again on the move with no say about what I like as all my life I am treated like property not a human being by the state/church who think they know what best for you and sell you on without any choice washing their holy hands in placing you far away from the school and your school friends to have no contact with ever again. Within three months of being used by this farmer as a slave and treated worse than his animals living in an outhouse sleeping on a worn out mattress and fed from the house back door, given castoff clothes for work that he deducted my wages for was the catalyst to why I stood up to him and shouted you can't treat me like this and make me work all week for nothing. I have right and you are unfair and cruel knowing I have no one to turn to or get myself heard against you. You are not being fair in the way you treat me and I have no one who I can trust in a system I'm already beaten by the authority who would take his word over mine as my guardian.

After three month working I ran away after I pitchforked him in the thigh that hiding a few days in the fields I manage to contact George my godmother's husband and ask him if he would contact a nun at Rathdrum Convent by the name of Sister Anne and check if she remembered me and would she help as I'm on the run and have nowhere to go for a safe place to live.

Sister Anne hearing my dilemma came to my rescue and gave my godmother's husband George an address and the name of a priest friend of hers for me to go and see, and he would help to keep me safe and warm with it place to stay. Having to go on the run from the farmer and the police was because of his unfair treatment to me and the blatant abuse of him taking me for granted in working for pennies. That in the short time I was working for that farmer I was meeting other young farmers in the pub and listening to their gripe about life and what they would do to change their lives began to play a big part in my learning as to how I myself had to stand up and believe in myself and change the direction my life was going, as those young farmers too had also dreams of getting away and trying their hands at something new.

I was fascinated as they talked freely about others and what was wrong if you did not stand your ground if you want to be respected and not be taken advantage of which I knew I was at that time then you have to take action, what action I had yet to work out. These thoughts milled around in my mind for days and when I next was paid I let my feeling be known to my farmer boss and told him if he did not pay me my proper wages I'm entitled to, I would kill him. He just laughed at me and told me to get out of his sight and get on with my work calling me a good for nothing bastard who should be grateful he took me in.

Be that I said I would kill him was more bravado to show him how serious I was and that I would no longer accept being used and paid less than what the school said I would be paid when they placed me into his care. I should be paid a fair wage of one pound seven shilling and sixpence a week not half a crown and full board. I made up my mind come hell or high water that he would not get away with using or taking advantage of me ever again. So I carried out my threat and was now running from the law as a minor criminal after I pitchforked my farmer boss in the upper leg who used and abused me for over three months who took no notice of my threat after I warned him, he still under paid me as if nothing registered with him. I believe there was no point in making a threat if you didn't carry it through otherwise it an empty threat and life for him would just go on unchanged. When he held back most of my wage the next week not paying me what was rightly mine I left him screaming on the ground holding his leg as I ran away.

Often in Taylors Pub, come post office shop by day friendly advice about my right was freely given in how my farmer boss should treat me and the general consensus was that I should speak out and nub the situation before I let it go much further. As a sixteen years old just out of Artane Christian Brothers school that all in the pub on hearing I was an Artane boy thought as with most people in Ireland who hear you're out of that school ask that stupid question were you in the Artane boy band not that anyone cared for the hundreds of inmates that never saw the light of day as the school traded on the band's fame that every Sunday during the county seasons were heard playing for the GAA at the hurling and football games in Croke Park. They were the school celebrities that went everywhere and treated like pop stars unlike the rest of the school boys who grafted and were beaten day in and day out. I soon learned their very little opportunity of escape as the public transport is non-existent and very few people had cars in what was a tractor world.

I been told many times in Taylors shop/pub you're been taking advantage of because you are an orphan while he send his own children to the posh boarding school in Roscrea to have the best of Irish education and you an eejit are paying for them. Whether they were being helpful or just pulling my leg I was not to know for as a boy with no understanding of working life outside the school walls everything I heard and saw was new and I wasn't clever enough to process what they said to be the truth or not, leaving me mad, and as I got madder and madder at how they viewed me a right oul eejit in their eyes and them playing me for the eejit I really was.

Often I heard young farmers talk about getting away to England as their brother or sister had done and how well they were doing making good money enjoying a freer life than they had here in good Old Catholic Ireland. This England was mentioned a lot as if it was Ireland's best escape place to fame and fortune as was mentioned another far away country said in wonderment and excitement America. All was not great after I made my escape as after a few days of being on my own and eating from the street table and getting by as best I could I began to feel more confident in approaching people for their odds that is loose change and a light for my miserable pick up dog end cigarette, often asking the same strangers if this is the way to Dublin as in the country many roads have no directional signs as to which way was what as local just knew their way about.

With my new contact's name in my head I was heading for Dublin and onto Wicklow near the seaside town of Arklow on foot. I had a name given by Sister Anne to my godmother's husband George in which by hell or high water I was to make my way to a place called Glenart College for trainee priests near Arklow in county Wicklow. After many days walking and the odd lift into the Dublin area I eventually got safely to where Sister Anne had told me to go and was finally under the care of Father Mc Cullum the superior at Glenart College. He asked Father Maurice a very kind and elderly priest to look after me and that the priest name Sister Anne gave my godparent as the person I should ask for and did.

As providence would have it, it was into his hands that I was now put and he would be my overall new boss for the foreseeable future. Some college student came to my rescue in helping out Father Maurice who asked the student to move me into the castle old tower that before I arrived was the storeroom for the egg boxes that the college earned good money from the sale of its battery hen eggs making the college a little bit self-sufficient. Students like Kevin O'Shea sorted out the light and the electric as others like Paddy Walsh and Dennis O Donovan made good my new room to live in and strengthened the wooden ladder that got me up and down to my room. Many other student befriended and helped me to settle in and made me feel wanted and safe.

It was Mick Bracken that Father Maurice made my main working boss in the seminary garden and others like the Maher brothers who lived on the Arklow/Avoca road as if their cottage by the seminary entry made them the caretakers so I thought. While it was the cottage on the right where Mr Fitzpatrick lived who was the caretaker living on the college property. The Maher brothers became good friends of mine in my time while I was in Glenart that they taught me much in growing up at sixteen that would help me later in life as in their funny way they changed my wild outbursts into fun by making me laugh at myself in not allowing silly rubbish to get the better of my mind.

They taught me how to act and take control of my teenage anger and turn it into a positive for good it was while I was living in Glenart College under the priest protection that my life began to have some meaning toward other that it was making me a nicer person to get along with. I was learning a lot of positive things that I should have learned had I a proper family upbringing and if the school brothers had taken more time to teach what was important as opposed to their daily beatings and us paying for our food and board with the long hours we all work to make the school self-sufficient in their not asking the state for a begging handout it was entitled to.

It would have been hard for any man to go out on his own and take on the world never mind an eejit like me who knew nothing of the real world its pitfalls how people generally got by and how they survive day to day living on their own without the support of family. With no street wit or knowledge to guard me against charlatans, crooks who would take advantage of my orphan and needy position that I was easy prey by my lack of street knowledge and wit and more innocent than a new born.

I was beginning to see the way people interacted with each other how they not feel put upon by the simple art of give and take in everyday things and work. Not to react as if you are being set upon because I never did learn how to know or trust people I've just met and what it is in my mind that says yes to trusting someone or not.

Having no post school experience of life in the working world in how to handle money or what to say when meeting new people that if you can believe what they're telling you and believe they are not taken advantage of you, that skill street kids know and are aware naturally without ever asking how it is they just do by instinct that cannot be taught or ever learn inside an industrial school walls as this natural learning of been with other street kids in the neighbourhood is taken for granted as how street children live and know from birth what it is they take for granted without ever giving it a second thought.

Understanding general behaviour and attitudes, and working out the wrong and right of others especially with people you never grew up with who have no institutional knowledge of why we are different, maybe it because of my prison mind behind grey walls that we never learn as children in being street wise and only had ourselves to spark and learn from.

Me 10 years old centre in front row 1957.

Chapter 2

It was 1957 at ten years old that Brother Farrell came up with a godmother plan to have children with no visitors or family to come and sponsor a boy he asked his four nieces in Dublin to start the ball rolling and to take a few orphan boys who they would come and visit on Sundays when they could and take us on a day out once or twice a year to their home and spoil us. The few pennies we got from our godparent was taken away from us and given to the black babies who had nothing so the school brothers kept telling us. Having never seen a black baby or for that matter a black person in my early life I like the rest of the boys were left a bit confused if it was a word more than a fact that we heard about these black babies every day that we had to remember in our prayers.

I wander to myself if the black babies were told the same story in Africa where ever Africa is that there pennies taken from them are sent to us white babies in Ireland who have nothing, and the black children pennies were taken to feed us as our pennies were taken to feed them. I could not have made my way in the world without the small tips given by those who wanted me to succeed after a bad start, as everyone in Glenart College from the student to the kitchen and estate staff done much to make my life grand. Just sixteen years old and already a wanted person by the authority and the gardai/police.

In my runaway mind I knew nobody was going to believe or stand up for me that what I done was because of an injustice against me being treated as a slave and not paid my proper wage for the hard honest work I had done for that miser farmer.

Now that I'm safe and cared for by the seminary superior I can backtrack the event much more clearly in my mind and know he did me wrong not me to him. I truly believe looking back from my safe hideaway in this seminary that he deserved all he got for cheating a poor orphan child like I was out of his rightful worth. Hiding away under the church umbrella in a seminary for trainee priests seemed ironic as it was the church that beat me in the institution and now it is the church that helped me to get my life back together.

In my mind I'm a young criminal not by choice on the run to where I don't know as there was no doubt the gardai/police would have been looking for me as there was no way right or wrong my action in law would justify me stabbing my employer in the upper leg would go unnoticed if he reported me, and if caught would I be given a fair hearing by a cruel one-sided system that never would back an innocent child's plea of innocent against a grown-up word. As a young boy unwanted by his family that the church and state come to rescue by taking and locking away in their institution to work and pay for his miserable existence of been born out of wedlock. You learn very early in life that nothing is free and the state makes sure you knew and were made to pay by your sweat especially tears.

In those early years you shed rivers of tears yet never been allowed to question anything they said only that you should do. Whatever my reason good or otherwise the state would not accept what I had done and there certainly would be some sort of search for me if he reported my attack.

I knew from years in the state care no one would take the word of a sixteen-year-old boy that had been given by their thinking every opportunity to work and earn an honest living with food and board to boot. Be that it was a one-sided system that would see the farmer as the generous one in taking me in and me the bad seed ungrateful should be punished.

It would never be said that this stingy farmer who offered his services to the school as an employer would be getting a boy farmer for less than the going rate for the state did not give a toss or care for my interest as long as it looked good on the government papers that the school releaseed me at sixteen to my new guardian who would take care of me until I became of age the state could wash its hands like Pontius Pilate of it dirty work as a job well done.

Orphan like I was without anyone to champion my rights or look after my interest was in all intense and purpose a one-sided transfer of their property to an unscrupulous employer who offered himself and knowing he was onto a good scam that benefitted them both while the farmer got away with using me on whatever job he wanted done. I had not a clue to what I was really entitled to and no one in the state-run system from the Christian Brother to my new employer was going to say anything if a cheap slave like I was to be had any working rights.

Human right as we understand them today was low down on any boss's list in 1963 it was more to the farmer that his cattle and livestock got the best treatment as they returned him the biggest profit. My worth to the farmer was what he could get out of me for the least pay an orphan against a farmer's craftiness and meanness was not a fair competition that in the twenty first century thought was yet faraway for a dreamer boy of 1963 that newspapers today would hang out to dry such greedy and corrupt boss for taking advantage of their position when they should have been honest and glad to give an unfortunate boy as I was then a real helping hand in learning the ways of the world and doing good by me in his dealing of work and pay that the school and state expected him to do.

My farmer was at liberty to use and abuse me as he felt fit with no recrimination from neighbours or family he freely accepting praise from others for his generosity in what he was doing for such an unfortunate as I was who would work as he required night and day without questioning his abusive authority.

In a romantic novel these things in themselves would be good if the employer really had my interest at heart then yes I was ungrateful to run him through with a pitchfork in the upper leg but as it was he couldn't care less about me and that why I did what I had to do. I had made no plan the day I did the dastardly deed it happened so quick when I stood up and shouted at him where the rest of my money and he just laughed in my face as if to say you got all you're going to get with the usual expletive of my status in life and now you can get out of my sight and back to work you good for nothing ungrateful bastard.

I was so angry out of my mind at his attitude towards me that I grabbed the pitchfork and went for him as a wild child hurt, I saw red and prodded him running as fast as my trembling legs would carry me. It was escape on the hoof with no plan made and no thoughts of how and what I should do or where to go and where could I hide. I didn't know who to trust or for that matter who to talk to about what I had done. The problem about not thinking things through is the full consequences of your action loomed larger and you're so frightened more because you don't know what to do, where to go, who will look after you.

I had not a clue where my next meal would be coming from where I might stay and what was I going to do next. With no school friend's addresses or a place to rest and hide until I knew the coast was clear and wait for the storm to die down as I aimlessly ran. On the other hand the farmer been a crafty man may have recovered enough to let it pass and phone the school to say I had run away in order to cover his own miserable backside. Of course he would contact the school knowing I would not go to the authority about my attacking him to report the injury I caused him he'll covered his own backside and probably accept another farm boy in my place.

Where was I going to stay and where would I go that I could find the right help I was very afraid feeling that the eyes of everyone who looked at me knew I was on the run from the law with a guilty look so scared was I that my imagination was running away with me in that I believed everyone I met saw in my face the guilt of my pitchfork attack on my farmer boss and that the gardai/police would have an arrest warrant out for me as a runaway minor for committing a dangerous act in injuring his farm employer, and anyone who knows my whereabouts should phone the gardai/police, and report my whereabouts to them.

Now alone and on the run to nowhere without any school friends who I knew would understand my anger and would have reacted in much the same way if they were treated like an adopted dog without any pampering. Any Artane Boys would have done similar in my position if they were made to work for a tyrant greedy farmer the school passed you over to on behalf of the state/church having sign away their responsibility of you as property without any protection with no rights other than beings the slave of this new guardian who thought orphans were good to be used as he wished without any come back of how he treated me in my work and give me what he think I should be paid against what the school told me I would receive.

Orphan children released from state industrial school system into the adult work places in the early sixties and before were thought worthless and used in a word without any government help and proper protection. Letting new guardian employer loose to have the best interest of their slave as a live in worker a top priority in treating them fairly was just like putting a fox as a security guard to look after the chicken it was a mad idea and on its own was a nonstarter.

Having no family or school friend on release to my new guardian as a minor to work for until my eighteenth birthday. That is what I and all the other boys without family were told by the brothers on leaving Artane Industrial School to work hard and do what your new guardian ask until you're eighteen which meant two more years, when the state believed you are capable of going it alone to stand on your own two feet as a responsible person in Irish society after which I would be free to make my own choice in what I want to do and free to leave without been answerable to anyone ever again.

Now I'm on the run and I knew if I was caught it would be gaol for the rest of my natural life as the world I grew up in did nothing nor cared for children the likes of me born out of wedlock bastard that should have been locked away forever was the Irish cruel authority mindset of state/church at my birth in 1947 that good decent folk could feel safe and the family good name protected of their daughter mistake to rid and hide the shame of her unwanted sin.

How I made contact with my godparent I'm not quite sure or how long since the incident had past I was able to tell them of my plight and what I had actually done. How I got by and how I lived other than there was much food growing in the fields that I could eat raw, like onion, cabbages, carrots, and the hedges shrub trees we call bread and cheese because you could eat their leaves and the red berries.

My good fortune also while making my boyhood escape was the farmers' outhouses were left empty while the cows and other stock grazed elsewhere. George my godmother's husband with his loud Dublin accent head shouted a few Dublin obscenities as he had no love for injustices or Culthie' that is farmers and those who lived and worked the land and anyone who was not a real Dubliner in his eyes.

For God sake and the love of Jesus, Mary and Joseph, don't you even think of coming here, he said to me, as this will certainly be the first place the guadai/police will be waiting for you to come too as the school brothers no doubt will have told the gardai/police of you having godparents while at the school and your only real contact you may seek to go for help.

If I'm honest I don't remember how I really survived those immediate days on the run sleeping in fields, outhouses when it was wet, scrounging food and caging cigarette to smoke, especially picking up butt ends of the street was a habit we all did as when we went on our school walk around Dunnycarney on Sundays afternoon if not raining we found to smoke.

Often I asked for a light of a stranger and because of the meagre butt end I had some took pity and offer me a whole one that I lit in their presence and nick out half way to have another smoke later on. Being homeless by today's standard was to me then in 1963 nothing but freedom, yes I was on my own scavenging and moving about with no real plan other that I must get help from where I had not a clue. It never occurred to me I was homeless for never having a home to be kicked out of onto the street by a mum/dad that I had none did I feel homeless.

But as an orphan this way of living was a new freedom to do and go where I like without beholding to anyone or anything especially the church/state authority. I felt going it alone was not too bad as it never was a thought I worried about as I was getting by and other than my godparent I could not trust anyone as Ireland in them days which was completely under the spell of the Catholic Church and what I had done was a mortal sin maybe even against the fifth if he died. My godparent did contact Sister Anne who I ask them to find if she was still in Rathdrum Convent and asked would she be able to take care of me as her name from my childhood memory was the mum I missed, and I needed her help now if she could be found. For in my earlier life she took care of me at Rathdrum Convent for eight years and I really believed and thought her to be my nun-mother.

Without really knowing the word independence and it meaning those first days on the run were the beginning of a freedom I not known before and with grateful thanks to Sister Anne in Rathdrum Convent she gave George an address and a name of a priest friend at Glenart College near Arklow, for me to ask that would take care of me, it was Father Maurice Kavanagh. I walk and hitch-hike my way with not a clue as to where Glenart College in Arklow was but it was a place and I was to find it by asking my way to Dublin and then into Wicklow County.

This was the first time in my life I was to go or travel with no money or means for I ran in what I wore and nothing else as I owned nothing and this the holy truth. I found my way to Glenart College and while been afraid and not knowing how I would be received I must have looked a sight and smelled terrible from days un-washed and the street perfume. But I walk up the Treeline Avenue to what look like a king castle that stood large in beautifully care grounds that I went straight up to the big brown doors and bang the door knocker that was open by a beautiful young woman who asked how can I help you. I told her I was sent here by a nun and to ask for Father Maurice Kavanagh she took me in and asked me to wait in the hallway while she found the superior to see what I'm about.

Father McCullum heard my story and was very sympathetic to the treatment I had gone through and asked the young lady that opened the door who he called Maggie to take me to their kitchen for something to eat. I was handed over to Father Maurice who was an elderly man and much a grandfather in his look and appearance and so very kind in his ways and more so in his eyes. He took me under his wing, and for the next six months my life changed from a miserable start of life outside the school walls to the happiest I have ever been. I soon learned that the God in the seminary was a different God to my school God that the student priest chose of their own free will to serve were always happy and unafraid to celebrate the life of the church. They cared for me not like the Christian Brothers God who thrive on beating, humiliating the children in their care who through no fault of their own had no family to protect them from the black skirted brute that beat us day in and day out as if for sport or to inflict pain on us for our parents' sin against their lord Jesus Christ.

After living in Glenart College for many months I was sent by Father Maurice Kavanagh to place near Ballymahon and Glasson to work for a Dublin invalid man at East Hill House near Athlone a town in the dead centre of Ireland as seen on a plaque in the middle of Athlone Bridge where the river Shannon flows beneath. I felt ready to go on my adventure whatever the price as for all the stories I heard over many months I was filled with a boyhood urge to see the world. I was ready in my head even at the young age of near seventeen to take on the world and make my next move and start out on my own adventure alone.

I made my way to Dublin to my godparent's house where I always stayed for a night or two and Dorothy would make me an full Irish breakfast before going anywhere in those days when I visited them and got to know a little more of Dublin on my visit that it became my main address of where I lived in Ireland. It was there house in Ballsbridge that I stay before I made my escape on a boat to Scotland in July1964 to start my new life. Never been anywhere or know any other country it mattered not to me were my boat leaving Dublin went. It did not bother me where the boat was heading as long as it was going somewhere and I was on it and to get started in my new adventure wherever the boat was going on leaving the grey Dublin North Wall.

Travelling into the unknown was really ok by me as wherever the boat lands that is where my life adventure would begin, and I must take this gambling chance after the swashbuckling dream I could not stop imagining that were taking hold of all my waking mind. I believed in my head nobody would be looking for me since the day I ran from my farmer boss in Tipperary that now are best forgotten. As in truth it would not have been hard for the gardai/police to have found me if the farmer was at death door. I also believe the farmer would have covered his own backside by reporting me to the school as a runaway with no mention of anything else that might call for other serious question to be ask.

Having made new friends at Glenart College and no contact with other Artane School friends that I spent my school days with it was hard not knowing where they are how their doing or to know if we'll ever see each other again. The school system broke us all up and scatter us all too different jobs over Ireland without any means of contact as the school gave no information to where you'd be going or gave your school friends our address to write letters.

You were just cut off abandoned without any concern that if things did not work out with your new guardian for any reason then hear the school's number to get in touch with us if you need any help. Asking the school for help was the last thing on my mind as the saying goes I'd rather be dead than ask the school for any sort of help. I knew no one else other than my godmother family I could put my trust in when I found myself alone. On leaving Ireland a country that I grew up in and yet I could not call home as home is where you are supposed to feel secure and safe. My Ireland experience of growing up was one of great fear from the daily brutality that orphan inside the institutional walls were subjected to with no protection from the cruel Christian Brothers guards that in my early years when I was eight were most cruel and only eased off at age twelve years old when as a boy/farmer I worked long days on the school farm out of site and in the care of our farming boss Brother Gerald O Connor who treated his farmer boys fair and square, unlike his namesake that was the brutal band master Brother Joseph O Connor who micro managed his band boys, and the school best advert to all in Ireland from there playing at Croke Park at all the GAA Games.

Only for my time in Glenart and the nice job Father Maurice got me as a shepherd boy looking over a small flock of sheep for my new very generous guardian who was an invalid and used his wheelchair to get about his big house and grounds. He was a rich Dublin businessman who owned this big property near Ballymahon and Glasson called East Hill House not far from the centre of Ireland Athlone town.

To me it was my great escape from the government and the school control that I still had just over a year before I would be free of the state hands I would disown them of their responsibility to me before reaching my eighteen birthday. A little mention again here and a special thank you to my convent mother-nun with the sister of mercy called Sister Anne who I never forgot and she me from those days in her care at Rathdrum orphanage 1947 to 1955. It was to her dear friend Father Maurice Kavanagh that kept me safe until I was ready to move on some months later when all agree my time of hiding was over and I was ready for the big wide world to go and face life difficult challenges on my own. If love is a mother gift then Sister Anne was always my nun-mother and although we never saw each other since I was eight she has always been part of my life every day that even today more than sixty years on I think of her and thank God for having put her into my life with Brother Columba, Father Maurice Kavanagh, and my godmother Dorothy the important people of my early childhood including the Maher brothers and Mick Bracken that I keep always in my prayers and now I believe all rest in the arms of the lord.

Life in Glenart College was happy and carefree among the student priest who took me under their wing, I learned in a very short time at Glenart College the true meaning of the word love for love was different from my love/pain that I had only known and suffered at the hands of the Christian Brothers in Artane Industrial School especially in my early years as all the boys were beaten badly as this was the school way in scaring and breaking all newbies into submission and making all toe the line in their harsh regime. Your welcome to hell which it was for most whether you tried to be good or not didn't matter as the school thrived on its beating and the power that they gave to monitor who were boys of fourteen and older that became vicious brutes themselves in doing the brothers discipline work.

Glenart was a beautiful place my first Shangri-La hidden in the green hillside left of Shelton valley were the Avoca river flowed and was being poison by a new monstrous monster they call a fertiliser factory that was colouring the once silver clean water into a sickly red-yellowish colour like salmon spawning before dying. I have great memories of those I knew there that sixty years on I'm still in touch with some of those students especially Father Kevin O Shea and Paddy Walsh who some years after he became a priest left on falling in love and is happily married while others are celebrating like Father Kevin their fiftieth jubilee priesthood in the Vincentian community.

There were many other great influence in my early life at Glenart College not least the Mather Brothers, Denis and Paddy my new boss Mick Bracken head gardener, and Molly Condron the college cook, and those two beautiful sister Maggie and Lilly Doyle. Secretly my first girl/woman crush as a teenage boy of sixteen being in love or infatuated as any young adult becomes when they don't understand their body changes that leave you act like a lovesick dog whenever near or in their present.

My eyes would bulge wide open totally mesmerised at their prettiness that words never came out right when trying to play my James Stewart roll in chatting to them on how I should act or what to say to girls in my asking them out. Never have I known the company of any young girl and how they work was really very hard for me, as up to now I had no contact with the opposite sex ever, and their teasing me only made it worse in my learning how to play the boyfriend part in winning over a girl to be a proper girlfriend of mine.

I needed their advice and their teasing did help in ways that I didn't see until I was relating with a girl about being myself and able to laugh at the silly things we do or say is something all young teenagers have no understanding of this mystery they call love that in a lifetime we all chase never stop wanting for love is truly the greatest mysteries God has given us.

The Mather Brothers both bachelor's men were as the saying goes two peas in a pod, Paddy the older of the two brothers was a retired merchant navy man who told many a wild tale that he would have us all laughing our sock off till our toes tickle. His knowledge of the world and places he had been to was my real understanding of geography and the world that I never known or understood while at school. His telling of places were as of dream coming alive in me that many a night he was the answer to my swashbuckling dreams that I could not wait to go and conquer all there was to see in the big wide world, that he open up in my mind eye and made real my boyhood imagination.

Denis on the other hand was the funnier of the two brothers in look as he always reminded me of Bugs Bunny with his two big front buck teeth and his lanky height, always cooking and making tea, and a great teller of Irish jokes and of everyday life as told by good story teller that in Ireland and in the Irish language are called Seanchai. In my boyhood Denis was the first real story teller and the best I had known and I listen to his words story the book I look forward to hear rather than a comic or rubbish books to read.

I passed most nights in their company as they had an open house to all that wanted to drop in, and it was in their little cottage that my real education of people and how they like to be treated came in the way that they never shouted or got upset with each other. The fantastic way that they took me under their bachelor wings for two wonderful men rich in tales and fun made me want to stay forever with them, that their kindness and warmth knew no bounds and nothing was ever too much inasmuch that they became a great part of my teenage memories the reason why I survived the odds as a child not brought up in a good family home or taught well to read a book. I must confess at sixteen I could not read well and the Maher brothers word stories substitute for my short comings with their mind books full of adventures and travels, made my boyhood dreams come alive.

In my long life now of seventy-six years I wonder back to those school days and how different people in all walk of life behave and were so unlike the Christian Brothers of my youth in the way they treated us cruelly to the difference good people make you feel when you're treated right, fair, especially with dignity and proper respect.

I never wanted to leave Glenart College and the new friends I had made there but the consensus was coming from all in the college that I should go and look for my own life far away as I am young and there much to see and do in God's wide world than just hanging around living other's dreams, and believe more in my own self in finding my own adventure making my dreams come true, and if I fail then I can always say at least I gave it my best shot and can try-try again.

The Maher brothers were living on the left side of the gate I'm not sure if they own the lodge type house that was to the left of the college gate as the Fitzpatricks who were the official gate keepers for the college lived in the lodge on the gate right side, and as a family they were good to as well. Both houses were built of the grey castle stone that in the bleak years many big house had that natural grey quarry look and the grey slate making them stand out with that very early Victorian look the cottages were a beautiful perk that went with the job as gate-keeper that along the way the castle must have rented out for private use.

Mick Bracken my gardening boss during the day and a great teacher about all things that grew in pots or in the ground had the Midas touch in everything green that he touch. Fruit he grew was in abundance and I remember once he caught me looking at a certain big red tomato with interest in the glass house and he ask me if I ever had tasted one, I said no, but in my mind I was planning on having it anyway as the temptation to eat it was strong due to it beautiful red colour that was taking control over my weakened resistance that like the serpent tempted Eve in God garden I too was weak and thought when no one is looking or about it would be all mine to eat.

It was my eyes that became the temping serpent in wanting to take and eat it I was being tested to my limit when Mick Bracken took the glorious big red love apple call a tomato off the branch and with his pen knife cut it in half given the bigger half to me it was still warm from its growing and the taste was like none I ever known before that to this day I still chase that first taste that has never ever been repeated for tomatoes as a fruit or a vegetable I love to eat, and a tomato for me is always better if fresh and virgin warm from its living plant.

That tomato was my apple in my garden of youth for it was so red and beautiful that if Mick Bracken had not done the kind act of sharing it I would have stolen and faced the punishment whatever my boss thought, but knowing him as I did he would have fed me more because he was the kindest of men that it was in his nature to be a father to all and over many years after I left to see the world he was always on my return the same to me. Mick Bracken smoked a brown briar pipe and always looked the picture of a man contented and very sound who had a beautiful family. He was to them a dad, a grateful and thankful loving granddad was as fit as a fiddle due to his daily ride on that old contraption of a bike that each day you would see him push to work from Kilcarra up and down its steep hill showing of the strong muscle in his arms and legs.

If I was to put an age to him then he must have been a young seventy years old with fantastic blue eyes thick crop of snow white hair and his skin un wrinkle even though he be out in all sort of Irish weather showing off a golden like Mediterranean tan. I kept in touch with him and his family right up to his hundred birthday and visit him a few times on my return to Ireland over the years of my going on leave from the Irish Guards tailing of a bit after I got married because of family responsibility and money being very tight. Another sad reason because of the situation in Ireland and the troubles getting worst made it impossible for Irishmen from the south serving in the British Army were open to IRA threat and their families if they went home that it was better for all to stay neutral and safe while the temperature and risk was too high.

At the height of the trouble the commanding office put out on battalion standing that anyone going on leave to Ireland would have to have permission in order that protection was in place, and the local gardai/police in the area your visiting had to have knowledge of your been home for security and protection. I did see Mick Bracken for the last time in the early eighties and was quite amazed to see him looking as good and composed not as nifty on his feet as he once was twenty years earlier, he was ageless and although near a hundred one could say that the good lord gave him more than most for his love of land and family as well as a personal thanks for his kind service to all in need especially the student priest who found great wisdom in their chat with him of a grandfather nature.

Molly Condron a stout and lovely lady that ran the Glenart kitchen and was for me after a few days in Glenart College the most important person to know if you were to eat and be strong. She was a fair person and made me work for my meals by letting me wash up the kitchen floor or do some other little task that she needed doing, especially when one or both of her girls were on a day off. I remained a friend of hers till she passed away which was a few years after I left Glenart to her heavenly and richly deserved home. Molly as a person was a quiet saint that walked life path alone having retired to Ferry-bank a new build area near the coast -line in Arklow. She lived out her last year's watching the sun rise and the evening sunsets over the thriving fishing waters that kept her busy when walking on the sandy dunes and coastal paths. Her good cooking and soft approach with everyone made her many good friends, and from that love of people as all the Irish have when they stop and chat, and take time in other people welfare knowing how they are, and if there is anything I can do she would say please don't hesitate or be afraid to ask. Helping one neighbours was for her a joy she just loved given her time if in need her biggest gift of all.

Maggie and Lilly Doyle were the prettiest girls and sisters who I first fell in love with I did not know the real meaning of love pertaining to the sex game or how a man and a woman open up to each other in a way that it got you going in the courtship game of becoming a boy with a girlfriend or vice versa. This stepping out with a girl or going a courting as the way it was named in my youth was a matter of watching and learning how others behave in the dance hall of Inch and at the Arklow centre point ballroom at the weekend gig to the extent that I often put my foot in it when asking any of the young girl for a dance out of a long line as they waited on their side of the dance hall floor to be asked for a dance, and worst again when it was lady choice and you were left standing on your own.

The thing I found the worst was when you wanted to dance and you had to walk over to the girl's side in the hope that the first one would say yes. It was often embarrassing that as I asked the first girl I got a shy no and as you pass each one trying not to show disappointment you walk on asking all of them if you would like a dance in the hope that one, no matter her look or size one would take pity and give you a yes, for the soft nos were like been shot in the heart making your face redder and redder as each refuse you politely and giggle shyly when you pass.

Completing the wallflower line unsuccessfully there was little else then to walk the floor of shame with your tail well and truly between your legs back to the boy's side without a winner smile feeling totally mortified and humiliated and in need of a mineral or something stronger to drink, and to die and cry silently inside. Knowing how to chat up girls and being able to slow and quick dance was number one in a girl saying yes as they did not want to be embarrass with a no hoper which I was that couldn't jive or do the twist, the smooth waltz, slow fox-trot dance without stamping on their delicate toes.

Making good small talk with a confident smile was another secret in winning a dance or getting another date. You could not beat the lads who owned a motorcar as that was the biggest key to getting the girl to and from the dances, and their friends would also be looking out for the same lift home. An orphan like me brought up in a prison school had very little of life skills with no real understanding of the opposite sex, knew nothing about the opposite sex world as none of this was taught by the brother who kept the secret of what girls and boys got up to in forming relationship a secret and was for us in Artane School a huge no-no.

What boundaries a boy ought to know that won't get him into trouble with a girl or her parent that he should watch out for was never taught and in the area of sex knowledge we were greener than the grass of Ireland. Real life was never going to be easy for a boy like me who knew little of earning a wage having never paid for food and board. Now buying his own personal need that each day multiplies as you learn that the money earned does not go far and you are always on the back foot in not understanding how to manage your weekly wage that none of us leaving school knew much about. How a boy is to win a girl and have her stay in his company was not easy as often they laugh and tease leaving you in girl-less limbo.

As a teenager with much to learn about the softer sex ways and thinking which changes faster than the weather I question myself as to what it is a boy has to do that will entice the girls to say yes. A skill I have not yet learned and also how this love game work in been able to read the complicated signs that changes from one girl to the next. Tips in chatting up a girl is what I needed as well as the secret formula of what make girls tick in respect of them been on an equal footing like boys to have as a friend and fun to be with. This trying to make contact with girls was not easy. I was out of my depth in asking girls out as not having a brother or a best friend of my own age that as a team we could role play our strategy as it was I was on my own in learning without a guide book.

Like a dumb fish out of water when it came to understanding or having a clue how girls mind or bodies work. Exploration of the opposite sex body was not going to be easy when you'd been brain washed in the church's teachings of hell and damnation that if you stray off the path of purity your next stop was hell. In truth I was afraid of girls and the fear the church had instilled in us all at school through years of being told it's a sin if you look or touch first your own body never mind a girl, having impure thoughts whatever they were frightened me so much that the years of rcligious indoctrination reminded me daily of how Adam had fallen into sin because he took the apple bite from Eve.

The brothers told us when she offered him a bite of God's forbidden fruit from the tree of knowledge he was weak and should have told her it is wrong to disobey God. The danger of my getting up close to a girl at sixteen was as far away as the moon from the earth that at night any temptation on offer I would have missed as I had no sexual understanding not a clue of how or what made a boy different to a girl's parts as I had never seen a girl naked to know what makes us different other than them been softer skin and much beautiful with long hair. As to matter pertaining to the birds and bees at sixteen and what they do that is about sex I had not a clue in the slightest. Unable was I to make the first move or know what it is a young man does with a girl and them to us in this game of love and how to play the love game, and to avoid committing sin would not be easy as any handling of a beautiful girl body put you on the wrong side of the sixth commandment by thought and deed. Understanding the dating rules and how boys with girls should behave and what girls expect from boys was more confusing.

My dream girls of the kitchen would have known the boyish feeling I felt and would often played on my teenage inexperience that not quite a man I did not fully understand the whys or the reason of my fumbling when in the present of girls in general. The Doyle sisters were in their early twenties and looked visions of heavenly angels to me they were more beautiful than most screen actresses I saw at the local picture house in Arklow on the weekends. In those days I lived out my weekly dream which were brought to life by my film heroes winning charm it was those pictures that excited my imagination in reliving again and again my secret wish of having a real time girlfriend, and the way I should go about winning one as my own.

The beautiful Maggie was the dark haired sister and it was known locally that she had won the Rose of Wexford competition, and with winning the Rose of Wexford she was the catch that any young man from her home town of Enistcorty and from far and wide would be happy to fall in love and ask to swing arm in arm to the alter of love as Elvis in his song mention. Having had no mother and father to talk such things over with like relationship about girls and the sex thing that a boy of my age should know about and to ask about the weird feeling I was having and how best I can control them, as my teenage emotions were off the scales that my every thought left me afraid to act on and stupidly confuse.

No boy in Artane School that I knew ever mentioned anything about girls and what they were about the only talk was about boy's stuff who won the feisty fight, the handball match, or some other yard games we played and what boy had received a beating and from which brother. Beatings were a lottery in you never knew why you were single out and worst their reason in carrying it out with a thick leather on the spur of the moment mostly for no other reason than for them to amuse themselves in scaring everyone to behave on the playground this they did as if catching a sheep for shearing grabbing any boy and pulling his trouser down trapping his head between their knees and given him six or more smack leaving welts and severe pain that for many hours after was an angry boy who learn nothing more than to hate and hate God's Christian Brothers more.

School left most of us with no idea what girls' body-parts looked like in comparison to our own body shape and the difference in their function to us. Boys in our group mostly orphan never had a chance of knowing any girls up close to see what a girl really looked like with no clue other then what we saw when our godmothers came up to see us the obvious difference you saw was in their body shape the softness of their voice, and the sweet smell of perfume that was very noticeable on those Sundays when they came that it left you knowing young girls would have smelt pretty sweet too as opposed to us boys that had an earthy smell of wild oats wheat and barley.

Whenever the opportunity to be in girls' company at the local dance or in a public bar my mind would let me down for with no life experience of how to approach a girl it was no good opening up with a rubbish line that would not work in getting her to say yes to a dance in which I could hold and take in the soft perfume of a girl into my nose and savour the closeness especially if I was lucky to hold one in a slow dance. Usually it was the last dance of an evening that was your last opportunity to impress and win over if you were going to get a dance, and if luck was on your side to walk her home and see her again.

Chatting up girls and casually opening conversation with a good one liner would break the ice I had not yet mastered this art of making a girl feel at ease and never had a backup girl plan in my no back up armoury to show me how experienced lads in the dating game field really work. This let me down always and the fact I was very young may have been another reason why I could not break the refusal line of nos at dances in getting a soft smiling girl to say yes.

It equally could be that they saw me as a nobody without money without a car or the honest truth be known that they too were themselves inexperience in the love game and too young that they too were looking for a more mature man in the art of temped love to teach them the way through the forbidden ropes in this new awaking in learning how to play the love game without been caught.

Ireland of the early sixties was still in the dark ages when it came to boys and girls in the courting and getting to know one another in a sexual way and its pleasure was denied no matter how innocent it was. It secrets was held back so the youth of those sad days remain ignorant as to how sex between a man and woman was whispered about as the prerogative of the special few that were married.

Chapter 3

Teenagers touching and heavy petting and experimenting in the sex game having sexual feeling they could not answer or complete for the church had put a mine-field around sex that only the married found its delight, and they too kept the sex secret of making love to themselves. It was mainly people of both sexes that left the church and Ireland and those who came back from being away around the world that spoke of it pleasure braking the taboo and speaking honestly that having enjoyed the bite of this forbidden fruit said it should be part of family education and not hidden as if dirty but to be open and honest in understanding our sexual function that the church could no longer control for the young saw the times were a changing as more and more learn it secrets and freely tested it.

Maggie and Lillie laugh as my innocence awakens in my questioning them how will I know if I'm in love and if the girl I find is the right one for me and how will I be able to tell. What is the secret in the art of kissing how do you place your lips to hers, open or close, and what is a girl's secret to kiss you back as you see men heroes in the films win and get. Maggie and Lillie always behave properly in that they were good in making me feel welcome and molly-coddle me like a lost little brother that needed girly guidance and encouragement. They were fun to listen to and they shone like stars in my sixteen-year-old eyes that never dimmed of them throughout my life.

Looking back as I do now sixty odd years on I do believe in hindsight for the college the sisters were the best thing to test all those young men who were given up there life for the priesthood and fore-going the love of marriage in order to serve the church. If men are attracted to beautiful woman then the temptation to the priesthood was well tested with the Doyle sisters for they were the best test to the student priest's resistance. If attractiveness of the opposite sex was ever to be tested then none other were better suited to that job than the beautiful Doyle girls that could not go unnoticed by any red hot blooded male holy or unholy.

I had a small run in with Des Mordant not his wife who was always nice to me but for some reason or other he took a dislike to me being friends with his children especially his oldest daughter as he was very protective of his children which at the time one was a little younger than me about fourteen. He often found us playing in the woods when he came back from work, and because of that and what he himself knew of teenage sex judged me wrongly in my knowing about sex when in fact I knew nothing other than I played innocently with his daughters.

His thinking of me the way he did put a wall between us that I did not understand and why he told me for no reason that he did not want me playing with his children and not to come near his house as I was no longer welcome. His wife though was a lovely lady always calling me in to have supper with them which now was a puzzle she wanting me at her house and him saying stay away. I was a bit confused as to what is right and wrong in playing with his children as he had me mark down as a bad influence a bad apple for some reason that he never divulge and I began not to like him although I had no problem with his family who were ever so nice to me.

An opportunity arrived one day when I saw him swimming in the make shift swimming tank and not being allowed to play with his children I took it upon myself to punish him in the only way I knew in that when he tried to get out of the homemade swimming pool I hit near his fingers with a long stick to make him circle round and round like a frustrated gold fish that my laughter and his plight alerted staff and student of my prank. I was sent for by Father McCullum superior of Glenart College and he reprimanded me in a soft priest way about the incident and said that I must apologise to Mr Mordant and never to play near the pool tank again as it could have went badly wrong considering you cannot swim, and him needed rescuing it could have turned sour and I must never let my boyish foolishness ever happen again.

That stupid incident with Mr Mordant was my realising I should leave as it was becoming clear to me that my days in Glenart were numbered and it would be better for all if I left before another silly outburst got me into serious trouble. It was again Father Maurice Kavanagh came to my rescue in talking to me about the big wide world and that my days of hiding away must end as he thought I am ready to move on. To where I had not a clue but Father Maurice been the clever mentor and a grandfather type and a good friend he had become over the last six months arrange another place for me to go to which he felt would give me another and better new start working for a lovely gentleman he knew well and who would give me work, full board with a small salary of thirty shillings a week.

My departure from Glenart had to be my choice and it was becoming a problem for me to stay as I was breaking free of my youth and really entering manhood with many growing pains for those about me to try and understand my changing moods that what was happening left me feeling out of control for reason I did not understand or know how to control.

I was a growing adult boy and probably like all teenage boys and girls we were all going through some form of transformation to manhood and womanhood without any of us knowing or understanding what it is in that causes our rebellious outburst as nobody spoke of anything and we were left high and dry in the madness of our bodies doing strange things that our brain are also at a loss to tell what it is that is happening in these changes to our bodies and inside our mind as these development occurred. Having hormones running wild around our bodies that is more understood today than it was in my youth which we knew nothing of or anyone else for that matter, and the reason why teenagers acted in the way they did that neither our parent nor elders knew little about the causes of teenage restlessness and their growing pains that even today is not fully understood.

It would seem looking back that both sexes were kept in the dark like mushrooms for sex and its pleasure was only acted on by the rebellious and the married. That first consented sexual experience of pure sex must have exploded the gate of heaven wide open in that love and afraid moment of them seeing each other for the first time naked as God had made Adam and Eve and their tender hold of togetherness as they lay in conjugal love that the pleasure to know and enjoy in the sacred act of married union on their wedding night revealed it own secret that in truth was worth waiting for in which newlywed man and woman become one.

It was time to leave Ireland and for the first time I also thought about what I would like to do even to the extent of handing myself in to the gardai/police, telling them my side of the story I should have told many months ago that I was afraid because as a mere boy against the system without anyone to stand and defend my corner I was going to go straight to prison and be punished just as I was put into Artane Industrial School when eight years old that I thought it would be better to be a runaway than spend any time in Dublin Mount-joy gaol.

I had asked Father Kavanagh a few times about my becoming a priest and how I love the way of life in the seminary and that I would put my whole interest in staying good and become like the young men I've watched over the months seeing how happy they all are in their chosen path of wanting to serve God. He reiterated again as he had on many a conversational walk before telling me that the life I had led to date was no reason to believe this was a calling because of the student in the college and the staff had been kind and very good to you. It was not on its own a good enough reason in wanting to become a priest as there are other practical consideration to be sorted out first. Your lack of education and that you are only sixteen years old and to make a lifetime commitment when you have no real experience of people and life would be against you in the full meaning and understanding of what it is you really want to undertake that I would encourage you to find another way, another life, away from Ireland and for you to seek the life our good lord has in mind for you.

If it is him calling you to follow in his footsteps then you will know, and if after a few years away of seeing the world you still feel the same way and you would still like to become a priest then I will help you as will any of our priests here for you to fulfil that calling. He said all this with a heavy heart you have no education, no certificate but if you really want to get on in this life and join us in the future you will need to start back at night school gained some certificate that will stand you in a good position of getting to university for a good job. All this information of what to do in going back to school be it at night after a hard day's work was not in honesty part of my plan as he told me that Glenart College was only a place of safety until I was ready and able to move on. That taking the next brave step of finding my way on my own out in the big wide world would have to be mine and mine alone.

That leap of faith into the unknown was a cushion in my mind and made alive with the tales of Paddy's travels and his adventures stories and the names of foreign places that over the months of friendship with the Maher brothers those faraway names and places had become familiar in my mind that I would remember and use in my knowledge of life as if I had never been an orphan. I would live in the shadows of his stories as his shipmate on the seven high seas.

It dawned on me in Glenart that I had to remake myself anew and not lie be that it is what I am really going to do in order that I can survive in a world that did not understand hard luck stories or care where you came from as long as it did not impinge on their day to day life as you soon learn the world is a cruel master and does not cry or care for the weak and fallen. It was with a heavy heart that my days in Glenart College were coming to an end and I had been prepared by my student friends to go out and be that self-assured boy I've become while working and learning with them to look after myself as I made my onward journey to Athlone and East Hill house of my new Dublin boss Father Maurice Kavanagh said would look after me making my going a lot easier by his kind words.

The day I was going I was surprised when Mr Mordant came and wished me the best with no hard feeling about our little spat that Father Mc Cullum ironed out and made my time after the swimming incident a story to laugh about and not to lose control and be revengeful when angry.

On the train from Arklow to Dublin I called in on my godparent for a chat and a cup of tea and to let them know where I would be staying in Athlone as in my head they are my new mum and dad and their home is my home. It was on the train from Dublin to Athlone town I had my lightbulb moment in that this new start against the life I had live in Artane and my time in County Tipperary in that small village of mine six miles from Thurles town they be buried away for good letting my mind change past circumstances in leaving behind the bad part of my life my orphan days in the hands of our mother church and state that henceforth will no longer decide my future anymore.

I became a new man with a new purpose in going forward with a will not to fail but to be an achiever and make a success of whatever life the lord laid out before me and do as Father Maurice Kavanagh always said go forward and never look back.

Locking away the hurt of my childhood to make my mind see the new re-created me with a new mind- map forgetting all that I had been through and make pretend I am an ordinary Dublin boy with a family who grew up in the city and not in that throwaway orphanage in Rathdrum County Wicklow or the brutal incarcerated eight years inside Artane Industrial School grey walls topped with broken glass which marked the industrial prison boundary.

Saying to hell with my past and all that was part of the Irish government machine and the skirted bully guards who the church called Christian Brothers that ran my life in their institutions gave me a feeling of real freedom and a joyous lift in my soul that day I started a new chapter a new day in my life.

Born at sixteen

If I had to sum up my life
In words I had to write,
It would be that I,
Was born at sixteen.

The slap of freedom woke me up
The chains of state were broken,
Those solid walls that kept me in
Womb of darkness opened.

I yelled a scream that freedom knows
I breathed freedom air,
The tomb that I was buried in
Guardian crows became scared.

For years they taunted my name
Beat my flesh at will,
Clipped my wings so I could not fly
Imprisoned me with their skill.

At sixteen I outgrew their chains
Strong in mind and strength,
No longer suffered their inflicted pain
To their horror I would retaliate.

Blood would flow from my swollen face
But I would smile at their hate

Whatever they did to make me conform
Stubberance was my wall.

Kicking my body on the floor
I gave them no satisfaction,
Though my body was bruised and sore,
Laugh into their maddening eyes.

The more they beat the more I'd smile
Not a game I let them win,
For them it was a cleansing of sin
That as a boy I had no part in.

Those guardian of the state souls
Hid behind cassocks black as coal,
Power gone mad, out of control
Ears deaf to mercy were ignored.

At last I was free of their torturous rule
No turning back, as I left school,
The name Artane would always mean pain
Yet the band played on its masquerade.

Blanking and cancelling out all my previous thoughts to start again with a sure purpose of proving to these good people that I am better than the system that beat me into submission and made me afraid to speak my mind, and afraid of everyone in authority even at times myself of who I was is now dead and buried. It felt right to move on and no longer to look back as it was time to let go the past and no longer carry unnecessary baggage but move forward putting as the saying goes my best foot forward.

So hey-ho here I go forward and onward to start my new life in Athlone with my new boss a friend of Father Kavanagh who he said would take care of me and be fair to me. With his address in my pocket I was on my way to be a handy boy/man for this invalid Dublin man who needed help around his house and grounds near Athlone town the centre of Ireland with a paid ticket for the train and instruction of where he would pick me up on my arrival.

The house I was going to be employed in was call East Hill House and it was a grand colonial looking house that once was owned by a rich land owner who own much property and lands, the black wrought iron gate when open led you up a long twisting avenue that took you to a huge grey strong looking house with many rooms and loads of grounds for his wheelchair to move around and friends to parked whatever mode of vehicle they might arrived in to stay or just visit.

If I had the hindsight and knowledge then that I have today of how family inheritants and generous people like him as I heard happen to other lads that stayed with their good employer who hadn't any immediate family were exceptionally lucky to be handed the land and property they went to work for and made a great success and other lucky to marry into the family which employed them that they went on to have their own children and family.

I had a happy few weeks at this house and the room I lived in was so large about six beds width across and long. I measure all sizes by the school space I once occupied in the school's crowded dormitory. My job was to look after a few sheep and in general sweep around the front of house and be company for him when no friends or visiting family were around.

He was a very interesting man who once ran a big business before he became paralysed from the waist down he never dwelled on how it all change his life as he was thankful for every day and for him having a positive outlook in everything was the only way to be. He mastered the wheelchair as if he had a new pair of legs and with that it gave him back his independence and self-reliance.

He employed a few staff to take care of his business life that called in from time to time to let him know how business was getting on. I found it odd that none of his nurses that took care of him slept in and the estate manager had his own cottage a little distance away from the house, as did the head gardener. He asked questions of me in how I came to be with the Vincentian Fathers and my life before that and how I knew his dear friend Father Maurice Kavanagh who he had known through his work as a missionary priest and his life in a Dublin parish after he returned from China.

He was of the mind that when the time was right for me I should search and find out what the world has to offer as you never know what out there and what might become of you in the future.

Questions that could not be answer if you didn't take a chance or dip your toe into the dark water of the unknown. In my time at East Hill House the fair came to Ballymahon and Glasson and it was the first time I seen a fun fair up close with all the musical horses and other attraction the coloured light with loud traditional music blaring for all to hear and sing along too by lubricant throats.

Fairgrounds took the place of the pied piper in drawing all the children of the town to visit. These travelling shows of my Ireland in the fifties and especially the early sixties had bumper cars which for me were the best thing I had ever driven on as we bump into each other for fun and everyone behind their own wheel thought themselves a formula one champion.

Beside the local fair was the Ballymahon Glasson market days that bought and sold cattle, sheep, horses, pigs, livestock per se. Good farming banter was exchange after a lot of black stuff was drunk and bargain made and seal with a spit on the hand and a shake.

These market days were the best as you got to see the real work of Irish life and its economy in action, and the banter that bonded different people from about the local area and far beyond.

My time in the middle of Ireland was happy and it was a few years later after I returned to Athlone town that I understood a mystery that had bother me a lot whenever I visited Athlone area, why people back then when I was a mere boy used to nod to me as if they knew me all their life that I didn't know or fully understand when I was working at the big house in the early summer of 1964, that now many years on because of the close resemblance of my head to those of the local of that community in which my biological family belonged. It would be five or so years before I found out my mother's family home and all her relation lived only fifteen miles from Athlone town in a place called Tough McConnell.

The reason why my head was an acceptable head in this area of Ireland that leaned to the west were my family and those of my mother people hale from in the County of Roscommon. I was young, restless, and wanted to leave Ireland and chase the adventures that fired my imagination since freedom of mind taught me that no one was going to look after me but my own good self.

I said my goodbye to my new boss friend at East Hill House thanking him for his generosity and advice, and he gave me a few pounds before my heading back to Dublin be that he did not want me to leave as he tried telling me I have a good year or two before me and I should wait and not to rush, but take my time and to learn a bit more about life before starting out on your boy adventure for he wanted me to stay and give this new place a chance, he said, before you write Ireland off as a bad number.

It had been in my head for months to get going on my own and see the world and do what my mind vision of adventures was telling me and not delay as you feel when young if you don't start you never will get going. Making my way nearly eleven months on and the water under the bridge of my past and Tipperary well behind me and I hope long forgotten by the gardai/police and others. I felt confident in making my move and like our beloved St Patrick who was a captured slave I was ready and good to go it alone. Nearly seventeen years of been an institutional boy I was ready for my own escape, and take the opportunity to change the hand that faith had or not dealt me, and take my chance and go on my merry way.

I wanted nothing to stop my burning desire of seeing the world and finding out for myself what the world was hiding. Stubborn might be a word I would use of myself today, but then in my youth my imagination was on fire as only a teenager's mind is, fearless and inpatient. Their nothing in my mind that going to hold me back for in my head was the one thought if I don't start my adventure, and get going I might miss my chance, and with both hands I grabbed the travel bull by the horns and made a go for it.

The burning dream I had were partly due to my first boy adventurous stories that mariner Paddy Maher told of his great voyages of his life while serving in the merchant navy was the key driving force in my wanting to leave and see the world and find out for myself all the world secret that would enrich my life. To tell my own stories and fantastic tales around my own home fireside one day with my own family that I hoped to have and tell of my life and travel, and inspire them to take a leap in their dream when they my children and grandchildren are ready to conquer and explore bringing to life their own burning dreams when their time comes.

I left East Hill House a sad but grateful boy/man as the Dublin owner asked that I keep in touch with him and Father Kavanagh as he felt oblige to let him know that I left his employment to make my own way in the world. With my goodbyes said I made my way onward to Dublin and stayed with my godparent at their house in Ballsbridge, I spent a few days before I sailed having check out when the boats leave the North Wall, having checked destinations, and leaving times, not that any of the places the boats were heading to meant anything to me like Scotland, Liverpool, names to throw at George who had some knowledge of the world more than me. George being George not having much time for anything outside of his little world said sure them two places are much the same as here and with that he said ah you know you'll be fine, you'll be all right, and don't worry.

I asked them both if I could use their address as my home contact in case of awkward question that might arise along the way that I would be able to answer without making up and say as easy as I have in using their names that would trip off my tongue and not be a lie if the authority ask any awkward question of where do you live and with whom.

The realism of my family story that I could use would have to have authenticity as people are quick to pick up on untruths and become suspicious of what you're about if they see a slight hesitation. I made my way to the North Wall to check the time of boat-sails at the dock I hoped to be catching and the number it would be leaving from. The weather on that day was its usual grey colour that never change and remains as Irish as the green grass that's always wet. The boat I would be catching the next night was leaving for Scotland at eight o clock not quite sure were Scotland was as any place outside of Ireland for a boy adventure who had not a clue of his own country and its many counties was thinking only one thing in them days to get far away from this God forsaken Ireland that did little in making my early life happy.

I followed Father Maurice Kavanagh advice and the Mather brother Paddy who fired first my mind to travel and see the big wide magical world and what it has to offer. It was going to be a long and arduous trip for a near seventeen year old on his first boat trip from the North Wall dock Dublin to Scotland. Question in my head kept going round and round would I be able to cope on my own with no idea of what Scotland had to offer and what would I do when the boat in Scotland has docked. This opened a can of worm in my head that made going on my own scary and cautious if I had to explain myself to stranger that might ask question be they friendly who may show interest and would deduce quite quickly I was a runaway from the gardai/police, home, or family, for I did look under age and very young to be travelling on my own and indeed had the looks of an gormless eejit on his first adventure anywhere.

Which made me fear being stopped that my guard was up for any likely Sherlock Holmes type who might ask to many personal question using their power of deduction in sniffing information that might give them rights to report my travelling alone as a runaway with no mean of support, no family or adult supervision, that would give the boat captain the power to detain and hand me over to the gardai/police for further check as to what I'm about on investigating my reason for why I'm making this boat trip alone to Scotland.

I would lie and hope that my God would forgive me later in the confessional for any small white lies I might have to tell for I thought right if it got me out of a jam and onward in my quest of my new adventure in seeing the world that burn bright in my dream head, my God would be OK with that. If asked by anyone friendly or just in passing how I am, and where are you heading, I would just say I'm going as a seasonal fruit and potatoes picker I saw advertised a few weeks ago in a Sunday newspaper. And I thought I would go try my hand at that staying with my imaginary family relatives over the summer who themselves went to Scotland twenty years ago and made a good life and are happy that I should come and stay with them this summer.

My imaginary aunt says all young people should try and better themselves in making extra money doing a summer job as it gives one so she always saying, the opportunity in gaining work experience before making up their young minds if they want to go onto higher education, or just enter the workforce in learning a proper trade.

I'm surely one of the biggest eejits that ever left Ireland to venture away when I did without a clue of what Ireland itself had to offer by not staying with my Dublin boss near

Athlone who wanted me to stay a while longer, and to be honest was a good employer more a friend in the way he looked after me, as a true friend of Father Maurice Kavanagh who he kept in touch with. Leaving on the hoof was a bad decision on my part but the travel bug in my head was too strong to fight against as my imagination for adventure said go for it and be brave, and to that end I went full leather ahead to fulfil my boyhood dream.

Not knowing many places outside of the school other than my short time in County Tipperary, six months in the seminary hid away in Wicklow and my short stay in the Athlone area was the limit of my knowledge of my Ireland, my home, my country.

With no real preparation for going alone and worst travelling into the great unknown of another country without knowledge of their language, colour or creed, if I was ask any question about my own Ireland my knowledge would be much the same nothing. So much did I not know and yet my mind pressed me on as if I was fighting with my inner self, for my mind was not caring what I knew it just wanted to go forward and fearlessly travel. My getting away on my own would have to be convincing for many Irish family who have a boy of my age probably made this trip once or twice in the past with their parent and would have had their permission to travel on their own to visit a family member living in England, Scotland or Wales that will be there to meet them on arrival.

Named places that would become familiar to me in the years ahead were for now places I had not a clue, as I was inside my escape head with one aim to get away from this Ireland that in reality never was home, and with no family history to fall back on that I could use in pretence of my family great achievement I was desperate in my need to know the world and time was short and pressing. I was ready in my mind eye for all the challenges that as a teenage dreamer I believe were not a problem and gave no real thought to what could go wrong.

I had no plan if any problem arose like every day living inasmuch as having three square meals and a place to sleep, how I would deal with everyday living that up to now others took care and looked after. I myself never asked that important question how much it took to look after oneself for as a child of the state and church my welfare was there responsibility until my eighteen birthday and to that end I never may any inroads as to how I would get by myself.

For now that was not a problem to worry about till it happened as the adventure I sought was about to begin and I wanted to get started in my going, and brave in facing head on my first fearless step into the unknown. I was ready in my youthful dream head to make real and bring alive my own stories of adventures as in the tales of Paddy's life that he told around his own warm fire in his small cottage gatehouse at Glenart in county Wicklow which spurred me on to be my own hero in my own film of my own life.

This was to be my cover story if stopped by anyone in authority that thought I might be a runaway because of my age as an unaccompanied boy that looked too young to be travelling on his own, that I would be staying with relatives in Scotland as that was where the boat was heading. I had to make out I knew what I was about and where I was going if asked by any port authority worker to prove who I was without drawing attention even though I had no concrete alibi to back up my imaginary made up story. If found out that I was running away without the authority knowing it, for example from the Christian Brothers it would be a case for the gardai/police to handle as I was not yet seventeen for a few weeks and the law of the country at that time may have even been twenty-one as opposed to eighteen like in these anything goes days.

I had no real inkling as to what would happen if caught, and of the outcome to my running away if I had been challenge and detain by the gardaí or by those doing the right thing as according to there arrest of me. I was really lifted by the stories I heard from Paddy Maher and of course Father Kavanagh who told me many times to leave Ireland and seek a new life away beyond the institutional upbringing that bred me. And to go and find my own fame and fortune away from Ireland, and that there is another side to life that is not holy church or state control.

Their advice to me came from their own time away in different fields of life, Paddy as a sea merchant, Father Maurice Kavanagh a missionary in China, challenges that they both told me were the best experience life had given them, and I too should when ready find my own adventure.

I manage to purchase my ticket and stay close to a large group when the official checking the ticket to passengers going on board was very busy at the boat boarding steps, I made my way gingerly up the gang way, sticking close to a large family group that pushed onto the boat, and I boarded with them as if I had done so many times before. Like a church mouse I would remain quiet and steal away until as they say in the movie the coast is clear pardoning the pun in my case the Irish coast could no longer be seen.

This in reality was what I watch with great anxiety and fear as I was not free until the boat had moved out into the sea away from its pier and well on it way to my new destination. Then and only then could I give a big sigh of relief at my being safe and truly on my way into the future that this boat of the B and I line would take me to my first new country called Scotland and its wonders yet to be seen and explored.

When you are young and afraid, especially alone you think that everyone who looks at you knows you're from that school and that you are a runaway not only from Ireland, but from the law.

Your imagination worked overtime making you more alert to passing strangers that pretend to be friends as trust is not your first virtue to hand after my sort of upbringing I've had, that all in authority believe they have control over you because they are class responsible as your elder and according to our church and the fourth commandment must be obeyed.

Keeping my wits about me was very important as any answer said wrong to any busy-body who by good intention might put pay to my plan of escape, in them thinking they are been a good citizen or a good Samaritan in reporting me as of special interest to the boat captain that you are travelling unsupervised and probably a runaway. I did not have much money and I was thankful for the few sandwiches Dorothy wrapped for me to eat on board the boat. With no money to spare for buying food or for that matter a drink on the crossing I was a force miser as I did not have a clue how much it would cost me to live and get by on my own for a few days before I'm earning some money, and making my own way in this new land of Scotland.

It was exciting in so many ways as I walk about the boat looking at all the people's faces and listening to the many different accents of passengers that I had a thousand question in my head of who and where do those not from Ireland and visiting Scotland come from.

There were people who engaged me in conversation as to where I was going saying how great it was to be travelling on my own and remarking how wonderful an opportunity your having a summer job and their trust in you will make your family very proud.

Boat are funny places after you've done your walk about to know where everything is, like the bar, the toilet, seating lounges, and as I was a low fare passenger there was sign of those without sleeping berth ticket not to enter, and other sign for first-class zone with a red rope tied barrier with a card sign stating no entry to unauthorised passenger. You see other people children big and small running around as all on board know there no way off unless you jump, pushed, or decide to swim.

People after a while begin to settle down on the boat lying about on the boat floor in all sorts of position, and even worst the people who are sea-sick holding on to the outer rail of the boat as they churn up their delicate stomach and its content earlier ate in the day that become food for the fish in the sea. It going to be a rough night crossing said many of the passenger and to me as a first time traveller this was the norm and much in line of what I had been told around Paddy's cosy fire in Glenart that waves swell causing the boat to roll. I was pleased I was not sea-sick and remember Paddy Maher's words of how the sea or the ocean cannot be tame and when it rough you just have to go with the prevailing wind and go with the boat's tips and sways to ease the motion of the sea, saving yourself from getting sick.

I was looking out into the darkness of the night as my mind wander to what in a few hours would be my first day in a new country and the start of a new life, and how I would get by as I had not thought through a plan of action, mainly because I knew nothing about Scotland, its people, geography, for everything forward from now on would be trial and error and whatever happen in between.

Irish people in themselves are a friendly lot and it doesn't take long on the boat for someone to want to know about you to have a chat, this man about fiftyish a frequent tripper to and fro to Ireland came over and asked me are you travelling on your own, at first I was a bit careful about my answer in asking why, when he told me you get to see all sorts when you do this trip as much as I do. I knew he been watching me on the boat that carry a few hundred passengers that after a half hour of walking about on the boat you get to know where everything is as well as recognising other faces that are not settled down in chairs or having secured their floor bed place. I restlessly walked around the boat until the lights and the noises soften and then took time to think and breathe easy as I watched the night gently pass by going over in my mind am I mad or what.

He knew well I was travelling alone as he had been watching me walk about looking for a quiet place to hide and past the trip. Which is not easy with the summer crowd going on holiday he told me that he like quite places himself on the boat in order to keep away from the rowdy drinkers who sing loudly making what one could say right-ould-eejits of themselves.

It takes a while for people to settle down and sleep where ever they can find a seat or a floor space, especially those who could not afford the overnight sleeper. I had no intention of sleeping as I did not want to find the few belonging that were wrapped and tied in my brown paper parcels gone.

I hadn't much but at lease it appears I had belonging as opposed to walking of the boat in what I wore carrying nothing, as it would arouse suspicious if a port officer was to call you over and ask a few enquiry questions that may end up with my going nowhere.

This man was a gift in as much as he told me that where we are going there was plenty of work and that Scotland was a second home for many Irishmen and women who left for the same reason as me, no job or opportunity of work at home and had to leave in order that there family received money from abroad until opportunity at home become better. I had lowered my guard a bit as I felt this person was someone I could trust in that I told him I was trying to make it on my own in order that I could send money home to my fictional poverty family who at this time are finding it hard to live on the little that my dad earned. I kept to relatives meeting me on arrival and how they were going to help me to get a job picking fruit and potatoes that season pickers prepared to work and put in a full day's hard work can earn and get by.

He mentioned a name to me called St John's in Ayrshire a few miles away from where the boat docked and said when he was a young man many years ago he went working there during the summers of his youth doing just that. It was to me an omen that I too should make my way there as that was the only name of a place in Scotland that I heard and knew from him that existed. He told me too that like my story of wanting to make money for my fictional family that that two was the main reason why countless thousands of Irish migrant travel from Ireland in order to find work and support their family at home. The Irish by nature are gypsies, he said, they love moving around and for many find it hard to settle in any one place to call it home.

He said that the reason so many are feeling bad and sick is because this boat that is so ancient and skimmed above the waves rather than a sharp knife that should cut through the waves, as it was first used to carry livestock many years ago but now it carried passengers and commercial freight instead. I was glad when he said he must get a few hours sleep as that was my opportunity to get back inside my escape head and dream away looking out into the darkness of the sea.

I was captivated by the shining night stars that again in Paddy's tales he told of his time in the merchant navy and how many a sailor is guided by and knew how to read with practice the stars that I hope to master in the future myself.

The rest of that night went quickly and as dawn was early at around four after midnight people started stirring and getting themselves busy packing away their make shift beds, and repacking their clothes in their suitcases making full use of the ablution in taking away the tiredness from their eyes before leaving the boat at seven.

There is a peace that is still and I felt it present in the silence of the dawn I also sense a new hope in that today I must live for the now and this secret moment. I could see were the boat was going and I watch for hours the waves create back wash as the boat bounce up and down to the strong music of the sea, and in the distance I could see land approaching and people on the quay side waiting to unload us and the cargo that this boat carries.

I laugh now nearly sixty years on of my first disembarkation and how I arrived in Scotland not knowing anyone or a single thing about the Scottish people, their culture, language they spoke. The little I learn at school was of the Catholic faith and Irish history from the Christian Brothers' point of view, and why it was that the English church broke away from Catholic Rome because their horrible selfish King

Henry the Eighth had made himself head of the English church to satisfy his own gratuitous lust.

History of our closest neighbours, Scotland, England, Wales, and of free passage without any form of identity was amazing as I walked through unopposed as against today's travellers because of open borders with all our European partners identity cards or passports must be shown even if you are a native born living in Ireland or visiting from another country.

I followed the crowd ever sceptical that I might be asked what business I had in Scotland and where might I be staying and with who. Question I had no honest answer for. Once through the customs and not being stopped I made my way out looking at all the signs in the hope of some miraculous inspirational idea in how and what I must do next that will set me on the right road to my future.

Dock areas are the same everywhere in the world that they smell heavily of the sea and iodine and the men that work on the docks are a weather beaten lot with leathery faces that the elements have carved. I followed the way most of the passengers were going as seasoned travellers always know their way out of these places. I with my brown paper parcels bundle under my arm made my way with my head held high, and walked straight out as if I had been this way many times before. I was buzzing inside with the excitement I felt having arrived in this new country call Scotland I at last was totally free.

I asked the way to St John's in Ayrshire, and where I could catch the bus as that was where the stranger on the boat had told me that when he was young it was there he went as a pickers of fruits and vegetables. I decide to do likewise in the hope that I would get a season job to start me of on my road in seeing the world by earning a few shillings first if you please.

If luck was the byword of the Irish as many believe it was I can only say my being born Irish certainly did not help or favour me nor did I find that luck spoken off in reference to the Irish that this poor boy really needed. For in my thinking this is another one of those created myth about Irish luck that was not on my side and having found the bus to St John's in Ayrshire and having made my way there was dejected and disappointed in that of all years the harvest was not good and there was no offer of work for any summer pickers who came looking. It became all too obvious that this was not a good year as nobody was hiring and without any contact of family or friend to stay with, I ended up walking the beach given me loads of space and time to mull over in my mind, and to think things out in what I should do next.

It was important to keep my spirit up and think positive in order to survive and not to look miserable and homeless. Be that is what I am and if I'm to win my way in this world I must be more proactive even to the point of that Irish luck that has as yet not shown it smiling face on me.

I ask myself how long could I live and survive with the little money I have all of twelve shillings and sixpence. Not being an Einstein I was able to work out that I could not afford to fork out any of my little fortune for rent, food, until I learn how far I could get by from slumming it on the beach and looking for handout from passers-by and pennies found became my daily routine until I could work out a plan to move on. I would just have to get by on the street and sleep on the beach until something turned up while praying the rains keep away. The little money I had would have to be used sparingly and for easy food if no money is found on the streets and beach front.

My adventure had started and now those warm days of Molly Condron best foods were the hunger thoughts tempted and come to mind as I shelter in doorways and derelict places that became my new temporary home. This way of living I told myself a thousand times a day is only until I get onto my feet and am able to support myself. I had promised the priests especially Father Kavanagh and a few of the students who looked after me like Kevin O' Shea, Paddy Walsh, Denis O Donovan in Glenart College and my godmother Dorothy a letter when I've got myself settled and working earning my way including my nice boss at East Hill house who showed real interest in me that I would let them all know where I'm living and forwarding my digs address when I am settle so that all of them would have no need to worry about me and know I'm ok.

It so easy to talk of what you'll do and speak about your dreams that have not been tested when you are in a warm and comfortable place without having any real idea of how hard and cruel the real world really is. When I didn't have the backing of a family support machine, friends, or a job to rely on to give me a helping hand. I walked the strand and slept for hours as a way of passing the day so as not to stand out as a homeless runaway who knew no one. My accent then just of the boat was raw Irish not yet blended into the Scottish/English spoken that I did not understand and the truth be told maybe they too would have found it hard in understanding my tongue. I spent a week in St John's in Ayrshire by the sea having found no work, and knew in my heart it was time to move on and I thank God it was late July and the weather was not too bad it was summer and I reminded myself while walking along the sea front watching the waves splash onto the sands that my turn would come as my mind wander far away of thoughts to other countries hidden beyond the vastness of the blue greyish horizon that I knew existed because of Paddy's wild sea shanty stories that I still heard loud in my mind and kept alive my dreams and I would only survive if I stay true to my travel ambition.

This country called Scotland was for me my first foreign place out of Ireland, and I found it as poor and its people struggling to survive as the Ireland I left. I began to think really hard of what I must do to change the way I'm living and what option there was in my getting myself out of this predicament of no money, no work, no place to live, no friends, no family, in fact, taking drastic action to make the world know I exist.

I was learning each day like a new born baby the way to survive by the little handout given by passers-by in that it was obvious to them I was a road-stray without a home, and not to put a finer point on my situation would know from the smell of myself and my clothes that the sea water could not hide.

Every day I awoke in the same clothes as my wardrobe did not need any hangers just a shake, I had only one trouser, two shirts, a jumper, worn socks with holes a heavy pair of brown brogue, my Donegal tweed coat that was my prise possession along with the brand new suit I bought in Talbot street for four pounds for job interviews and special occasion with one white shirt as advised by Father Maurice Kavanagh I should wear when going for a job to make a good impression. I kept my interview clothes parcelled up and tied in the brown paper wrapping that I brought safely from Ireland with two holy pictures of our lady and the secret heart with an extra trouser and white shirt was all I own. I stored in the railway lock up for a few pennies until the time was ready to continue my travels in seeing the world.

How to change my dire situation and seek help was nearing fast in that I may have to give myself up to the authority as the adventure was not going according to my dream plan nor was it exciting as the dreams I dreamed in my Irish bed would be. It was not the romantic dream that as a hero I would be a winner instead here was I a hungry destitute without anyone to help and at my wit end and really feeling down in the dump and sorry for my poor little self.

The Sunday story I heard of the prodigal son were coming truly alive in my brain but I was worse off than the bible tale in that with no family in Ireland I would not have a waiting father running to meet me and prepare a feast for me, my welcome would be more or less the gardai giving me a cell and cup of tea to welcome me back. After a week I was seen the same old faces that like me were life outcast for reason of family breakup and drink addiction as no one here care whatever your circumstances that brought you to this low way of living, and with a like-minded stranger in the dry doorways for mutual comfort and help it had been security in number.

It never crossed my mind to use the church because of past dealings with the Catholic Church in Ireland I made that decision to myself as a nonstarter it would have opened a can of worm for me in them been the only real home I had known back in Ireland and at the industrial school. Worse would be my own shame of having fail on my first trip and having to crawl back to ask for help I would rather drown myself in the sea than go begging of them anything was the better option. It was by luck that I got talking to an elderly man in a café and he suggested I might try looking for work in Liverpool.

We talk about my option over a cup of tea which he bought and told me to make my way to Glasgow city and see what jobs are about there and if nothing shows within a few days don't hang around move on to Liverpool. You of course would do better if you go to Liverpool as most of the people who lived and work there are originally from Ireland and to us who know Liverpool well we called it the capital of Ireland because of the many Irish who have settle, live and work there.

Chapter 4

I was on fire and once again I was fuelled with new place names and the possibility of something turning up as faith has a queer way of changing your direction by information received, and from people who without knowing it at the time were helping me on which new road I should take as they became my watched signpost that you do not want to ignore. On the strength of that old man's advice the next day with my brown paper parcels collected I took the bus to Glasgow for under two shillings clean from a dip in the sea I went forward on my adventure in seeing the big wide world.

I arrived in Glasgow bus station on a miserable wet day and found the lock up for my brown paper parcels that for a few days would be safe until I have to move off again if no work found for that other place call Liverpool. Glasgow in some respect was like the Dublin I left grey and without colour it had a drabness that seem to pull the poor together as I walk about looking for work and a good place to hide away for a dry place to sleep when night comes. As that seems to be my daily priority as well as where I might find easy food to get by I found that you notice warm hide away quicker when you are homeless and you notice others that are in the same situation as you.

A few weeks out of Ireland and it was coming home to me that if my circumstance doesn't change then I might be better returning to Ireland and face the music even if it meant going to prison as life on the road living as a feral-bum is no fun and not anyway easy and more worst for me as an orphan who had no life skills and was not very street wise. I am badly in need of the Irish luck that so call Irish luck to change this dire situation that seem hopeless right now. Seeing the world like this is not living up in any way to my swashbuckling adventure my mind envisaged and the exciting exploit of my mentor Paddy Maher stories that still drive my dream of travel on, and burn bright in my mind as his fire in their cottage by Glenart College gate.

Not having any real understanding of money and the change from a Irish ten shilling on paying the bus fare was totally different and my handling of cash was not very good as I never had or seen more than a Irish pound note as money in my life, my total worth as I sparingly spent was now about eight shillings left of my fortune after having started out with a few weeks ago of the twelve shillings and sixpence I left Ireland with.

It does not take a genius to work out that I will be looking for good dry doorways until lodging and work are found as there is no way on earth I can afford a bed and breakfast place that the eight shilling I have left would get me three night leaving little change for small things. It was the summer of Cliff Richard and I know this from the fact that in our world then you needed the pictures to cheer you up and escape life miseries if only for an afternoon especially a wet Glasgow one the picture that was on in the picture house was called Summer Holiday which I thought this too is my first real summer holiday on my own and this here picture could be a good omen.

The poster outside the picture house was of a fresh young happy face pop star called Cliff Richard and his pals on a big red bus that parted another tuppence dwindling down my fortune to have a few hours of pleasure that I went in and took the opportunity of getting in out of the rain and while away my dream of travelling the world if only on their bus for a few happy dry hours. That picture Summer Holiday if I am really honest was my only real association with Glasgow of 1964 as it was the only happy memory against the misery of loneliest I experience in been homeless and hungry living of the street for now on two weeks was making me re-think my position if I should give up and return for one of Molly's hot cook meals that now would be well appreciated.

This first adventure of seeing the world was not living up to my over-acted brain that did not question life hard going and what the future has yet to unfold for me. I was down in the dump and my mind was playing trick bringing to life a Dickenson stories of life in Victorian days that this grey Glasgow city was without colour and poverty was ripe with no real job prospect that I could see on offer.

Glasgow was a drab wet and grey place with little work opportunity much similar to my Dublin city which I left for better opportunity and along the way hope of making my fortune that right now was looking very bleak realising nothing was about to change.

I think those nights on the streets of Glasgow where I met other young and old people whose dreams were dead as I lay down to sleep the night besides for protection, as one old saying goes birds of a feather flock together so it is with the homeless as they look out for each other with the little they have. I heard many a night their stories when they had better days and how life and circumstance change their lives without them having a say inasmuch as a marriage breakdown or one's addiction to drinking and gambling that separated them from normal society leaving them homeless without friends and family to care about them.

After a week on Glasgow streets and nothing much happening it was time to move on now that August push July away and the days were much warmer and maybe to my luck would also change as one always live in hope. That holiday film with Cliff and his pals on the big red bus travelling around Europe made up my mind that I to should be on my way and do what that old man in St John cafe had said, if nothing happening move on to Liverpool sound advice now that the few bob I had left was running low be that I only bought mugs of tea and the cheapest of sandwiches, I knew I had to make my way to Liverpool before I was totally penniless.

For all the hardship and bad-luck I found and seen it was amazing that those who have as much as me and that was nothing gave from the little they had, and in some cases their life experience was worth more to me than the morsels of bread we shared as it gave me in those dark days of wandering about this foreign country living on the street with people whose life stories are not all the same for ending up like this while my life to date was not a bed of roses eider. Others' lives I heard about were worse in that they spoke of their marriage breakdown, family abuse, having to sell themselves to make money to support their drinking and gambling habit what they sold of themselves in my naïvetés I did not then fully understand other than that what they said they did you just accepted their word for if it was nothing else you can believe it true.

My last night in a Glasgow doorway shelter and again I was told by another friendly homeless man bedding down for the night, what's a young fellow like you hanging around this horrible place, and living on the street of this city when you be better off with your own kind in that capitol of Irish people Liverpool, there's as many of your country-men and I know for sure you'd stand a better chance of work, and if all else failed, you could jump on a boat back to Ireland even if you have to work your passage to get there.

You knew that these other homeless people who gave you advice had your best interest at heart when they wanted you off the street before the street owned and destroyed you.

The poem below I had written in memory to all I met and my own time as a ground rat of many weeks living on the street when I had nothing.

Street Walker

The old coat upon his feeble frame
His blanket for warmth at night
Matted and torn for years he had worn
Was won as a prize in a fight.

His memory of love and roof overhead
Of carefree days and spendthrift ways,
Are picture now in others he sees,
A mirror of once what he had been.

His eyes sweep the ground no longer proud,
For the hope of a better day scrounge,
He stumbles and trips cut his lips
Kissing the pavement, trodden on by the crowd.

Sad eyes that show the depths of despair.
He puts out for a helping hand,
The heels of his shoes are filled with yesterday news,
Turned away from every open door.

The city's bright lights make it always twilight,
Never knowing the day from night,
Alive as a hive, as people try to survive,
While others like me are left deprived.

He steadies himself with shaking hands,
From a bottle too many the night before,
Begs his way through another day
As he's done now for twenty years or more.

Back to the main bus/train station early the next morning. Collected my brown paper parcel and with less than six bob in my pocket I was again on my way from Glasgow to Liverpool that ate up a few more shillings. This time I was feeling more upbeat at what lay ahead and my spirit too was lifted that whatever will happen I'm in God's hands. I had passed my seventeenth birthday a free boy/man and as with all birthday before they were nothing special days other than I was closer to the age where I no longer would be a ward of the Irish government.

In myself I was ready to take on this new place that many say is my best hope for finding work and if successful save some money that I may be able to continue on my travel quest in seeing the big wide world. I made my onward journey by train to Liverpool. It was a beautiful day and for some reason it looked like I had arrived at the busiest place on earth or so its seem to me for Lime street station was huge and the crowds milling about going here and there made it as if the push was by fans cramming into Croke Park on an all Ireland final day.

The station was bigger in my mind than any I knew in Ireland and yet the crowds were friendly you could hear the loud laughter and chatter of passer-by. It was as if I were back again walking down Moore Street in Dublin multiplied by four were the hawkers selling their wares are the stars. There was a happier upbeat feel about the movement and the pace in which people went about their business, and it been the height of summer and I'm seventeen having gone near on four week since I started out from Ireland I felt as with the August summer breeze something new was about to change and I could feel it maybe the Irish luck was to be found here and please God it will find me.

Amazed was I on coming out of Lime streets station I noticed a pillar-like statue of a man not as Lord Nelson that stand on O' Connell Street proud and well dress in his naval uniform that I asked a passer-by who is that up there and was told that is one from your country himself the Duke of Wellington, another one I knew nothing of or even heard about. Here was this Dublin man by the name of Wellington standing as tall on his column as did the English naval officer Lord Nelson who stand proud and tall on his column that is sighted on O Connell Street in the heart of Dublin city and a great meeting place for lover especially stranger to meet up, and known to all as the pillar.

A reversal of great men in that Wellington came from Ireland, Dublin born, and on joining the army made it to the rank of general. He beats the French General Napoleon Bonaparte at Waterloo and is thereafter England greatest hero. I was to learn more in time of this great Irishmen in that he became not only a general but the prime minister of the British Isles. For in Wellington time all Ireland was under British rule and to all intents and purposes was part of England that today only Northern Ireland has remained of what now is called the United Kingdom as the other twenty-six counties became part of what is the Republic of Ireland in 1921.

I was flabbergasted on leaving Lime street and walking aimlessly about when I saw above a big stores entrance by the name of John Lewis a full grown naked man statue that left little to God's imagination, I thought what must any decent lady out shopping having to walk by or into the shop may have to lower her eyes from seeing this most outrageous of naked poses for it left nothing to hide. This nude man was showing the world and all who passed his proud manhood and physical prowess and for the life of me I could not equate it purpose to a clothing store other than he needed to cover up.

I looked of course until my neck ached not believing such a naked statue could be publicly shown without offence and for all to see in realistic form and size when I remember that I'm now in England and this is the country I was told at school King Henry VIII of England desired to have another wife which the Holy Father in Rome forbade his royal request due to him having a wife that he broke away and made himself answerable to himself and founded his own church been unsatisfied with the pope refusal declared himself head of his country church and changed its laws to suit his amorous appetite for kingly sex.

The English church under his daughter Elizabeth did not like the Roman Catholic faith that she caused a great persecution against those who did not conform to the new protestant faith that she now has become its head. I was now among these people who I had to take care not to corrupt me as I was pre-warned by Father Kavanagh before leaving Ireland to be on my guard and not let anything get in the way of my faith and keep close by attending holy mass on Sunday as there no great respect from other than one who is true to their strong faith and belief.

August was a much warmer month and I think in some mysterious or magic way things seem to be changing be it the weather or the happy atmosphere of long summer days that brought out the best in people as opposed to inclement days I knew in grey old Dublin. Keeping time or wanting to know what time of day was never a thing I worried about as I got by without having a watch a luxury I never had owned before the age of twenty. In my life so far a watch was an expense I couldn't afford therefore time on my wrist play no part in my timekeeping for time information I would check a street clock if one was showing it face otherwise I got by as I always did knowing day is bright, and night is blackness. In my boy farming days I could tell the time by the light brightness in the day and better if the sun was in the sky that is a farmer's watch.

Those days of my youth and starting out in life of my boyhood travel a watch was not something I bothered with having never wore a watch that was beginning to be owned by the masses but wasn't a must have when I was hungry and had nowhere to live.

Although I did not know it at that time there certainly was a social revolution in motion I knew from walking about Liverpool and the different in the attitude of the young toward their elders that was more free than the young I saw in Scotland and the difference again was bigger than the young in Ireland in my days of freedom that I see here in this vibrant crazy happy go lucky city of Liverpool. The social revolutionary change was faster than a moving train that was happening, and unknowingly quick below the war population noses that complained of the young's disregards for discipline and work.

How they wore their clothes and the unkempt hair they walked out and about scruffy like as if they did not care how they look or presented themselves in the public square.

There was a buzz everywhere of a new group called the Beetles and the Rolling Stones and other breakthrough groups that ware changing the music sound. It was described by some in the media especially the political class and the establish church as very evil satanic and certainly harmful to the youth they are managing to collect as followers of this new wild craziness.

The Beetles were new and making a big splash about the music industry although there music did not appeal to me at first but the more I listened to the words of their songs the message they put out to be heard I began to understand. They moved the young in a way that was not known before in that their songs sang about freedom that in the beginning was awakening new mind to a utopia on love against the old concept of marital love that was being lay bare to enjoy by the new youth. With the aid of a new pill that was changing old mindset that girls no longer have to fear sex if like boys they take the magic pill could go the whole way with their boyfriend.

This pill changed the dynamic and gave girl a new power and protection against unwanted pregnancy from intercourse with boyfriends and protection on a one-night stand were a female might giveaway to a man met at pub, club, dance, her treasure gift.

This new pill gave the sexual revolution especially the youth love without the worry and girls craved the same freedom if they wish as boys never having to carry an unwanted child if they had unwedded sex.

My music of the day and still is today the Irish big bands and Irish country with reels thrown in rather than this new head bagging stuff. Some of the new music was beginning to enter the Irish dancehall before I left with the like of Elvis and Chuck Berry, rock and roll, and Ireland's own Elvis type the great Brendan Bowyer with his hucklebuck and his introduction of those great Elvis hip movement was the beginning of the dance change taking over in the young Irish minds from the siege of Venice, the waltz and fox-trot, added to the American dance moves of the twist and jive both very popular energetic dance workout. I saw in England a rising young Welshman by the name of Tom Jones make a music impact with a huge voice and hip moves that sent the female world wild inasmuch that he was adored by the number of knickers ladies threw upon the stage as kisses of their love. I had the opportunity to witness in 1967 Tom Jones at the Atlantic ballroom Woking and many years later at Lakeside country club in Frimley green run by the Atlantic owner and entrepreneur Bob Potter.

Liverpool was vibrant and so alive that it picked me up in that I could feel just maybe my luck could turn for the better as she love you ye ye ye was in the air and Liverpool young were crazy for the Beetles and their every new song. Their lyrics cry for change that was about to happen and the young went along willing to catch its fever that in their clothes and hair fashion they wanted to be rebellious, and push into the establishment face that the times in the words of Bob Dylan the great America singer song he sang, the times they are a changing.

The reason I believe about this epic change was the youth of the sixties had a new spring in their thinking and a new get up and can do attitude that this is our time and we want our future to go in a different direction. The rising youth felt it was time to say goodbye to those bad old days their parents and grandparents allowed themselves to be dragged down and kept down in what upper society believe was there proper place. They were a beaten people after many years of war and rations with low esteem and depression of post-war years that the young felt they needed to turn everything up on it head and sod the consequence come what may. For now it is our time and we will not be treated anymore as servile to blind obedient for we want change and we want that change now in a freedom to choose and take a new look at doing and living differently.

The depression and the greyness of life of the post-war young growing up in those bitter years of hardship and rations was the crux in why many wanted change from years of shortage and little money the young just wanted to break the dull living and feel the rising mood that was lifting spirit to something that was not yet understood and yet was happening. This change of the angry youth was breaking the slave chains of servitude that was the mentality of the men broken from two world wars, and the young of the changing sixties would never go back to their father's abeyance without question, as here was a new awakening of a freedom that had yet to know what it wanted and the young would push as far as it could go as there is a race on now to change everything, and be as outrageous that one can think of and be.

The cry around the world of change with the young was the same everywhere it timing as unpredictable as a child inside a pregnant woman growing. This unstoppable energy train of the young to where it was going and what it will be was anyone guess as it was like a roller coaster free-wheeling without a driver to a unknown destination whatever its outcome it had to be better than what has gone before. The outlandish clothes and long hair was becoming the new look. The old generation thought scruffy and the young revel in as it was their time to say in street language that we are going to be different for we are free and will do what we want as a people that no longer believe in the establishment setting out its rules for others to obey when they themselves do not live by their own strait jacket laws.

Once again I heard the old man voice in Ayr at St John café by the sea, said if nothing turn up in Glasgow don't hang around make your way for Liverpool and if all else fails you can at least catch the boat home to Dublin.

So after a few days living on the street in Liverpool I was getting by a little better than I had in Scotland be that the weather was warmer and there was more happening in this city that the thought in my head said check out the chance of working your passage back to Ireland if all effort failed in finding a job or a place to live, with little money left it seemed a better opportunity of getting home if I played my cards right and got myself clean up and spend the last of my money on a bed and breakfast. Yes I would be going home with my tail between my legs and my dream of conquering the world shatter at lease I could with hand on heart say. I had given it my best shot and after nearly five weeks of surviving on my limited wit it was becoming obvious that I would be better off with people I knew including handing myself over to the gardai/police and face whatever punishment I deserved for running away without informing the school that were still my guardian for another year.

Whatever the outcome I would be better off the streets ending this dirty scrounging around like a ground rat living on the streets for whatever crumbs and pennies that could be found. I learned the hard way and should I do this adventure again I will be better prepared knowing I need to have a lot more money and where job opportunity are especially head for the Irish stronghold like pubs, church, and clubs among my own kind that can help in the big cities like London, Birmingham, Manchester and Liverpool.

Now having made up my mind that I should return to Ireland over the next few day I took a chance and booked myself into a bed and breakfast for two night given the landlady every penny I had which I think was about three shilling and sixpence she gave me a small room with a wash bowl and she said the bathroom and toilet is a shared one that you can lock when in use.

The land lady was very nice and without any more charges she gave me a nice cup of tea and a ham and cheese sandwich which was much appreciated. I gave myself a good scrub and a bath and put my new suit on that I bought in Dublin and my new white shirt and set off for a look around of any place with a sign offering work looking clean and tidy. The landlady was very helpful in pointing me in the direction and said there are plenty of sign leading to the docks and if today is you're lucky day you might even find work there. I walk along the street making my way for the ship office to see if I could work my passage back to Dublin for free if no work could be found.

I began to prepare in my head what I might say, I tell them first I'm an orphan who ran away from Ireland five weeks ago and have been living hand to mouth on the streets without any money and finding no work anywhere, I'm very tired, and fed up sleeping rough in doorways, on the streets, and I just want to go home if there any chance of my working my passage home to Dublin, as my dream of finding work be it season work has not borne any fruit. I also thought in my mind if that fail I would tried been a stow-away and if caught I still be happy for they would hand me over to the dock police to sort out and as a juvenile runaway they would have to protect, feed, and look after me while sending me back home under escort by the port authority then handing me over to the gardai on arrival in Dublin.

I picked myself up and was again ready in my head to face head on whatever the day would throw at me for when you are at rock bottom there no farther you can fall. I walked as if I had not a care in the world as today was going to be my break or make day. Laughingly I was not ashamed anymore only hungry and as no one knew me weather I was a tramp, rich, poor, having walked the streets of St John in Ayrshire, Glasgow, and Liverpool it was an easy lesson I had learn that whatever you're doing you are on your own for nobody gives two hoots about you because no one here is looking or watching out for you.

In all reality I was just another face added to the thousands of faceless young walking around be you a stranger, a ghost, or a local lad going about his own business. Who really knows anyone going about their way and to that end who cares as long as you are not threatening in your look or attitude and up to no good or mischief making? It mid-August 1964 I'm happy in myself for the weather is great warm and everyone out and about wearing their happy faces which make me somewhat happier about my own poverty disposition, insomuch that I stroll around for hours thinking my life is grand, and so it was for those hours in my head as I watched the young girls out and about looking beautiful, carefree in their best summer clothes be that many are showing more leg than I had ever seen on girls back in Ireland on the streets or ever in my life.

Here in Liverpool the young laugh and chatter with their throwaway don't care attitude that only they know best how to shrug off when not having a care in the world as they skipped along with their friends happily knowing they belong.

In my dream head I was hoping one day this new change that is happening and the summer warm air adding to the youth wanting a new way in ditching the drab winter grey that post-war years of ration, poverty, and servitude will no longer hold them back as they break free to follow their own dreams, in some small way is matching my dream of a better life that I went in search of when I took that boat to a new future wherever it maybe believing in my dream head whatever I'm looking for would be easy to find and be ok with.

I'm seventeen years old and although I have no name for my sexual feelings that I can blame on my looking at these flighty beauties as colourful butterflies that make me feel gidish in myself. I know one thing for sure I like girls and their sweet softness that is opposite of manliness and man-smell I am in love with them all whatever their colour, height, size, curved and the hidden rest. Oh to have one as a girlfriend and know the joy of this summer day with one. I thought as my mind played a long game of want and choice of who would I spend the day with if they were candy it certainly would be down to the eyes, hair colour, curvy trim in choosing what girl-beauty I would pick.

Walking in the August sunshine window-shopping I marvelled at the beautiful and attractive display they show and how I loved and wished but could not afford anything in them lovely displays windows, as now I'm just a dreamer and like any teenager with no money I look at these new clothes that dressed the plastic statuettes on display imagining how if it was me wearing those beautiful tailor suit. For me it was a great way to pass the time and it made me think if ever the day came that I could afford to buy their new shirt and trousers or other clothes the window shops dressed and had on show I will have made it and I am rich. After a few hours of walking and having looked in a thousand window-shopping my eye caught a sign in a big open display window which said "why not join the Irish Guards today". I was fascinated by the poster and it words and the picture shown that my thoughts went racing as to what or who are the Irish Guards.

Thick as two short plank and without much knowledge of such things I only knew the gardai/police at home in Ireland and they were only refer to as the guarda so how come this big notice in the window is saying why not join the Irish Guards today this was very confusing and puzzling to me as to what this shop was selling and who were these Irish Guards that this shop was asking of men to join.

Being homeless for now on six weeks and having got by so far on my own with next to no money and finding no work made this freedom of living and travelling on my own very hard. I had been living hand to mouth on the streets using the public toilet for my daily need and washing as best I could do under the circumstances of a homeless street walker and I really had had enough. The freedom of being homeless is only good if you have plenty of money and you can eat and keep warm. I certainly would give this Liverpool city a better chance if I found a job as it was a vibrant place and my being homeless was not so bad because of the generous passer-by that gave me their odd penny for a cup of tea and toast more than I received in St John's in Ayrshire or the grey Glasgow drab streets.

It was loneliness and always feeling dirty that made up my mind in calling my penny-less days and this first adventures to an end, and the indelible smell of the street perfume on my clothes that washing could not wash out. Knowing I could return to my old boss at East Hill House who I knew would take care of me and if not there then back to Father Kavanagh who again I knew would give me his protection, food, warmth, and rest. Sleeping rough on the street begging pennies from strangers made me realise how low I had fallen and was not part of my adventure dream that money earn and saved would need to be part of my next planed adventure. Now that I have at least experience this fail dream it has made me wiser of the real pit fall in what to expect if and when I do it again.

As it was I had made a good go on my own in three different places over the last six week and as a total stranger, young and on my own, knowing no one or nothing of their ways if going home was to be in my head there was no real disgrace as I was a much wiser boy/man in my knowledge of what been homeless and living on the street was all about. Having learned money is the real key when travelling, and of course for any young Irish who have family contact this is by far a winning ticket in getting started on any new adventure in life.

One of the greatest bible stories is of the prodigal son, and this came to mind when thinking my decision to return home be that I did not have a father waiting for me. In that great book the prodigal son was able to go back home when at the end of his tether he remember how his own father look after his family and servant, and seeing the food the pigs were eating was more than he was having that made his mind up pretty quick that the servant on his father farm were treated very well, that he say to his father on his return "treat me as one of your servant and to that end I be happy." This too was my key thought in going home to Ireland and eat humble pie that for all that was wrong with my Ireland it was the place I could go back to as it was home.

My decision to go back if nothing turned up with no rich father waiting on my return I knew in my heart of hearts that I would be at least safe. Liverpool was my last opportunity for work and if that failed I would make my way back to

Ireland on the Dublin boat. Standing and looking in that window I was memorise by all the colour pictures on display that I was like the proverbial rabbit caught in the headlight and glued to the spot. With nothing else plan for that day I just stood and dreamed if I could would this be my way out as I had not a clue as yet to what this window meant and the offered in its slogan "why not join the Irish Guards today".

The words were printed in big large white letters on a colourful backdrop of Buckingham Palace and a photo of the changing of the guards. Afraid to ask who and what are Irish Guardsmen and the type of work they did that look exciting by the photos on show in the window. I must have read every word over and over again that that window was offering and look at the pictures quite confused as to how so far away here in England are they asking for young men to call in and become Irish Guardsmen. This was not Ireland and who were these people that were looking for Irish men to join them.

My thought went back to Ireland and the Garda Sichcana (Irish police) thinking to myself that my education and knowledge about Ireland was really very scant and if this shop was a recruitment shop as part of an overseas office for Irish boys in Liverpool to have a career as a garda in Ireland I never would have believe if not seeing it for myself. After all I have led a close life and what in all truth did I know about my own Ireland and what went on in how people in general got their jobs.

I knew little about anything other than the places I had been to work and my godparent's place in Dublin. Every day since leaving Artane and working in all-weather as a farmer, gardener, a shepherd, I watched day by day people who I learn lesson from in their different jobs that I had work with and more importantly taught me how to behave.

My time on the street and the good advice people gave me especially those in no better a situation who still cared as they hope I would do well and who share what little they had even if sometime it left them with nothing. The shop window picture were of men in red coats, blue trouser with a red stripe down the outside, wearing huge big furry black like hat with a bluish plume wearing a golden chain below their lips on their chin, and wearing very shiny black boots or shoes. There were other picture of big green tanks and men wearing greenish clothes as if they were camellias camouflage to blend into the woods as Robin Hood men wore in the forest when hiding from the soldier of the Sheriff of Nottingham.

I don't know how long I stood reading, digesting and looking through that amazing window when a big uniformed person from the shop came out and started talking to me about what I was looking at and ask me about the interest I was showing of their display in his shop window. I told him I don't know anything about this or ever see anything like this before, and was in all clueless as to what they were selling and why are you looking for Irish Guardsmen.

He said why don't you come in and have a cup of tea and biscuits and I tell you more about the life in the Irish Guards. The offer of a cup of tea and biscuit was just too good to refuse. I myself he said have been an Irish Guardsman for many years and this shop as you call it is in fact a recruitment office in which I and my staff offered young men like yourself an opportunity to see the world and make a fine career in the army.

After I had my cup of tea and biscuits he started asking question about where I came from and how old was I and a lot of other question about where I went to school, where does your family live, and how I came to be in Liverpool, with no reason to lie to him about myself it wasn't a problem as I had made up my mind if nothing change today I was going to return to Ireland as soon as possible and make my way to Wicklow or Athlone where I knew both places would receive me well.

I really was on my knees at this stage and not cut out for this adventure of seeing the world with no money, no clothes, and no proper contact to direct me on my way. Having survived the last six weeks on my own and with the help of others I met in the same gutters who told me to go Liverpool as my best opportunity for work for a young Irishman. I made it to Liverpool after weeks of rough living on the streets and as nothing had gone right from the beginning I was now at my wit end at this sleeping on the ground and huddling inside doorways for warmth at night, as sleeping rough had got to me and if prison was on offer with bed and food I would as sure as hell right at this moment give it a go.

I told the man all he wanted to know about myself and my limited education as he mentioned I would have to do some form of exam to know if I can read and write not two skills I excelled in as my handwriting was rubbish to read and worse than a doctor signature to decipher. I could read as best like a seven year old hence my taking so long to understand a little of your window display. He told me his name and that he is call Sergeant Smylie and that this was his name and rank in the Irish Guards and that it was the best regiment in the British Army, it may well be but who was I at seventeen that knew nothing of the world or anything about anyone's army that I could agree or disagree with him.

He then told me that if I was accepted on passing the entrance exam I might one day be like him a sergeant in the Irish Guards. Sergeant Smylie was very impressive in stature and smartness and vocally precise in that his enthusiasm show through in his happiness in been an Irish Guardsman and all that he said the regiment did for him. I was so impressed by his whole manner and him been very kind to me an unfortunate boy/man as I was then who dream of seeing the world was near an end.

Sergeant Smylie was a very nice person in that he knew from the beginning I was a probably a runaway by the shear fact of his Sherlock Holmes deductions and his fatherly knowledge of young men that pass in and out of his work through the years. He knew too if he handles this situation right today I would be added to his list and be on my way as a new Irish Guardsman to the guard's depot in my becoming an Irish Guardsman.

We talk about my life and why I left Ireland who would miss me and who should know that I'm all right who could vouch for me in Ireland and be able to prove who I say I am. From the outset we got along well as he told me how the regiment got started and that it was a tribute to others the like of me that came from Ireland over the decades and fought for the queen and her country.

This was a bit confusing for me as I had never known anything about Irishmen going to any war other than the history of the 1916 rebellion and our freedom won against the English in 1921, or any other war that Ireland had been in was not in the history book of my days in school not that I learn much for I spent my school days milking and looking after cows and pigs from twelve years old on the industrial school farm.

Not having a regular family like many did in Ireland I had no one that I could shout about that had gone and left in emigrating to England or any other place around the world like Canada, Australia, and America, it left me with no first-hand experience of any family hero that had fought in any war or for that matter ever left Ireland to work that I could pitch from. Other than my friend Paddy Maher who had sailed the seven seas and his stories of the places he seen and the culture of those people and places he visited while a merchant seaman and Father Maurice Kavanagh the quiet man from China missionary I knew no others that had ever been out of Ireland.

Sergeant Smylie could tell that my education was not much as I'd never done much schooling that would be worth talking more about for I had no certificate of any kind to show that I stayed in school learning until I was sixteen and what level in education that I achieved. The fact I could write my name was a plus and the only plus for beside that my handwriting was illegible and the signature just a bad scribble. Sergeant Smylie then got down to been serious and told me that I could from today be a paid up member of Her Majesty queen regiment the Irish Guards forth of foot and no longer would I be alone, as in the Mick's as he kept calling the Irish Guards which is a family regiment should you sign today you are one of us for as long as you live.

For the first time in my life I was truly elated bubbling inside that probably all he was saying was too good to be true that I found it hard to control my thoughts for if this opportunity fell apart it would be a serious hard knock. I could hardly believe my ears that for the first time in my life I was going to belong to a very large family. Telling me that I would see the world was all too much that my head was in a right old spin I felt my spirit climb above the clouds that I was so happy. I could have cry for joy as my dream of seeing the world was at my fingertip and the travel I have dreamed of could actually start today.

My life up to now was horrible except for the months I spent in Glenart College in county Wicklow, and the eight weeks in Athlone area. I was now in England been told by this father figure by the name of Sergeant Smylie that from today if I sign up I would no longer be alone but a member of a close and strong family. I couldn't wait to sign it was a dream come true not only having a family but seeing the world to boot for free.

As with all good things and opportunity there is a but first there was an immediate obstacle in that I was not the correct age and I would need a sponsor because I was only seventeen years old and the sergeant pointed out keenly you would not be able to sign for the army today without a sponsor while under eighteen. You need to be eighteen or over Sergeant Smylie said a few times to sign on your own, to join the British Army as an adult soldier you must be eighteen years or above. Sergeant Smylie was a very smart cookie and a real man of the world who knew of my dilemma that if I left the chance of my coming back were very slim if I bother to come back for in his book an Irish man was a real prize for the Irish Guards as it gave status the more blood that was a hundred percent rather than fifty or twenty-five percent, enriching the regiments Irish-ness.

He was quite impressed with my quick thinking mind in that I propose an, if, to the sergeant, "why don't I pretend you never saw me" and I left walking back in again an hour or so later as if for the first time in order to fulfil a life time wish of seeing the world.

It was because of Sergeant Smylie friendliness and warm manner that I returned and the prospect of belonging to a real family for the first time in my life was a chance I just could not miss. Having lived rough for a few weeks it was time I did something for me and as it had been my birthday a few weeks ago this joining the Irish Guards would be a great gift to myself and truly the best brilliant present that would answer all of my birthday wishes in one.

Sergeant Smylie had been very straight and courteous to me and instead of sending me packing because of my age and with no reference of family to vouch for me he treated me as an equal, and as a person who really was in need of help without my asking for it. He welcomed me on my return as if it seeing me for the first time going through the recruiter patter learned by heart and offer a warm welcome and would I like something to drink asking can I help you sir. Is there anything that we can do for you today sir, replying I would like to join the Irish Guards and see the world.

Chapter 5

Again we started all over with my listening to his prepared spiel that recruiter knowledge know by heart in encouraging and making exciting all the reason why any young man wouldn't want to join the army and make it a career with opportunity of bettering themselves in discipline and life skills, the opportunity of promotion through the rank if it turn out to be the place you want to stay and most important of all to travel and see the world for free is open for any young person that want a good military career.

When the sergeant asked the question of me why do you want to join the Irish Guards, I said I have come all the way from Ireland to be an Irish Guardsman. I lied hoping the good lord would forgive me when I next go to confession after all the sergeant did not know me from Adam and as I was quite big and strong lad for my age without anyone knowing my real age other than the school that I had been a prisoner in I was not going to put the school down as a referee. It would make no difference to my godparent if they were told or wrote to and notify by the army that there god-son had join the British Army as an Irish Guardsman.

They were my only Irish contact in Ireland that I knew who would give a credible account and I knew would stand by my decision right or wrong. I was happy to lie about my age in becoming a man that could sign on freely into whatever the Irish Guards did. My godparent I believed would give their consent willingly and would sign any papers saying that I was eligible and that there was no reason on earth why he should not join the Irish Guards if that what he want to do.

My godparent knew my real reason of escape and the fact that Ireland held nothing more for me and they understood my leaving the horror of Ireland past behind me and those days in Artane under the Christian Brothers harsh brutal regime as a means of going forward in my dream of travel and wanting to see the world and to make good of myself. My godparent would think my joining the Irish Guards was the best start any young fellow could do and if he wanted to be a soldier in the army that was brilliant, and so it was for me too.

Changing direction and blanking out my orphan days to go forward with my new birthday I be part of a new family called the Mick's as this was a well-known nickname for Irishmen as was Paddy outside of Ireland. But to be honest both names were new to me for nicknames as a shelter boy who knew little about life of the Irish abroad and what they were call was also new to me.

I was ignorant of the simplest things and totally naive to most and everything that many Irish knew and took as general knowledge while I was learning little things that amazed and excited my mind like a newborn baby learn to walk and run I was learning at seventeen how to be independent in life skills absorbing all new information I thought would enable my own knowledge to understand this new life as an independent free person standing on his own two feet.

I had no fear if the army were to contact my godparent letting them know what I had done it would be good for me as it would let them sleep in the knowledge that I am safe and well that after six weeks away alone and not been able to make contact with anyone that I promise to write was now no longer a worry as now I had in my head this big news that if all goes well today in joining the Irish Guards they will all be glad to hear that I am safe and well, and all would agree I made a good choice in choosing a life in the army a great starting point for any young man especial an homeless orphan who needed a family and home.

With little information about my life of my real family to offer those who would ask question of this and that outside the school the knowledge I acquire since knowing my godparent family I was able to use as my own true family life story that I fed from. Before I left Ireland I now know it was a God blessing my asking their permission to use their home as an address of contact should there be any request of referee or family permission needed in respect of my character. My godparent did not mind my using them as a contact address if any person of authority wanted information about my character or require references, they said I should use them.

It was that day at the recruiting office I decided I might as well be eighteen years of age within reason that others would believe I was as an orphan. I really had no one to disprove or prove otherwise for truthfully I had no real idea how old I was other than what the Irish state say I was on leaving school a year before when they told me now that your sixteen years of age you are eligible to leave the school and be employ earning your own living to that end only did I know I was sixteen.

The brothers gave no information of my family history or what education I had acquire under their care other than a piece of paper with my date of birth and the date I came to Artane from Rathdrum Convent eight years before in 1955, and with nothing else wrote on it other than the name of my new employer I was sent to work on his farm six miles outside of Thurles town in County Tipperary.

In those days travel and following up information was terribly slow that people like me were able to slip under the proverbial radar. I only had the school's word that I was sixteen when I was released with no paper document or Irish identity card on leaving the prison school a year before. I never knew anything about proving yourself to anyone or where to get a birth certificate nor was I handed any official document to say who I really am. I knew nothing about me in so far as how or why I ended up in the care of the state and church nor told if I had any living family, no information whatsoever on been release at sixteen that might be of interest in wanting to know and care for me if directed that way by the state now I'm no longer a burden in their care but release as a young man/boy with farming skills after years of working on the school farm to stand me in good stead as was the case with most boys who had not been claimed in those long years of enforced incarceration that having been rejected by one mother and family, and hidden away as a ward of the state until eighteen years old.

After an hour and half of question and tests I had done all the paper work I had signed on and was now excited my insides were bursting with joy and happiness that now I did not have to fall on my sword and return as a failure no longer was I worry about handing myself over to the garda or the authority over my little indiscretions with the farmer that it was not worth mentioning at this time as that would have put the kybosh on my ever going forward in my new adventure as an Irish Guardsman.

Today I gave myself a new birthday present as I go forward with my new mind, my new start, my new birthday, no longer am I an orphan, with my new family the Micks making today the best day of my new life, I no longer had to go and check out my return to Dublin for as of today I'm on my way to seeing the world for free thank you very much Sergeant Smylie.

This birthday present that I gave myself was all down to a lucky chance and that wonderful caring man, Sergeant Smylie who prompted me well, and gave me the opportunity of a new start in life a thanks he never know how grateful many years later it was for me. I got through the recruiter examination paper and the little paper work over a few hours and was ask to wait in the office while they finished up their side of my paperwork in joining the Irish Guards my life was taking a new twist, in now I was going to be an Irish Guardsman and the regiment I was going to be a part off were at my joining in Germany, another new name that stirred my onward travelling thoughts of where is Germany. Having no great schooling I was becoming aware that life and meeting new people like Sergeant Smylie were my new teachers who were educating me in the ways of the world and their genuine interest in me made me happier than I had ever been.

It amazing that in all my years to date I had not an inkling about one of the biggest event that occurred and ended just two years before I was born and the amount of people who had die, and the atrocities that the war made possible on both sides of the world to human being and the denial of their war crimes of those that were part of it. Because Ireland as a country took no part in the war I still find it bad that we children were not taught the cause of it happening and why the horror of it cruelty towards the Jews and the disable including those the state believe different were on mass killed, and class as less than nothing, which for a boy like me and the fact I was nothing to anyone until now came home in my new learning as each new day turned.

Being vulnerable as I was without any support was notably observed by Sergeant Smylie who took upon himself to look after me as if I were one of his own children, his asking me to sit and wait was him working out a strategy to make me safe and keeping me well till my train to the Guards' depot goes from Liverpool in a few weeks. This new man/boy on the twenty of August nineteen sixty-four had signed a contract to serve in the Irish Guards for twenty-two years with the option of release or to purchase his discharge whatever those word meant then which I let fly over my head. I was hearing other words like family, job, and will received money as of today and if after three years or worst get thrown out of the Guards' depot if I could not past the army probation period another word I knew not it meaning.

Having signed on the dotted line for the Irish Guards not really understanding all this queen and country stuff of England and United Kingdom and her other territories bit, for me at that moment it was a case of belonging and having food and shelter provided as I was on my knees and with no family, no friends, no money, and dog tired of living on the street over the last six weeks which have taken their toll on me. In that I was a real down and out making do with what I could find on the street eating what the vermin rats did not want and was at my wit end to what I have to do in order to change my circumstance for the better. This was the best answer to my daily prayers and the start of that Irish luck often mention that is accredited to the Irish.

Sgt Smylie was as a father figure and very wise and ahead of his game he saw I needed a minder and a proxy brother until my call from him to make my way to the Guards' depot training centre in Pirbright Surrey is what he told me. It was as if luck would have it that there was on that same day another fairish head looking young man that too was keen on joining the Irish Guards and who was to me my own street dodger as in that film Oliver twist by the name of Eddie King and it was to his charge that the recruiter sergeant made responsible for my welfare until we got our rail warrant for Pirbright in Surrey wherever that is.

I left the recruiting office with Eddie who had a world of knowledge and it did not take him long to know that I was inexperience about life on any street and in almost everything he asked, like have I got a family, a girlfriend back home. I told him about my foster family and what information I had picked up over the years when I visited my godparent about their children who became my adopted brothers and sisters, how I work for the priests over the last year and of people and places I knew about not much for an new eighteen year old who had no real account of life in Dublin and never as yet had a real girlfriend waiting for me in Ireland.

Eddie had known and done lots in his city of Liverpool and him a proper raw product of his world, and his knowledge of how to get the best out of anything even if he had to make something up on the spur of the moment came natural. All of this was the start of how my life with Eddie started and how the way forward was going to be in future. I would never tell anyone of my time in Artane or about my short working life for the Scrooge farmer the school made me work for and what I did to him that made me run and escape from his charge, that chapter of my life to date would be confined to my mind vault and would remain locked away forever as a time now best forgotten.

Eddie was a great laugh and a really good friend to be with, in that he said right from the off let's go he said shouting and laughing out loud we are in the army now and let go for a liquid lunch and a Liverpool special chip and butty sandwich curtesy of course of our newfound mother and father Sergeant Smylie from the piggy bank of the Irish Guards. I had great fun with Eddie and the antic we got up to were big kids stuff him been a real Liverpool lad who was at ease on the street and his knowledge of how to circumvents small problem of getting a free meals or extra money from the employment exchange to tie us over until we could make do on our own was real magic and for an eejit like me a real eye opener, and the art of his getting money for doing nothing on a thingy bank the unemployed call the dole.

On seeing how Eddie operated may me wish that as a real dim-wit if I had a quarter of his street knowledge and wit then the weeks I spent living rough would have been easier to handle as he knew how to con a meal and draw money from a sort of free hand out bank call the dole that those in need can received money if they don't have work or as Eddie call it collecting the social all this was over my head and one I could make no sense of as to how it all work. I knew nothing of these things that Eddie said if you don't use it, you lose it, and only goes to waste as it is there to be had and you got to oblige and take what on offer especially as it was free.

This was Eddie's city and he knew all the moves in getting about and how to survive without costing himself or me a penny. Never in my wildest dream would I have thought half of the things that Eddie got up to and did without blushing like him signing on the dole because at the time he had no work. Eddie looked after me for the next week or more calling at my digs in Green Lane which the army were taking up the slack and paying the land lady who by all account was a very good friend of Sergeant Smylie.

The landlady washed the little clothes I owned and pressed my four pound suit for the journey to the depot, all in all life was better when sharing with another of about the same age as Eddie was in having fun and looking forward like me to seeing the world. Doing something exciting was important and better than hanging around the street scrounging a living or in Eddie's case creating fun for the hell of it, and yet my seeing what Eddie got up to for a laugh was no different than the thousands other city kids that Liverpool made and were well balanced and happy.

In my mind there was a little bit of remembering the pals I use to play around with in Artane Industrial School like the McHugh brothers Gerry and Bubbles, Snowy Ryan, Colm and Seamus Rock, Francis McDonnell who I thought was my brother because of our same surname, Danny O' Keefe, Timothy And Michael Flynn and Billy flood just a few of the boys I play and laughs as a kid for eight years in the school that been with Eddie brought back to mind and made alive. How I missed them and so cruel it is that none of us have any whereabouts of each other as on my leaving the industrial school at sixteen you are again cut off and punish by the force separation of no forwarding address or information to your school friends of where you are been sent to work but just cut off unable thereafter to keep in touch with each other to keep alive your childhood friendship forever.

Liverpool was a new awaking in the way its people behaved and I understood a little why it was said this place is the capitol of Ireland, because the Liverpuddlion have a similar humour and way about them that the Irish craic was everywhere and if you close your eyes and listen bar their accent you could be mistaken and think you are back in Dublin. It was also noticeable to me how they look out for each other and family in their tight knit community.

The street noise had a happy sound you could hear it in the air, and the change in the young you could feel was ineffable that there was no stopping this runaway train they drove without tickets and ride through to its end destination flying on its great high. The young wanted to be free and make a different life letting this new change find its own way with its no care attitude that said let's see where it takes us.

There seemed to be a positive atmosphere with all that was happening overnight, the music, the street fashion, the new looks, the new scheme of hire purchase, buy now pay later, opening a world of have anything you want now and pay on the never, never, not understanding these things of how people could only get credit if they have an address and a sponsor like a priest or a professional person to sign for them. I received word from Eddie that I would be making my way to Brookwood station in Surrey and from there on foot to the guard's depot in a couple of days' time, I was sad and yet happy in that I would be going on my next trip with a sense of purpose and a reason to be leaving Liverpool to a family I was looking forward to knowing and be part of.

This set me thinking if there was anything I had not worked out to my life storey for now I would be meeting many other men that would also be as Mick brothers for life, and be like Eddie was when we first met and our getting to know each other by those intimate questions of family and the usual where do you come from, how many sisters have you got, and how pretty are they the usual get to know you hundred question that when answer is not spoken of again.

The one question that always ask how come you join the Micks and what you knew about them that made you sign on. Most recruits into the Micks came by route of its own recruitment office firmly established in Liverpool making it fertile ground for Micks that had and a father or brother that serve in the regiment and still do. Question I myself would now ask as each day I was learning the way of the real world and thank to the time spent with Eddie and his easy manner of a street wise grown up I too learned to have for the first time in my life a true friend in the years ahead our friendship would mature and strengthen and no matter what the future hold he would remain a true friend for life.

Sergeant Smylie assigning Eddie as my first Mick brother/friend was an astute move and one that made my waiting time in Liverpool the best time that the weeks of roughen it were long in my pass and no longer bother me. My perseverance paid off as now I have a true friend and in the words of Sergeant Smylie the Micks are a family, and true to its name I enjoyed this newfound brother who was learning me in the way of the street survival ways in a strange land that would stand me well no matter what city I went to or came from.

This Mick brother Eddie was Sergeant Smylie way of teaching me to trust others in making me aware about having a family member and one's roll in it, and the great reliance one has to have in any family especially trust in your brothers as it is this that will saved your life if you show them the same commitment in any situation of need that you can be relied on to do what is right when either back is against the wall. I knew that from now on my imaginary family and their way of life must become mine and the story I first gave of myself to Eddie would be the same and as real from now on with no diversion from that truth.

Leaving Liverpool was sad as it was the place that found me loss and now gave me hope that my dream of seeing the world truly came alive and in this new job as an Irish Guardsman my dream of seeing the world is near on realise. I received my rail warrant from Eddie and he was asked to explain to me how and where I get to my destination and what changes and places I should watch out for. Especially he said on arriving in London where it will be crowded and anyone not familiar with as I was not could easily get lost, and missed catching there connecting train to the guards' depot in Surrey.

My big day arrives and I was having a last cup of tea with Eddie in Lime Street Station going over once again the route and were I need to take care before I see him in a few days as he not travelling until the Monday as he wanted to spend his last weekend before making his way to the guards' depot into the army with his family and friends at a goodbye party.

I said my goodbye to Eddie at Lime Street Station and I must confess I felt terrible lonely going on my own as I had got use to hanging out with Eddie as every day we had a laugh which cemented our brotherly friendship as if we never known another way. I was sad leaving Liverpool for over the last two weeks I had experience the most fun and a fast growing up that as a young man I no longer look at myself as a boy because now I'm in the army and been with Eddie made me appreciate what having a brother really meant. I was no longer alone and it taught me the meaning of having a genuine friend, that brought back vivid memories of friends I was missing from my days in Artane Industrial School who like me were out in the world on their own having to make the best of what life has to offer and to learn on the hoof how to survive after their time incarcerated within the state/church walls.

I was feeling a little bit scared and yet on a big high as I have a rail ticket and was on my way were I was wanted and in my mind if something was not going right, I was told to make for the transport police and ask them for help giving them the information that I am just over from Ireland and looking for my connecting train in getting myself to the Guards training depot in Pirbright Surrey.

The army warrant was a great way to travel as you felt important belonging to an organisation even it at this time you knew not it full meaning of what lay ahead, and in my case ignorance was truly bliss.

The train journey from Liverpool to Euston station London was about five or six hours and I could not believe they had food and drink for sale in a service carriage in which you could buy a train meal or just stand in the bar and get merrily happy as was to be a journey I would make in the years ahead going on battalion leave. Many times with members of my Micks family going home to the north of England or in my case to Liverpool dock and onto the boat to Dublin to see my godparent and from there I went in search of my real and biological family that after many visit on army leave I found came from Roscommon in the west of Ireland.

I made it to London Euston Station and from there I enquired on where and how I should get to this Brookwood station, I was told I would need to go to Waterloo Station on the other side of London and that I could get there easily if I use the underground train totally confuse and knowing I'm Irish I thought how can you travel underground. It all became clear as I watch and saw the moving stairs that took you down with the many thousands of people that travel that way every day I was thinking to myself that never will I get used to these moving stairs that went into lit tunnels and for want of a different name an underground city as I saw more people milling about in there than went to Gaelic football matches in Croke Park.

London was fascinating and vibrant in what I could tell from the short time of what I saw of it in be-between two major station and the crowds that cram together like sardines or as busy ants going to and fro up and down on them moving stairs, and in and out of the train warren buried below the ground. I have to be honest the first time I use the moving stairs I was frighten and could not fully understand how it all work and the speeding trains that went through dark tunnel as if moving inside a large underground cemetery with its human rabbits that ran about from one tunnel to another.

It was late on that Thursday evening when I decided to stay the night in Waterloo Station and continue my journey the next day on a morning train when it would be better for me to start out in morning light rather than arrive late evening and nobody knows you're arriving.

Little did I know about the army been a twenty-four hour a day job and had I had arrived in the late evening after dark the army would have been ready for me as I was one of many new recruits it received daily in which the army trained to be a fully qualified guardsmen soldiers.

Train station are great places you could hang out without being noticed as homeless or for that matter a lay about tourist waiting for a later train that fifty-nine years ago the security in the station was not under the eye of armed police. Then there was no closed circuit television and the George Orwell world of 1984 that you see today was not yet a reality. You could lounge around sit and watch travellers coming and going and in itself watch life unnoticed without been approach as to what your business is.

Unlike today were the railway security police ask question such as where are you from and the blind obvious question that station security ask where you are going. And if there not satisfied they go for the jugular question what are you doing hanging around in this station that after all it is a public place scaring you to move on.

But security is the byword of today because of much tension and retaliatory grievance from the days of IRA bombing in the seventies through to the nineties and the treats from countries invaded by the superpower to eradicate an ideology that not tolerated by western powers against countries like Afghanistan Iraq, Iran, Libya and their unjust standby of the Palestinian question and people since the 1967 war and Israel's illegal occupation since that has become a thorn in the side of the west of the treatment they know and see is wrong, yet say nothing to change the Israeli rule of taking and given nothing to a people they treat badly and really should not after the brutal treatment they underwent in the war as a people maltreated that they do now to another themselves must consciously see is totally wrong.

I passed that night waiting on a bench as a laid about tourist with a destination to go to and not a street bum looking for a roof over his head. I was dry and warm and I could use the station facilities for free in cleaning myself up before catching my Brookwood train and buy myself a strong mug of tea a toasted sandwich before catching my train to begin my new future in the army.

Chapter 6

I caught the train for Brookwood Friday morning and not seeing the first-class sign, and not understanding the train warrant as to which class ticket I have to sit in I found myself jumping into a six person empty carriage as they were in those days of the pull slam doors, and sat myself down. When a big portly gentleman got on board who was wearing a pinstripe suit which I never heard the word pinstripe before I would have just said suit as in my childhood all men wore suit be they different colour or style I had not a clue about this gentleman who had a blueish suit with a short coat under the other that I was to learn later is call a tree piece when a waistcoat is added and worn.

The word suit was said without any reference as to it style or pompous trade naming and he was also carrying a black umbrella and a funny black bowler hat that I often saw in the Laurel and Hardy films I wanted to laugh but did not in case he take umbrage at me been an eejit and certainly I do believe he would not have seen the joke.

I learn later that such order of dress was fashionable with city bankers and gentlemen in the city of London as well as officer in Her Majesty services, and city worker in or around London. It was a type of uniform worn by the establishment and those working in government and of course army officer on duty not in military uniform as a civilian order of dress code.

PHILIP ANTHONY McDONNELL

I got into conversation with this stranger who smiled and did not mind as I told him of my intended future that I am on my way to the Guards' depot and that I hadn't got a idea what to expect but that this would be a new start for me and that I was looking forward to what lay ahead as a new challenge in my young life. This person was very nice and he agreed with me that the army was a good career move and a very good place for any young person wanting to make something of himself. He knew a lot about the Irish Guards and told me that the Irish Guards had a great reputation as fighting men making the regiment I was joining he said to be one of the military finest fighting machine.

At my stop at Brookwood he too got out and because I had be-friended him, he ask if I would like a lift to the guards' depot as he was going that way. I was more than impressed as the person driving him had a smart black car beautifully clean and the driver was equally smart in a press grey suit. I was so green that I did not even know what you call a manservant who drove his master about.

He opened the side door for my new train friend who sat in the back of the vehicle while I was placed in the seat opposite the driver. Not much was said by the driver other than yes sir to me when I asked him a question as to how much a car like this would cost. He told me that it was not his and to own one was way beyond what he could afford with a force smile stopping the motorcar at the entrance of the guard's depot.

The driver told me to go over to the guardroom and report myself to the on duty police sergeant who would direct me by way of the receiving room. I got out of the shining black motorcar after thanking the rich gentleman and made my way over to the guardroom with my brown paper parcels under my arms when the sergeant smartly pull in his feet and gave me a welcome salute before I could ask him where I should go as a new starter of the Irish Guards. He waited until the car drove away and ask what had I just ask, I repeated which way is it for me to go to the receiving room as was told to me by the rich man driver. He went berserk and the vein on his neck bulge to near bursting with a litany of expletive and names he called me and other words I never heard before flew out of his mouth as to who did I think I was. His screaming words and expletive could be heard by all in the guardroom and miles around.

This ranting when on for a while as to don't you know who that was in the car that brought you here, I said, I did not know, No we just met on the train and that he was very nice gentleman that offer me a lift to here because I had not a clue to where here was. To which more expletive follow that I will certainly in future not be as clueless as to where here is in the future. I told the screaming sergeant nervously that I had this lift given to me because I had got into conversation with that kind gentleman and I told him of my reason to be going to Brookwood to join the Irish Guards which impressed him, but not the screaming guards' depot police sergeant, which I said was his reason for dropping me of at the guardroom entrance.

Well I can tell you he said with another mouthful of repeated lashing of loud expletive that I'm certainly not impressed with you been any sort of Guardsman Irish or otherwise. As to whom he is and what he does for work he never said we were both stranger who met on the train and other than that I don't know him. I never before saw him in my life and what he did for a job he never said or told me. Well let me enlighten you stupid so and so but much more angry and different, his words were limited in that he only knew bad words and many I never heard before as he splashed my face with spittle and hot breath.

It was then he told me that the gentleman as you so called him was the guard depot commander and his name is and don't you ever effing forget it as he spitted more into my face Lieutenant Colonel Scott- Barrett of the Scot Guards, and reiterated again with more expletive that at no time was I to be seen not moving my arms and feet unless at a speed of a hundred and eighty paces a minutes.

The good police sergeant decided that my entry to the receiving room should be as good as the lift by the guards' depot commandant driver that he had one of his regimental police corporal rift me to the music of loud angry shout of left, right, left, right, said so fast, that my feet were unable to touch the ground at the speed he called out that I must have look worse than a waddling duck out of water on dry land.

A police sergeant giving away a free salute to a nobody like me was what made him mad and my having a lift from the depot commanding officer is what really got to him. No way in a month of Sundays would an officer in the guard's lease of all the depot commander in the mind of the police sergeant give a free loader without a case carrying all he own in two brown paper parcel a lift and to that end himself given me a smart salute is what made him madder and hot as hell.

I often think in hindsight that the guard depot police sergeant on my arrival was not gifted with any Irish charisma and gift of the gab as it was I who had the lift that in a million years would never be offered to him, because faith was with me that day and what happen was meant to be that I and the guards' depot commandant through honest conversation on that train were at ease with each other, and his generosity

I fully believe in offering me a lift to the guards' depot showed genuine kindness on his part in given me a lift as a future Guardsman in the Irish Guards.

In the receiving room the duty sergeant went through my life history confirming again all I told the recruiter sergeant who signed me on that this now was all about the nitty gritty of myself, who I am, what am I about, where do you come from, who do I have at home that would vouch for me, the army could approach of my joining without any permission if they wish to do any background check on what is now for their military record.

What relation or family name that could be contacted seemed to be an army priority in as much that the army would make its own check as to my eligibility in having joined the army of my own free will, and had I the right to do so. All was under threat if my storey could not stand up on its own and it was another test to my new age and my godparent not saying anything different to what I have now said.

I had just turned seventeen a few weeks ago and with no parent to stand by what I said my chances of staying would have ended that weekend if found out. If that was to happen I knew that the police sergeant would be only too willing to show me the way out with a little help from his eloquent used of words that trip of his tongue so easily he would have found great delight in sending me on my way with a few choice words that all would know I been found under age and kick out before I even got started.

I have to thank that wonderful Sergeant Smylie for taking me to the side and going over the in and out of my new birthday and my reason of why I wanted to join the Irish Guards. Thanking him again for his foresight in helping me an orphan boy who had been through the mill of state industrial school and farm work whose need to travel the world and get away was what most young person with dreams wanted to do, and the army by its nature is a great starting point in travelling and seeing the world for free, at the point of doing only what the army require.

The few weeks waiting after I joined the Irish Guards in Liverpool gave me a chance to tell my godmother about my new birthday as to not be eighteen there was no way I could have signed up on my own, so for future reference here is my army birthday the twenty-six of July 1946 that may need authenticating if the army write as I know they will on question of birth and family as quietly advised. Over the next few hours we went through all the medical and other check that were necessary for the army to be thorough on whom they enlisted and that they have all the correct information in written form. Because of my church upbringing I had no idea about any document that could prove to anyone of where I was born and really prove who I am.

I had no real knowledge of proving who I am myself never mind anyone else, as Plato once said "I think therefore I am", and that believe it or not in 1964 was as much proof of by been here that I am, and because I can think, therefore I exist.

For now everything was going honky dory I have just passed through the reception centre and am on my way to where I will be billeted for the duration of my training which I'm told will be about twenty-four weeks. And if successful I would then join my battalion which at this time is presently station in Germany, and are due back within a few months and will be stationed at Chelsea Barracks London. I was taken with some other that I notice spoke like foreigners to me in that their accent even though it was English of sort was quite confusing to my ears that knew no other tone than the Irish brogue of different counties. Here were men from

Wales, London, Birmingham and Liverpool are known as scoucers which Eddie said he was. Understanding each other was another part in getting on as a squad, a bit like Pentecost when the Holy Spirit descended upon the apostle with fire off tongue that they spoke in different tongue as I heard my new recruit brothers.

The guards' depot is a cocktail of mixed young men from all part of the United Kingdom that I had never knew existed or heard speak in my life who after being process and trained by their regiment they have sign up to be in. I was enrolled into the Irish Guards, and the training squad I was put into was a mixed of Irish and Welsh guards recruit platoon. We were taken to our lines and it was a type of prefab building in the shape of a box that I now remember looking back on as the trained soldier told us all was of a spider design. We enter and there were four big rooms that the corridor in the shape of a plus sign that the room's front door acted as your cull de sac at their respective end and above each door was a name pertaining to a battle honour the regiment had won its Victoria Crosses at.

As with everything we would do from now it was all about the Irish Guards history and how my joining as young new recruit would keep alive the survival and upkeep of the regiment great past by maintaining an attitude of ongoing service in the vain of those that we follow.

I was by far the youngest in that new squad of Sergeant Mick Kinane who himself was a son of an Irish Guardsman that had died in World War Two and was adopted by the Irish Guards as I heard later on in my career that took care of him and his mother in Dublin. Sergeant Mick Kinane was known to all as Mick short for Michael but in the Micks he was simply named Mick synonymous to his father regiment that he loved, and was born into.

Mick Kinane was known as an Irish Guardsman through and through so much that he lived and breathed everything Irish Guard from his birth until the day he could stand as his father had as a proud Irish Guardsman he in all and every sense of the word embody the true Micks spirit. Life in the Guards' depot from day one was regulated and every hour of your day was timed and work. For me it was as if I was back in Artane with the Christian Brothers other than the army routine was a lot more fun, and the black clothes that the brothers wore was swap for a soldier mixture of khaki and camouflage green. For many away from home for the first time and living with another twenty men in a dormitory like room was a new experience and not easy to get used to as with all the other getting used to that your privacy of toilet and showers is no longer an individual private man thing you just had to get used to many sharing in those private matters.

Another great shock on joining the army for any new young recruit was your life was no longer your own when you are told twenty-four hours a day what to do when to do it you quickly realise that your life and freedom is no longer your own but the army.

The army becomes your mother and father demanding your total attention and to that end you are best to do what is ask and not fight the system as you will always lose. I knew from the moment that I enter my squad room that this life was for me and I thanked God that first night for taking care of me and giving me this new life of finally belonging. I was no stranger to living a dormitory life as since I was born that is all I had ever known and never having a personal locker that here I got to put away my army uniform was a plus to my old school that gave you nothing for you own nothing you had to have a personal locker for no spare clothes.

New people to this sort of living found it hard and wanted to leave as the thought of them having no privacy was something they never experience before especially with stranger that before long would become life-long friends that in a few days all will be walking in and out of the bathroom with towels wrapped about their waist or the more adventurous and exhibitionist sort felt proud they got more to show that walk in and out of the room naked.

The Devil O' Neill was a ginger hair Dubliner fierce looking and a well-built Irish Guardsman who was our barrack room trained soldier. His main task was to keep us all in order and to show us how to iron and do our kit especially our locker layout for our daily inspection, and to teach us the secret in shining our boots in the spit and polish way that needed a skill I never really mastered also to lay out your bed block according to the military manual of the day in a box square measure by the army manual and nothing else besides would do including ensuring all knew how to clean the toilets, baths, showers to a standard that the platoon sergeant expected on his daily inspection.

As the weeks passed in training one got used to spending all night cleaning their kit in the toilet and the laughs we had about the day training was the best part. But best of all was the getting to know each other in ways that only togetherness in the same situation of living so close can make you understand that your life in a bad place of action made be in their hands that these hours of extra work doing kit the platoon sergeant thought needed extra work enrich your mind to what being a brother soldier was truly about and reliant on each other is key.

The platoon sergeant had instructed our trained soldier to inspect no matter the time of night until we all got our kit to what he knew was a guardsman standard. Keeping your mind active while doing shining parade which went on for two hours each day from five to seven was the depot regimental homework time. During shining parade you were taught regimental history as I had learn my two times table in that you repeated and repeated until you could say it without thinking a form of brain washing to be really blunt. It became so repetitive that if ask when was the regimented from you could answer it and any other question thrown at you by your platoon officer even in your sleep. Like the name of the regiment first recruit and where he was from, how many Victoria Crosses the regiment had been awarded and in what circumstances the recipient earned it, and the easy one your army number.

Our platoon officer was Lieutenant Shaun O' Dwyer a very quiet and serious fellow tall with mousey brown hair, freckle complexion who had a good understanding of men, and although I knew no difference in the word class as a status pertaining to a person pedigree of wealth, property, reference money, people and the phrase use in the term of good breeding as it was known among the educated. It was all new to me and if I was to interpreted myself I would fall into the low of the lowest and maybe for once agreed with the police sergeant description for he was more on the button in some of the names he had mention as if he knew about my family situation and my school days as he had a lot in common with the Christian Brothers who use un-godly expletive when they too lost their control.

Lieutenant Shaun O Dwyer was a very good officer in that he was fair in his way of getting the best out of each recruit in making every effort to talk and understand all the men in his charge. When he ask when was the regiment form and why it was to be answered without hesitation. The answer was that Her Majesty Queen Victoria wanted to reward her loyal subject of Ireland that contributed faithful service in taking up arms on many of her campaigns that the Irish volunteer in droves went and served in Her Majesty's services that she in return wanted to thank them by creating another regiment of foot to be call the Irish Guards, the fourth of foot as Her Majesty special guards regiment to have close to her. Her Majesty's command came true on the 1 April 1900.

In my platoon of that intake of 1964 are a few I still remember even though it over fifty-nine years since those days of fitness and fun a time that preceded the age of everybody owning a star-trek phone, and computers. The following names that come to mind are Brian Hayes from Birmingham, Jack Nolan County Carlow, Eddie King my first Mick friend from Liverpool with Joe Salmon and Freddy Entwistle, others by the surname of Kennedy a Dubliner, Stone, Bell, Skillen, and Meehan from Belfast, Pat O Connor from county Cork, and a young potential officer by the name of Philip O Reilly from county Kildare, who spent only a few weeks training with us before going away on an officer short training course to Mons college, at Camberley.

Sergeant Tom Barry another Dubliner was our weapon training instructor and a bit of a screamer, and great at what he did inasmuch he made weapon training and shooting on the ranges exciting with all the shouting and unnecessary swearing as most instructors in those days use as another weapon in getting us recruits to understand that from hear on in we are to obey without question as your life in the future may depend upon your quick reaction that the army from day one want you to realise is the one thing that may save your life under fired in learning to accept military discipline and orders in all situation and condition without thinking or questioning the why.

Stupidly I got myself into trouble on my first Sunday in training for not getting out of bed 0630 hours as I was in my Irish Catholic head again that you must not work on a Sundays as it was a day of rest, and according to our Catholic teaching it was a grave sin committed if the work wasn't really necessary, as in hospital work or taking care of the sick at home.

Just weeks out of Ireland and mindful of my Sundays duties in attending mass and keeping holy the Sabbath day that was drum into everyone in Ireland of my youth that you cannot miss going to mass as this is the lord day as our faith demand we obey and attend holy mass not to go would be a mortal sin and if one should die in that state then you were damn in hell for all eternity as taught by the Christian Brothers in Artane Industrial School.

Sergeant Kinane my platoon sergeant was called to sort me out by my barrack room trained soldier who was the red head Devil O Neill a really tough boot of an Irishman one you would not want to take on in a fight sober or otherwise he was mad as hell at me, shouting expletive on what I will or won't do at my refusing to get up out of bed bursting veins in his neck as his face match his hair at my refusal to work on Sunday even to making my bed. It became a serious issue my obstinate to work and my insistence that I must go to church as it is the lord's day.

In the end Sergeant Kinane a Dublin man and I believe a Catholic by name although not sure if he practice his faith allow me to go to calm the situation as this was early days and because of my disruption to the training programme and my answering back to the trained solider I was put on a charge for not getting out of bed and causing a nuisance with the trained soldier in front of the whole squad.

I had to walk to Woking to St Dustan church which was about six miles away and return although the local bus ran through the depot road every hour to Woking I had no money to catch the bus and no one offered me the fare either to punish me for upsetting their Sunday routine.

It was as I was returning to the depot that I was put on another charge for leaving the depot without permission by the police sergeant who saw me coming in and once again gave me a little of his time in preaching his Sunday sermon which differ to that of St Dunstan parish priest father Seamus Hester in Woking, implying that I am always up to some sort of no good and who did I think I was. To me he said you're some sort of Jack the lad and thereafter my nickname Jack was born that became synonymous throughout my career not as Jack the lad but as Jack the press for reason of my job as the Hoffman presser in the battalion of 1968 when I took over as the battalion presser ensuring all were turn out smart for public and guard duty, like the regimental band boys who always look after the presser with a small silver coin so they could get away to their second job in some pub or club about the smoke knowing their kit was well press and in good order for their next day royal guard playing duty.

For now I am under the keen eye of my platoon sergeant, Sergeant Mick Kinane who agrees with the depot police sergeant in repeating the police sergeant words yes that what we got here is a Jack the lad who think he can do what he want and from that day the nickname of Jack stuck. I am of the firm belief that Sergeant Kinane was as wise a man as my recruiter Sergeant Smylie when he saved my life from trawling the streets and changed the direction my life was heading.

Sergeant Kinane was a fully fledge Dubliner who I know and believe knew me to be another orphan that had been in that infamous Dublin Artane Industrial School by virtue of its band that played in Croke Park during the Gaelic athletic season as I had shown him all the hall mark and signs of other who had join the Micks and had that unafraid look and would fight for the smallness of morsels. When he said to me one day you're another one from that place called Artane aren't you, as I told him he was on the money and that it was a tougher place than the army as he laughs saying you're probably right.

My introduction to the company commander was in circumstance that were quite unusual for him to see me on the Monday company orders as it not often he's confronted by a new recruit on a charge of leaving the guards' depot to attend church and another charge of not getting out of bed to work because of his Catholic teaching that only a few weeks out of Ireland was the practice he had always observed in attending mass and upholding his Sunday Catholic duty.

The company commander of number five company that I went in front of was Major R T P Hume who hearing my charge was a bit concern that my having broken military discipline was a bit of conundrum for him as he too was a practising Catholic, and putting on his Catholic head in dismissing my charge telling my platoon sergeant that should I ever failed to attend church he would want to know and I would be charged. As this was my first offence I was given a verbal warning only and from hear on in I was to be a good recruit that I can be in obeying those in charge without ever answering back as this is what been a good recruit is about and what you have sign on to do. Bearing in mind he said the fourth commandment apply here in honouring your father and mother which the army today is for you from now on.

My face was becoming noticed by all the instructors and training staff in the four billet and often without knowing all their names the other platoon sergeants, and corporals, if I was seen by any of them would immediately shout at me to move along not to stand still while making me aware that I was a marked troublemaker whose life they could make more miserable if I reacted wrongly to their over the top protected discipline.

It was obvious to me that I was on their hit list in their training office for everyone to take that special interest in my person that their ongoing attention shown to me made it concrete proof that they were on my case and watching. I didn't actually care as life here was easier than the nastiness and cruelty of the Christian Brothers, and having people care for you even shouting at you was great and for me it was another form of showing they cared and loved me.

The army I believe is made for a person like me with it twenty-four hours worked out for doing something that you never have to make up any pretence time to work in passing away idle time that the devious devil make good use of, had the army not been the great expert they are in making good use of recruits time. Lieutenant Shaun O' Dwyer in his own way tried to know each and every one of us by learning about our home life and what made us all tick like the time we were out digging on our first exercise in the nearby woods of the guard's depot. I was paired up with a Welsh man who was a coal- minor in a previous life and for me and him digging six foot trenches was a doddle as I remember our platoon officers asking what our trade were before we join the army. I told him I was a farm hand and the Welsh man said a coal miner to which he reply a good combination for the army and brilliant when we get to the exercise area on the Salisbury Plains.

Salisbury Plains training area was in fact a second home for a lot of military training and big exercise about the south west of England, and nearby was a great monument called Stone Henge which in 1964 on return from a few weeks' exercise we stopped off and were allow to walk among the giant stones in a time of no fences, no on site security or visitor centre, with little traffic that we just park on the road side verge and walk over to the stones. We were given a little history of them been the oldest free standing temple over four thousand years old. How they came to be here is still not fully understood as the stones according to archaeologist have come from a Welsh quarry, and how they got to be here is in itself another mystery yet to be solve. The people who worship hear were said to be Druid a pagan faith that worship the sun and Mother Nature.

Years after seeing Stone Henge I wrote this poem called

STONES

Grey is there only colour
Standing as shadow's against the green
Mysteries of untold years
That speaks to ears that cannot hear,
Thousands of years have stood these giants
Silent and in-intent meditation
Offering to the God of the universe
A door to man mind on this earth.
These inanimate stones of Henge
Who's blood veins have drained,
Dried by the burning sun
Scattered by winds and gales,

Stone monks in thought and prayer
Who never say a word?
Hide their heads within grey cowls
Their shoes buried beneath the ground,
Faceless and nameless they stand
Through the long days and nights,
Never growing old with age,
Forever stones of youth and height.
Those that pass, or see them,
Whatever the seasons or time
Are touched by their quietness
Especially at the God sunrise
Beauty does their present make.
Vitality and energy these stones generate
Telling you loud and clear
In their dormant sleep, they are awake.

Chapter 7

Life in the guard's depot was routine in that every morning you woke up at six and carried out your morning ablution before making your way to the cookhouse for breakfast. All in the guard's depot learn the bugle calls that announce reveille, cookhouse meals time, company and commanding officer orders and the last post that played each night at 2200 hours before night sleep. I loved the bugle calls and in time you find as the bugler playing without being prompted you start to hum along learning the difference in the ending each call makes, and the importance of being able to answer the call after the bugler has sounded.

To go anywhere outside the accommodation block require you to march at a very fast pace and if you have to carry your mess-tins and eating irons to meals then the free arm was to be swung in a smart march fashion, the guards' depot across the whole was a beehive of doing and going and I loved it, in that everywhere guardsmen recruit at different stages of their recruit training gave you the assurance that one day in the not too distant future you would be a fully fledge guardsman, and posted to where ever your battalion was serving on leaving the guards' depot after you have passed out.

Training over the six month was well broken down to period of marching and continuous drill hours of screaming one, two three one, one, two three one, and in every movement of the drill, halting, turnings left or right, about turns, and saluting while marching was also done by numbers.

Across the vast parade ground platoons and different squads shouted the anthem hymn that all guardsmen's recruit learn from day one when performing any sort of drill movement, I believe many screamed the timings in their dreams one, two three one, one, two three one.

Physical training or PT for short was another great laugh in that all worn these big baggy blue shorts and red or white tee-shirt, green socks with black pump, nothing was made to measure but one size fit all, skinny, fat, tall and small. Indoor circuit training which was great fun in all the layout games we were put through like parallel bars, jumping the horse, climbing a vertical rope as if it was what you did every day a feat I never managed to find easy but a good laugh when watching others try it, the infamous press ups and step ups, and other indoor exercises like catch or throw the medicine ball a funny name for what was a very awkward ball to hold.

Outdoor physical training was a must and a test of your mental strength when wearing full battle kit on tabs that weigh you down like a human donkey in that these run and marches were absolute killers, five miler and ten miler that in time you got better at doing, for the secret I found was to keep in-step with the person in front of you, and keep your head down while pushing on and treat it as a laugh, never letting your mind say you cannot do it, but just go through the pain threshold and persevere by pushing yourself on was the only way to win, mind over matter, especially when doing the assault course first in PT order than further in training full combat order. Sergeant Barry our weapon training instructor was excellent in his field craft and taught us how to handle different type of weapon and how to throw a grenade, and to shoot another type of grenade off the rifle barrel end of the 6.72 SLR which was called an energo, a mini looking rocket that flew into the target area not made for accuracy and shot from the standing position pressing the rifle butt end into your belly for more control, and of course the light machine gun known as the LMG, to be replaced when I reached the battalion by the general purpose machine gun, GPMG, a platoon heavy weapon.

Weapon training and shooting on the ranges was a great favourite of mine especially the different weapon we used, like grenade throwing require good skills and nerve of steel, as you held the grenade in your hand, pull the pin, throw grenade, count to five giving yourself time to see were the grenade land then duck quickly before grenade explode. We got to test other weapons and who was the best, who had a good eye and steady breathing when the shooting got going in using sub-machine gun, and hand control of the nine mill revolver that we were give some lesson in, but never issue as officer and specialist personnel only got revolvers to use as personal weapon. Signaller were issued the sub-machine gun as their personal weapon because of the A 41 radio pack they have to carry on their backs. I often got a good score and would in time shoot for my battalion in the 1965/66 London district competition, as part of the battalion shooting team that we excelled and won the London district championship.

Getting to the march and shooting stage was a sure sign that your days of training were near an end as to be at this stage in the depot you knew was well over half way, and by this time march and shoot were turn into an overall game when it came to inter platoon competition in which platoon was the best and the winners would be the platoon that won the most point when all the scores have been counted, including carrying a mocked wounded man in a fireman lift a hundred yards that the mocked wounded soldier did the same in order to complete. These march and shoots were no easy task with full kit and finishing with a man on your shoulder you had be extremely fit and I believe this probably was the fittest most soldiers are ever in their army career as it was supervise and that was the added bonus of being fit as the physical training instructor were a dab hand with lot of experience to get the best out of anyone. I love the end of each day when back in our billet we would all be back doing our shining parade which lasted for most two hours, chatting and laughing on the funny things we got up to and the bloopers any of us had made.

Halfway through training you knew the bonding of the platoon was really working as it was a case of helping each other in their weakness like weapon handling, drill movement, and at boot parade in getting that depot shine by working all together as one. The nightly runs to the NAFFI for the steak pie and pint of milk was to me even though we had to pay for it out of our own pocket a special treat I relish those special moment of self-indulgence each evening after shining parade.

Although for me who found it hard to get that finish shine require on my boots that left me spending many a night on the trained soldier inspection list into the early hours with matches holding open my eyelids till my kit was up to scratch in the hope that my nocturnal hard work pay off. It was the craic in the washroom that may those late night more bearable as it was a great bonding period in hearing and learning each other's story in how any of us came to joining the Irish Guards, and about our lives before we joined and from where we came from.

The depot days passed quickly because of the planned structure of each day doing drill, weapon training, indoor physical training including light and battle run. I could sum up these last few months as the best time of my life we were nearing the end of our training and not long back of depot leave as we are now in the early days of January 1965, knowing that I'm well on my way to completion and no longer worry or fear about been caught reference my real age as I was home in Ireland and my godparent mention hearing from the army and that they assured them of all the question.

I had a great Christmas and a fantastic new year at home in Dublin, I thanked Dorothy for telling the army I was free to be in the army and an Irish Guardsman if that what he want to be without question.

Our training came to abrupt end when our company commander informed us as one of the senior squads in the guards' depot that we would be going to London to Woolwich barracks for a week in assisting the visiting unit returning from overseas in cleaning there kit for the upcoming state funeral of a former war-time prime minister.

That afternoon we were bus to London to do shining parade for the navy, marine, including foreign troops hold up in Woolwich barracks for this great statesman funeral by the name of Sir Winston Churchill who had passed away and that the country wanted to give him the best send-off it could. Because this man serve his country well through the Second World War and in peace time as their prime minister lifting the country spirt during its worst days of the Second World War, and it is said that he stood firm with his country at it darkest hour and now his country wanted to show him how grateful they were by given him a state funeral and it most grateful thanks, for his boldness shone when the country needed true motivation and direction.

So here we all were in the big smoke that as we had now done more than four months in the guards' depot we were now allowed out in our civilian clothes and have late night and weekend passes that the Brookwood to London train was a giant magnet for any young person like me and my newfound friends that when opportunity and money allow we went to London for the lively craic.

So true were the words of my recruiter sergeant, Sgt Smylie in that the Micks are a family and the proof was in the eating that to this day fifty-nine years since my joining as a boy I've had a fantastic life and fulfilled my boyhood dream of seeing the world and more.

Our staying in London and not having to catch the train up for a Saturday night out gave us all a better understanding of how our life would be when our time comes to join our battalion that is now back from Germany and stationed in Chelsea Barracks a stone throw from the centre of all that this great city has to offer and if all goes well as I believe it will is my next stop. I will be a fully trained Irish Guardsman in two months' time working and mounting royal palace duties including the Tower of London, Windsor Castle, and the Bank of England guard all from the comfort of my new home in Chelsea Barracks London when I pass out in early March for the next few years.

The battalion were hit with their first big public duty test on that cold January day of 1965 as street liner for the great man himself the funeral Sir Winston Spencer Churchill. There was a platoon of Scot-guardsmen attached to number nine company Irish Guards in Kenya on active service that all rookies like myself coming out of the depot would love to be joining as you feel on completion that you are ready to take your place in whatever task the army has to offer especially an overseas posting in some far away country on your first assignment would be more than fantastic it would be just great for newly train guardsman to show his worth.

The battalion role had switched from a battle group battalion in Germany to it London Public duties role was as easy as water roll of a duck back and were well tested for that great man funeral the late Sir Winston Churchill that everyone on parade or marching wanted it to be just right. For now we are the guard's depot finest on funeral fatigues and be that it a sad occasion for the country I must secretly say it was a fantastic break from the depot routine and training. Our platoon seeing all these other soldiers of the world armies that came from Hong Kong, Nepal, India, Canada, and every other corner of the Globe with place names that sounded beautiful and magic was a sight to remember and treasure in the knowledge that I am part of this great man history be that it's because of his funeral and your playing a small role in the smartness of those on parade and that you were in London for that auspicious occasion that history will forever remembered and I will never forget.

I was screaming in my head oh if only you could see this beautiful turnout Paddy Maher my mariner friend of these soldiers and navy people that are here in London for this funeral, and the important of the man that has died, who was the United Kingdom great war-time prime minister Sir Winston Spencer Churchill, and that head of state and ambassadors are wanting to be seen as they too see history in the making and ending.

Although I had heard once in our history lesson at school his name and how he put the kybosh on the Irish question and that gave reason for some Irish to find a dislike of him on the then norther Ireland question in the nineteen twenties, as for myself I knew nothing really of the man and how great he was for this country as for any other matter of the big wide world I was ignorant too of the Second World War and the fact that the Irish government played no part taken only the spectator stand because it had no money, no army, navy to defend itself.

The colours of their different uniform and hat led many to use the opportunity of swapping badges and army trinket, souvenirs to remind themselves of this day in years to come and the historic value that never again would there be a state funeral on this scales for a non-royal be ever seen again so it was said then. Not knowing back in 1965 that an aristocratic young girl by the name of Lady Diana Spencer would married the queen's eldest son Prince Charles in 1981 I myself would be a sergeant street liner with seventeen years under my belt in Her Majesty Irish Guards and be part of that royal wedding day.

Who was to know that Princess Diana funeral would top Sir Winston Churchill by an accident on the thirty first of August 1997 in a tunnel in Paris, when the country would hear that the beautiful and young life of the un-seated royal Princess Diana life had ended in a car-crash causing disbelief and an out-pouring of unseen or known grief of a nation never before felt or understood.

That the upper stiff lip no longer applied as the country went into a bereavement never seen in England for anyone never mind a non-royal the bigness of Sir Winston Spencer Churchill himself paled into insignificant to the public crying that show no embarrassment of how much she was loved that the prime minister the honourable Mr Tony Blair read the mood well in calling her the people's princess.

Her funeral drew a crowd of over one plus million were Her Majesty was seen to stand with all her family by

Buckingham Palace main gate and the world saw her give a gentle bow of dignified respect as the funeral cortege pass by an unprecedented salute from Her Majesty. This out-pouring of love and tears from the people to feel so bereft and crying not only for Diana the people's princess as named by the then prime minister the honourable Tony Blair and mostly too for her two young princes, William and Henry called Harry of their mother loss for boys so young.

Sir Winston Churchill had lived a full life and reached a great age that his leaving was also a celebration of a man who done much for his country that the funeral was great and for someone like me to be in London on such a special occasion was a privilege to seen the whole show up close. The opportunity of seeing all the different soldiers and navy people not only from other unit of the British Army but from countries that were part of the commonwealth and her war-time allies that wanted and felt they should paid their respect to a great man that stood up for his country in war and peace time and was the man of the moment in their time of need.

The whole of London roads about Parliament square, horse guards and Westminster Abbey was close off for hours as soldiers, sailors, airmen from many country took up their position in the order lay out, and waited a long time for the procession of visiting military and mounted horses and carriages with those of the blues and royal including the artillery gun carriage that the body of the great man was drape upon in the colour red, white and blue to start moving. The funeral cortege stretch for miles on that cold dry January day that it took hours of standing before they got moving for the sheer number attending.

Our task on the morning of the funeral was to do the last brush down of kit for the street liners, and serve tea and biscuit were required, the street liner on that funeral day stood for near on five hours that day because of the great number of followers on horses and carriages and unit from around the world that wanted to paid their respect. When the funeral was over and the great man was taken home for a private burial we made our return to the guards' depot and within a few days of our settling into the depot routine again we were told to make ourselves ready for a two week stint of field training in that loved training area of the Brecon Beacons near Sennybridge in Wales as our last big guards' depot exercise before completing our field soldiering side of training before making ready for our final passing out drill parade.

Our return to the guards' depot as fully train soldier having pass the field side of training in Brecon with only a few weeks left in practices for our passing out parade and the drill routine of every marching movement learn and done without any shouting out of numbers as the timings is now inbuilt into our brain that whatever is ask in our drill movement of turn, and marching, left, right, about turn, a halt, is done as a professional guardsman. Sergeant Kinane stated that today is you're passing out parade in front of guest, family and girlfriends so be a first-class squad as you are no longer a recruit but proud Irish and Welsh guardsmen who will shortly be joining your battalion in a few days after passing out and a little bit of guards' depot leave.

Today is your big day having made it through the six months' training you will all be expected to carry out your royal duties as season guardsman when you join your own unit. There will be no second chance when out in front of the public carrying out your duties at the royal palaces especial at that most infamous of all her palaces Her Majesty Tower of London which houses the crown jewels.

All of you will get the opportunity to find out if those haunting story in the tower history are true and learn it history first-hand in knowing about the executions of Henry the Eighth's wives and enemies, including the story of the gruesome bloody tower of what is supposed to have happened to the boy princes and other stories to boot of the history and folklore that the Tower is noted for and has kept alive and somewhat wholly true.

We are today Irish Guardsmen and no longer depot recruit as all the lads are making time to ensure all there kit is of the highest standard not only for themselves but to impress our platoon officer and platoon sergeants that brought us to this finish line. After six months of hard and rewarding training we are fitter and more confidence in standing on our own two feet than when we arrive as awkward civilian now remade into proud upstanding Irish Guardsmen.

The depot commanding officer Lieutenant Colonel Scot Barrett who was my first contact six months ago and gave me that generous lift that had the opposite effect on the guards' depot police sergeant, who saluted me on my arrival and who I now know that the man who offer me the lift was the commanding officer of the guards' depot and the staff car that pick him up was the commanding officer personal car by his guards' depot driver. I have laughed many times to myself at the way I arrived and a real eejit I was, and how the depot police sergeant lost his head and the plot on my being a nobody that got out of the commanding officers staff car and he giving me an officer's salute.

Then to ruin my first day to the rant and language I never heard before that I was a shabby good for nothing that the army would soon sort out with words true to my status in his litany of military uses now as a trained guardsman the army has straighten out, and yes the guards' depot did sort me out and I'm thankful for all the fun that in the army great men like that police sergeant made me who I am today, and if I could I would return his salute a hundred times.

Having done my six months and now passing out I will see up close for the last time the man from the train who I know much better for he was very fair in his dealing with men, and over the six months of training I saw him only in his official role as depot commander inspecting all the squads on their passing out parades, and up close on my twelve week inspection when he quietly pass by saying nothing. But I sense that each time we met he knew more about me than I ever would have him and he smile that same soft smile I first saw when he himself told me that the Irish Guards were great fighting men and now he see that I have made the grade and will henceforth joined the line of Irish men that have made the Irish Guards the great regiment of foot it is and always will be.

To have seen him otherwise would have meant goodbye as it was for serious disciplinary judgement that was above company commander heads that he administered punishment and if he deemed you were of no further use to the army he gave you your discharge papers as he was judge and jury in military punishment that in my day a commanding officer power was absolute.

On my passing out day with no relative able to attend as in my godparent due to them having another newborn that I had just to do my best in any case for the squad. The commandant stood on a dais with all the invites guest sitting to applaud their sons, nephews, brothers, or just best friends on this momentous occasion of being upgraded from recruit to a trained Irish/Welsh Guardsman.

I'm not quite sure after six months and fully trained and looking every bit an Irish Guardsman would the commandant recognise me as the young eejit he first encounter from London those many months ago and gave a lift to having told me on the train to Brookwood that the Irish Guards were the best of soldiers and very good fighting men.

Well of course he did recognise me and gave me a personal well done and like the rest of the platoon a good report that made our platoon officer and sergeants very pleased at the commanding officer of the guards' depot satisfaction that you are all now ready to serve your regiments. I not sure if the Devil O Neill as a gas or a laugh had me pull to the side and I in my immaculate kit ready for parade ask me to start brushing down the other lad uniform. I had let go and forgotten my first weekend that he like an elephant had not and wanted his pound of flesh before I pass out in having the platoon laugh at me before leaving the depot square and after our passing out parade we left for depot leave and Chelsea Barracks in London for our next posting on return.

The depot commanding officer gave us all in his farewell address advice in never forget what you'd learned here and to remember to do the guards' depot proud in carrying out your duty no matter where you serve and be the best a guardsman you can be and with that singing in our ears he wish us all the best of luck in our future military careers. Having passed out we gave a squad present to our instructors and of course our barrack room train sweat the Devil O Neill that in early training you would never had put your hand into your pocket to contribute anything but now with a mature attitude and a squad that think as one we are all fellow brothers in the Micks it was a pleasure to say they are friends more than instructors and look forward to seeing them in the battalion when their stint in the guards' depot is through.

Now it was down to us to put into practice all we learned having pass out with flying colours which we all did on that early cold march day that a few weeks later we are standing on the battalion square in Chelsea Barracks on St Patricks day parade receiving from Her Majesty Queen Elizabeth the Queen Mother the shamrock which she present to all rank officers and men of the Irish Guards including the Irish Guards' depot recruit, and the old comrade association. The excellence music played by the regimental band and the pipe and drums has everyone tapping mentally as the shamrock is distributed.

My life in the battalion had begun and I am excited and ready for whatever the Micks want me to do as every day you are doing something new and learning to be better than the day before. The Micks jungle drum was certainly working for on my first day in Chelsea Barracks I was known to some seniors rank without I knowing who they were as on my arrival to the battalion in Chelsea Barracks on that cold March day in 1965 having just disembark from the depot bus, I heard my name being called and I shout here sir, and as a hard worn recruit of six months' training without as much as saying a word I am been rifted to the guardroom as a prisoner without knowledge or reason why other than some mistake made that will eventually be put right but for now I'm put into the guardroom known to all as the corner shop hotel.

After spending a little time in a cell I'm inform by the regimental police sergeant who I think at that time was the infamous Sergeant Ricky Nelson who told me that if I did not sort myself out that this is where I would spend a great part of the next twenty-two years. Now go as quick as your legs can carry you and make your way sharply to number three company accommodation and see the company quarter master sergeant as to where you will bed down.

I don't know who lay on that prank as a joke and I never found out who it was that pulled that stunt in having me lock up and played that joke on me on my very first day in joining the battalion. How real it was done and acted out made it so convincing and certainly gave me a right fright and a shock as to what life in the battalion would be like. Over my years in the Micks I learn there are many jokers and trick perform and not to take what happen to you personally although saying that it is never funny when you are the one on the receiving end of others butt-end jokes.

I was put into number three company number two platoon run by Sgt Harvey Mc Dermot who placed me under the watchful eye of a fellow Dubliner by the name of corporal Jimmy Kearns, now Jimmy Kearns as a man was first rate in that he treated everyone with the kindest of respect and in return he was love by all. Jimmy would help anyone if it was in his means beside that great quality he was a very conscientious and smart guardsman who live for the Micks and loved been an Irish Guardsman. Jimmy was a practising Catholic and it was obvious to all by his generous giving and understanding he would do you no wrong, and if he could do you a good turn he would. This I pick up in those early days when Jimmy look after me, and took me under his wing.

Jimmy was any Mick's big brother and he certainly took his looking after me seriously in always given me good advice in how to fit into this new life in London and the places I should avoid when out of the barracks as a newbie in Chelsea. He advise me that I should be aware when out and about of been approached by strange male or female for not everyone is nice and friendly as he said London is a magnet for all sort of attraction that may trap you into a life best avoided, drugs, sex, drink, bad company, that your innocent maybe taken by some devious sexual predators that offer money to tempt you to do a type of sins certainly not on the Catholic teaching list.

Jimmy was one of the nine company lads that returned to Chelsea and re-joined his old company which was number three company from an active and successful tour with the Scot guards that serve in Kenya in the time of the Mau-Mau unrest and were themselves well trained in jungle war fare, and close quarter contact. Nine company lads were the envy of many that had not seen any military action other than there posting in Germany that was a non-medal award. The British government as signatory to an agreement sign after the Second World War made by the winning sides in keeping troops to oversee the country peace and the United Kingdom number at a level of 50,000, or so as part of that agreement was made to keeping the security of Germany and weapons out of the Germany military hands.

The made up nine company of Irish Guards that went to Kenya received a general service medal adding a nice little bit of military jewellery to wear when on public duty that just look beautiful and shiny on the red tunic.

Chelsea Barracks prime location in London was unique and great for a young guardsmen like I was in 1965 on my first posting with everything at my fingertips.

My first memorable memory of Chelsea was being woken up on Paddy's morning by our platoon sergeant to a beautiful mug of tea with a drop of the hard stuff for good measure, and the sound of the pipe and drums lads playing and larking about on the barrack square in all order of dress while others shouted from the accommodation windows of rivalry to drown out the south lads song with them singing the sash my father wore all done with the humour that guardsmen north and south can enjoy the craic and no offence is taken. St Patrick's Day in the Micks is a great day kicked off with a fantastic parade with our queen mum presenting the regiment its shamrock and after the parade have lunch where a senior guardsman will make a royal toast to Her Majesty the queen mum that every guardsmen raise their glass and thereafter St Patricks day celebration really begin.

Chelsea was an open see through barracks its guardroom situated near the front gate that open out onto Sloan Street side to it famous square and was mainly use by officer and senior rank for easy access to and from Sloan Street station. While all other rank use Ebury bridge road back gate that led you down to Victoria station on route to Buckingham Palace that became the Irish Guards country walk to Buckingham and St James's Palace most days as a resident unit when they did their changing of the guard with whichever other guards battalion was coming of that day. Because of the Tower of London, and Windsor location after guard mount on the Chelsea parade, they boarded their vehicle that took them to Victoria barrack to mount Windsor Castle guard, while the Tower of London went to mount duty on tower green in the Tower of London. Guardsmen love the Bank of England duty where you mounted bank duty at the Bank Station then marched to the bank entrance big black door that each evening city folk watch knowing the bank gold not only safe in its vault but protected by a half platoon of professional soldiers ready to act if there any attempt to a break-in. Each evening whatever guard regiment was on bank duty received a newly minted half-crown that in it day could buy you a few pints of Arthur Guinness. Shortly after our tour of Hong Kong that Bank of England duty became redundant and as an old sweat now of six years I missed doing it if not for anything other than the new silver half-crown that was minted on the day.

On and off duty we use the Ebury bridge road gate to go anywhere out of barracks you did the same walk but casually pass Buckingham Palace then across St James's park and through horse guards parade pass great respected monument of war hero's into Trafalgar square and up into Haymarket, and the West End. One of my great walk I done often becoming very familiar in walking my London in those wonderful teenage Chelsea days.

Sloan Street side was the side that passer-by walking from Sloan Street Station towards Chelsea bridge on their way to Battersea Park or for a long walk on to Victoria main bus/train station. The passer-by could stop and gawped through the wrought black railings, the tourist bus drivers who learn the times or had a mole on the inside to keep them posted as to what was happening that most morning when mounting for queen guards duty and other battalion parade many buses would stop and their tourist would debus clicking away with their cameras to their hearts' content that no doubt the tour bus driver made an extra few bob from an inside source.

Chelsea Barracks single accommodation block was a long one three storey building of red brick with large white window that face onto the only big space that was the barrack square while at the rear was the cookhouse, company stores, garages and the armouries, with the officer mess to the rear of the barrack square at Sloan Street end near to the main gate that gave them easy access in and out to Sloan Street Station.

The long building frontage had two like arch-tunnel that led to the barrack rear, guardroom and back entrance gate, and the married skyscraper quarters of the privilege married that live in barracks. The access for the married was also convenient for they could just go in and out by the side gate of the guardroom, whereas single guardsmen had as in the depot days to sign in and out and were inspected by the sergeant of the guard or the police sergeant as to whether they were in good enough order to proceed and be seen out as befitting the high standard of an Irish Guardsman out and about in London town.

Chelsea Barracks had no athletic facilities for physical training in that the battalion was very lucky and fortunate to have across on the other side of the Chelsea Bridge a great green open space of Battersea Park, a vast space of green that house in 1965 a world class all year round fun-fare that for me in my youth was as if this park held the secret of all my Christmases and holidays of fun as an orphan boy I missed while hid away in that Christian Brothers school of Artane. Never did I know as a child but would live every day now that I was lucky enough to have on my doorstep all the fun of the Battersea fair the place Londoner in those years after the war felt was Christmas and Easter every day and not once a year.

Battersea Park was a wonderland and for the battalion stationed in Chelsea Barracks a great place to exercise in and to meet the opposite sex and of course a great place to relax on beautiful warm days in the heart of London. Free to enjoy when not on public duties and time off for there was much to enjoy in that open space of mature trees and green open space. A first-class sport track you could go and show of your prowess as an amateur sportsman and excel in your own personal fitness training as many young guardsmen were doing long before the running craze started in running around to keep fit. Keeping an eye on the local talent especially the young attractive nannies that walk round with their little treasures that help you in your first chat up lines as to how cute the baby they push around look and is.

In those heady days of the sixties before the world went jogging and power walking became a daily mad craze most army lad ran a couple of miles in the park in order to keep their fitness standard up to scratch. In my days of youth station in London Chelsea where the fashion changed hourly and mini-skirts turned my Catholic head to sinful thoughts. It really was hard to avoid when out the temptation of beautiful women you saw walking in the skimpiest and outlandish of dresses and the new hot pants craze been it said what it is on the girls' bodies made your eyes pop and unable to ignore. As young girls confidently and unashamedly walk happily shoving in your blushing face as a matter of course their temping curve and tight boob top imprint which left little to one's imagination.

In their pretend of un-knowing the mental damage their body appearance was doing to all the hot blooded males that could not hide their eyes as they flaunted and held your attention that often took you out of where you was going only to wake up and fight your new demon of the hot pant weakness you became addicted to following their shapely teases. This hot pants craze that left little to the imagination when you saw the scantiness of those pants which made your thought burn hotter than hell you knew hell was the road you were firmly on. It would take more than cold showers to temper your thoughts desire and curbed your physical weakness which was completely out of control. The fast changing pace of life in the early sixties with the new clubs opening and changing style of colour was replacing the drab grey that had hung around since the war, and now had it day that this dramatic change was taking hold and the outlandish haircut and mad new cult of faith, and street clothes design to shock was gaining attraction.

Another new craze of nose rings and eyebrow studs, body piercing on men and women was the new thing that you saw on the King Road as it became part of the fashion walkway and outright madness to be seen.

If you were anybody that wanted to be noticed in this new up and do fashion of shock and be seen, then the King Road with your innovative worn idea was the place to show off your fashion taste to be another top hit as a new street designer. It was the must be seen place to go and have your photograph taken, and if luck was on your side maybe you would be as successful and famous like the new Twiggy model who became an overnight success when spotted by the one and only top of the day photographer mister David Bailey who made Twiggy world famous from the picture he took and pre-empted her as a fashion icon not seen or heard of before.

It wasn't that Twiggy was a Marylyn Monroe type or stunningly attractive it was more her quirky look and boyish style haircut, her stick like body that fascinated David Bailey the photographer of the girl's unusual form that had all asking what it is Bailey photograph about. Where is the fashion going that is open as a free for all that this Twiggy an unknown from the street had become an overnight hit and an immediate new model that her image is been copied by other top modelling agency that went looking for their own type of Twiggy lookalike.

Whatever tomorrow shock would bring on the street is anyone guest as ordinary people moved the fashion along that the designer and the fashion gurus had not an idea what the next big following would be as the sixties became a time of anything goes. It offered great opportunity and challenges for any rising young designer with up and go to understand what the street fashion was thinking and were it was going to go next. Street fashion as it became known was an anything goes style with the outrageous been the new fashion and the more you could shock society and have everyone talking on the wireless and television won you the day. Leaving the old fashion houses scratches their heads and other part as to what sell and work and in vogue with the street fashion that has a runaway mind of its own that no named brand or fashion house could control but only pick up the pieces as they too went looking for the next big thing to challenge the street fashion.

It was the month of May 1965 when the battalion intercompany athletic and boxing competition got on the way for which each company had to find their best person to represent there company, and if fantastically outstanding they would be put forward for ongoing training as a member of the battalion elite athletic and boxing squad. I got paired off against big bully Blair of the signal platoon and I could see by his size and weight I stood no chance against him in the ring, so I cross over the canvas as if to say hello and punch out at him in his corner while he was still sitting, he defended my punch, spraining his thumb and I was disqualified my boxing career was over.

The battalion athletic day was usually held in Battersea Park athletic sport track although a public area it could be booked as was done whenever the battalion needed to train or hold an athletic day. With training practices we had to share the facilities of Battersea sport track with other clubs and units about London, and of course with the local schools and running clubs. The barracks closeness was very convenient to the park making it a great place to keep fit and relax when not on duty as a green space with a world class fun fair that was the best. This was London's answer to New York Coney Island in enticing tourist and Londoner alike to enjoy the recreation and all the fun of the fair right on their own doorstep.

Athletic was the battalion way in finding out who were the best in sports by competition of the intercompany sport day, and a way that was fair for competitor of all sizes and skill to show how good they are. And an opportunity to give new blood into the battalion a chance to make their mark on their company team and if really good an opportunity to join the battalion team representing the Irish Guards in other competition against other units of the British Army who are the best in their discipline and at the top of their sport.

On my first intercompany sports day as a young new member of number three company I was chosen or should I say volunteered to do a track event and I would be representing my platoon, my platoon sergeant Harvey Mc Dermot entered my name for a the first race telling me you only have to go once around the track and as fast as you can go which I thought to myself was an easy request and I was really happy to do as I thought sure I would win for been a fit young guardsman weeks out of the guards' depot and not yet into the relax demeanour that many of the old sweat had adopted.

Company Sergeant Major George Shannon who was overseeing the company day athletic, never mention that the race I was entered for by my platoon sergeant was a four times round the track and not the one lap I been told.

We all lined up at the starting gate and on the word go I was away like lightning and was flying round passing all the other contestant like a steed winning the Kentucky derby thinking to myself that I got this one in the bag for my company and in my head I'm doing great like my Irish hero

Ronny Delaney who was the greatest Irish miler runner for Ireland in the fifties. It was when nearing the end of my round and I was coming in to what I thought was the finish post and totally shattered I could hear lots of loud shouting and hand waving with shout of three more like that Jack and keep going, you are doing fantastic. It was then that I collapse ending my athletic future in the battalion or ever representing my company ending up as the biggest eejit who again was made to look a laughing stock as the other runner kept an easy pace while I died by the side of the track heaving up my insides and the laugh of the bystander was on me again.

Every day old soldier learn you lessons of life be it the hard way and not to take every one and what they say as face value. Still only young I have much to learn and for all my knock-down I was learning to accept and stand tall for I love it all anyway and my life in the battalion was going great.

As a new guardsman in Chelsea in 1965 I was caught out again by a few old sweat on a tried and tested neat move as he was a Dubliner and his friend from Carlow asked me if I would like to join them for a meal with a few other Micks from number one company. I was pleased to be accepted and like a real eejit had walk into their trap with both hob nail boots, hook, line and sinker, another lesson I learn the hard way as my story goes. This motley gang of old sweat whose names I'll never forget and will look upon as friends in the years ahead were Frank Williams Mixer Camilio, Kevin Treacey, Jimmy Haydon and Billy Lloyd all member of number one company who took me with them to the Mexicana in Sloan square a newly open Mexican restaurant, and of course I was very impress at the poshness of the place and very happy that as a new boy in the battalion I was being looked after by these brother Micks who had great taste in food and were making me feel welcome into their company.

It was a great meal and the drinks flowed not that I could drink in the same class as these season Mick that could down the Liffey water in great amount. When the meal was finish and idle chat was slowing down one by one each made some casual excuse of going to the bar, the toilet, outside for a smoke, that for a while I sat alone waiting there return when the serving waitress ask me where are the rest of your friends, and who is it that will be paying the bill, that when the penny dropped I'd been had big time again.

It was then I knew I had been truly screwed and with not a penny to my name I started working in the restaurant that night and for five further night when not on duty to pay for that meal doing what comes naturally when on cookhouse fatigues that is pan diving. I never did find out the price of that meal other than I worked twenty-five hours of free labour. I knew to refuse would have meant the police being called and for me a new young Mick in London that was a big no-no, and to be really honest I did not know those guardsmen well enough to be able to identify or accused. I fell for their scam and I had to laugh as in a number out of ten for been taken for a ride I would have to give it a full ten out of ten or a great big wash up ten. Besides the meal the craic was fantastic and another lesson learn in my learning curve that as a real eejit I've just got to watch out when been tested and hope to be a little wiser in the future and not fall for the blind obvious again.

Over the next year and a half the battalion carry on with public duties and when time allow for battalion holidays, company training in Salisbury, and Brecon in Wales these were great escape from the smoke and queen guards. Wales was a real challenge when it came to wet weather exercises in winter it was cold and miserable digging in and living of the land and keeping your kit and yourself dry and clean was another exercise in itself as shaving out of your mess tin without a mirror and cooking your 24 hour ration compo was a test that in the summer living of the land and doing your daily chores was much better. The Brecon Beacon is a fantastic place that many a platoon commander course is run and tested, and company platoon field skills are tested at the highest level.

As a reasonable good shot with the seven point six two rifle I was selected for the battalion shooting team and went to Perfleet in Essex for three month as a member of the battalion shooting team for intense shooting practising and to work on my personal marksmanship. The shooting team created a mascot cut out from a range target that had a paper tiger head glue onto it which we brought to all shooting competition for good luck. In 1965 we won many cups including the London district shooting competition that again we won the year after in 1966.

Another outstanding and probably the biggest event in the mind of all English football fan was beating Germany in the World Cup becoming the greatest sporting memory ever for the English team and the country as the year 1966 is forever immortalise especially on those who follow league football. For me who was on Buckingham Palace guard duty the day England won the World Cup it did not shorten my stags on the forecourt as the country had just gone mad and been on Buckingham Palace guard duty that winning day and into the night saw no end to the massive crowds that never left the outside railing as they entertained Her Majesty the queen. All that live and work in Buck house and of course us guardsmen on duty may not know who won the football match that with their love of football songs and impromptu choir singing, shouting, we won the cup was hard not to know and for someone to tell Her Majesty she should come out and join them in song on her balcony.

Me on battalion shooting team 1965/66,
winner of the London district cups.

There is no doubt Her Majesty was pleased to hear the football revellers sing their chant over and over again as this win could be defined in them words that Churchill said at the end of World War Two as the power to be in football reiterated today is England football finest moment in soccer history.

The vast numbers stayed and stayed and would not, could not sleep, just wanted to let all of England especially Her Majesty the queen that we are the champion as was the repetitious song they sung out of tune in hoarse voices we are the champion, we won the cup, we won the cup.

On that particular night it made no difference to the guard if we wore our day studded boots past ten pm as the guard normally change their footwear from hob nail boots to night shoe/pump on the post near Her Majesty sleeping quarters as was the custom for the guard patrolling beneath Her Majesty bedroom window so as not to make any great noise while still carrying out our duty in a smart guardsman like manner throughout the night.

London never quietens normally but that night it was hard to see if these die hard England supporters would ever let this event of winning the World Cup fade away without everyone knowing including Her Majesty, seeing that this was the greatest day in English football history that most people could ever remember since the great celebration of 1945 when peace had been declare at the end of World War Two.

I remember that it was also a special year for the regiment as we had in the month of May received our new colours from Her Majesty the queen in the garden of Buckingham Palace were afterward all rank of the battalion enjoy the garden party which was held in the grounds of Her Majesty home.

As a guards regiment there is a closeness of not only been forth of foot but that you are there in her present because of your guardsman role in guarding Her Majesty, her royal resident, and being part of all the big event that as a resident guards regiment you add colour to any state visit and other big occasion like the trooping of the colours, state funerals, royal weddings, special venues like beating the retreat and military parade like the state visit and the state opening of Parliament that bring in much needed money and loads of tourist for the economy to thrived.

I also remember that in our Chelsea days if any member of the royal family was going on a foreign trip or holidays a fatigue party from the in-house regiment was sent to Buckingham or St James's Palace to load their baggage onto the departure vehicle. This gave you an inside look of the inner sanctuary of their lives as was on the occasion in 1966 when the young Prince Charles was making ready to go on a trip that we went to his room in Buck house and he was there watching as we collected his bags and trunks acknowledge us with a shy thank you.

Been up and close to her Majesty and her family is a privilege especially when your regiment is receiving their new colours as witness by myself as a number three company guardsman on his first parade in her Majesty present at Buckingham garden in 1966. The new colours presented to the regiment by Her Majesty Queen Elizabeth the second, would be carried proudly by a junior ensign as a great privilege on the queen's official birthday parade when the Irish Guards troop their new colours in front of the other four regiment of foot, and the household Calvary regiments the blues and royal. Who look magnificent and so distinguish upon their horses immaculately dress in their red and blue uniforms wearing glittering breast plate, swords, and on their heads beautiful silver helmet with their blue and red tassels. Sitting on their horses gleamingly clean wearing their best polish saddle and halter that the horse's brasses so highly polish shimmered in the sun.

The Calvary mounted band also boggle belief at their outstanding dress of horses and men including their musician skill of playing and horsemanship control. That the outstanding stars were always the big base drummer and their trusting hoses that never falter under their loud drumming. The regiment laid up the old colours in the guard chapel were they are respected honoured and at rest.

1966 was the Micks turn to do the trooping of the colour a highlight in Her Majesty calendar and one the regiment would make the best of as this opportunity comes round every seven or so years, I was a street liner on that day and a very proud Irish Guardsman not to mention all others in the regiment on parade and on horse guards in front of Her Majesty trooping our battalion colours making all who had taken part in the regiment day a success. The closeness of the crowds that stood on both side of the mall ten deep without any steel barrier to keep the numbers back and the amount of police were fewer in number than are seen on duty today.

The public and the times have change that the police have to be ever more watchful for the unexpected opportunist wanting to claimed their fifteen minutes of fame in doing something mad like streaking, a madness that was becoming the new big thing to do when huge crowds gather like Twickenham rugby grounds. When the unbashful Erica became the infamous first lady who started the streaking craze at England top rugby ground showing all in running across the pitch in her birthday suit to a cheering rugby crowd that for the next few years the streaking craze went into overdrive and was tested at every opportunity by the extrovert that wanted their fifteen minutes of fame.

Chapter 8

It wouldn't do for a streaker to run out in front of Her Majesty while she on her horse, not that she would stop, as she probably would give the streaker a good walloped with her whip on their rear with her riding crop for the streaker to go faster as Her Majesty is known to see the funny side to most things, and it is known within her royal circle that Her Majesty has a great sense of humour she more than likely see the funny side.

London that year was amazing buzzing with all sort of going on and great changes taking place that one could agree it was a great time to be alive as the feeling of happiness and opportunity were opening for anyone, and the world at that time you felt was your oyster. Life could not be better for me as here I was now a seasoned Mick with two year under my belt and only nineteen years old/military twenty. I knew my way around London much more than I did the city I was born in Dublin, and was more alive to the Irish craic in London that in the sixties was much on par with all the craic that was happening back home with all the Irish upcoming bands wanting to be part of the London Irish scene, with headliner of the great filling big venue like Earl Court, the Albert Hall, and the Irish dancehalls that the Dubliners, Dicky Rock and the Miami and Capital showband with the like of Brendan Shine, Philomena Begley, Ruby Murray, and other of their day filled up the Blarney Club and other great dancehall like the Forum, Town and Country, the Galteemore in Crickle-wood to the sound of Ireland that made the Irish in London feel as if they have never left home.

Being at the centre of this fast unstoppable youth rebellion of change which I hope would not go as fast as life in the Micks was passing. I could not have ask for more out of life at this time for it was the happiest I ever known and with the vibrancy I felt in London and the new optimism of the future whatever it would be was very contagious as it was a fever I bathed wholeheartedly in without a clue where it would lead or end. For as a young guardsman stationed in London in the early sixties, life was just great as here was I in Chelsea Barracks on full board living in one of the greatest city of the world at the centre of this new sexual revolution that was challenging all that had gone before.

In its new thinking of what the future got to offer against the Victorian attitudes that was being torn to shreds, as this new awaking of change was cancerous to the politician and worse to the establish church that found it philosophy off the wall, and moving too fast. The power to be having no real answer to curbing this fast flow as the young of the day led this runaway train not knowing how it would stop.

With the passing of the Bay of Pigs a few years earlier and with other crisis brewing in Asia and Africa, today's young having grown up in the worst of austerity after World War Two were now breaking down every conceivable barrier that they felt needed knocking down and remade. If the end of the world was around the corner then they were going to have the best of fun, but not before taking all that life has to offer especially the new sexual freedom that was catching on without marriage restriction fears.

At that time in London I remember especially in the West End the in your face advertising of the sex clubs and the board walkers with bible quotes of the end of the world warning that most ignored and went into see the striptease live act in the Soho clubs and its enticement of gratuitous pleasure the bible walker cried out loud would lead you to hell. A majority of the passing crowd blatantly ignored as they hurried into see the scantily clad girls of the Paul Raymond review show, and other sex haunt were striptease shows of the sixties was a popular stop for the young and inquisitive of the day that I too an Irish Catholic failed miserably and in my curiosity to know enter and was amazed at the stripper routine and the beauty of girls naked I had never seen before. That left me questioning myself and this new awakening if I'm really honest I was feeling excited and wanting to know a lot more about the opposite sex and their hidden secret I have yet to learn and know.

The youth of the sixties thought if the soothsayer of doomed are right then they were just going to enjoy themselves breaking every rule that the establishment itself did not give two hoot in obeying for the new message on the street that was taking hold was, "live for today for tomorrow as it happen may never come." Another catchy slogan that began getting the young attention and one they like and wanted, make love not war, the emphasis of the day been on the word make love.

Freedom to be yourself and dress how you like was frown on by the old as the young became more overt in dress that were once perceived as only seen or worn behind close door, now street wear became more visible with a sexualise emphasis on see through dresses, and what in their appearance they could do with studs in the nose and studs through eyebrow and tattoos to shock. Society was at it wit end as to what was coming next as this door of sexual and liberal freedom was flung wide open that the birth pill brought another freedom which gave woman the right to be free in having sex without the fear of becoming pregnant and be in the free for all love game and do what men had been able to do in enjoying sex without any final commitment.

Two major laws passed in nineteen sixty-five was the abortion act which gave woman another escape from mother hood if she decided to terminate for reason of been single, unable to support a child or that as a mother she is mentally unfit, the law especially was in favour were a woman of any age was raped or was carrying a down's or other severe medical child, and Parliament decriminalise the homosexual act to allow consenting same sex person to be free without punishment that before meant going to gaol if caught.

At that time it seem that all the churches committed hari-kari having gone quiet and sort of gone underground in the hope that these satanic practices would be short live, and that the moral righteousness would again take the high ground and all would return as it had being before. Unfortunately the sex genie was out of the marriage bed and this freedom for both sexes and its taste was for more not less. It was the beginning of cohabiting without any strings no rings and having your married way of life without having to pay for a big white wedding and just live as you both agree to your own rules. The slogan make love not war was just around the corner and the push to break every boundary was being push as far as these new times would allow, and it was being said on the radio that this is the age of Aquarius and it was being hailed as the new age in opening doors that no longer were just for the married or what the Soho girls were offering or doing in private.

It was a new awaking for a new age where woman were coming to know the power they held in this new sexual freedom, that now any women for the first time had full control over their body, and could choose to exploit it in whatever way they wish without worry of them been lumber with an unwanted child, that before was not possible. Unlike men who forever enjoyed their free to do at will sex without ever taking any real responsibility or precautions in the sex act and it outcome that for the first time the female population throughout the country knew this birth control pill was a sex game changer and was to be grasped with both hands.

There was two opposing forces at work in that the young wanted to break free from all the drudgery there parent had fallen into without question, while the young wanted to change the hopelessness of following their parent lives into the same old trade and works.

Having fun and a better quality of living without begging for little to no money as there was more to life than been tied to debts that they saw their parent suffer and struggle trying to giggle the little they made to make ends meet. Well the youth believed that you are only young once and been young was first and foremost their time to enjoy and go with this new change and new music. No longer be a slave to work, but be open and free in embracing this new revolution for now is our time to help that change and moved forward into that new youth world against the old drab and grey suited authority era of the post-war years to the youth of the sixties was now dead.

This revolutionary change on the street was in many different hands that like the street fashion took on a life of its own with no one owing it, or able to predict what will happen next. It challenge the big stores and designer clothes makers, and went against the high street stale and staid the young no longer wanted to been seen in. There was a huge buzz on the street and this new fashion of the young painting their bodies as an art, showing of their new looks and dyed hair, with lips of different colours of green, blue, black, and purple, chalk white, and piercing of ears, lips, nipples, noses, cheeks, belly button, tongue, eye-brows, including area not on show for decency sake was wild and running more wilder as each day past.

A poem about lips

Lips inviting, lips exciting
Lips of heat and shades
Blue lips on a wintry day
Revitalise by the sun rays.

White lips on a wedding day
Purple or green to be outrageous
Scarlet, black, yellow or gold
Lips for fun contagious.

Wet lips upon wet lips
Held in timeless leisure
Deep, deep magnetic clinch
Fuses sexual pleasure.

Lips are the doors of love
They are found in many colours
When we find the right set
We pass by all the other.

The pain to change was visible in the young and the rush to shock was the new norm as tattooist and other jump on this new gravy train in opening their doors to easy drugs like LSD and magic mushroom type, illusionary drugs that the young were being coaxed by the attractiveness of this new world to experiment without having a clue as to the damage it may later cause them. For now it's go with the music and the lyric of the fab four with many other rock sound, like the Who, Rolling Stones, the Kinks, and many more that saw this new freedom in music as another way to change their young lives, weather they could play an instrument or not was just to be part of the change that was manic and unstoppable, and an opportunity to be the extrovert you knew yourself to be and take on board the madness without being put down as it was a time of anything goes and why not give it try and see what you could contribute to this new change that was in it infancies and was developing day by day and was challenging all what went before.

What was moving the young in the change was a desire to break all the rules and see if thing could still work by another means and be just as good for change was needed and yet untested as the old guard of industry and commerce were set in their old ways from the war years, and just stuck in the groove not wanting to rock the industry boat that was a well try and tested system to innovate with any new ideas.

The thinking of the old was this generation that is young have lost their way and the devil has them in his control, and believe that in time this radical phase will fizzle away and all would end in crying tears. The establishment honesty believed that in a short while everything would return as it had been before letting those in authority rebalance and steer the country ship back on course again.

Well their wishful thinking as to this rapid change slowing down never stop but speeded up that for many years the youth of the sixties rode on that runaway train never wanting to put the brakes on but ride it to wherever it ends.

Another great force came from America in the name of Billy Graham in the mid-sixties who packed out venues to audience that were ready to hear a real American bible preacher expound the name of Jesus and to have the crowds shout Amen to the lord's name, Jesus Christ. The devil must have been beside himself and very upset having thought he had a home run with the youth of the world going on his hand cart to hell that from nowhere come the great American crusader Billy Graham to put a spoke in his wheel. Billy Graham had come to stop the devil from having a field day in leading this youth rebellion and causing mayhem. For the devil was able to laugh his socks off at society totally breaking down on sex and marriage, the passing of the abortion act, decriminalising the homosexual act that would no longer be seen as a crime by two consenting same sex adult, all taboos were being kicked out by God-fearing people who were no longer in fear of God's law that these changes by Parliament were forced on its members afraid of an election change in losing their seat.

Here comes out of the blue an evangelist packing stadium as I myself went to see the great Billy Graham in Earls Court in 1966, and was deeply impress with his belly full of fire speeches, and his standing up for God only son Jesus who of late God's commandment were being turn upside down, and the Christian churches were being left shaken in their boots as the rapid change in the young hearts for an easier way to live without church and state and marriage was being change for a simple life of co-habiting, and with woman having the pill the door to sex open wider as another new slogan of the day became known as living in sin by those not afraid of hell.

The great crusader of the lord Billy Graham was a force that was prepare to speak out for truth and be the face for God's work, and tell loud and clear what society must do in order to save itself from final damnation, this man was the first true walking advert with the spoken word for God while the churches remain silent, and priest of the Catholic Church caught up in the new sex revolution left in droves in agreement with the pill, and that contraception question. The Catholic Church under Pope Paul VI waited for the answer in his encyclical humanae-vitae that reaffirmed the Catholic Church position in the value of gods procreation in respect of the married, and one body in not assenting any change that society wish for in the use of contraception that many priest were hoping the Holy Father would say yes and allow due to family poverty, struggling families, that as their shepherd they be able to give a yes to their married parishioner of it use, but the church says no to the use of contraception having given its reason that was not good enough to stop many priests from leaving who wanted the Catholic Church to be unfaithful to gods truth.

I believe Pope Paul VI saw the future and it consequences if the church went down the road of man and not of God, that breaking the love partnership God gave to the sacrament of marriage should not be tamper with as it is our true expression of marital love and of God love who made us all.

The evangelist Billy Graham told the huge crowd in Earls Court stadia at that meeting having it all without responsibility was too much to ask, telling the young ears that listen there is another way to live, for sin in any disguise is wrong, and his message to the vast numbers was you have the right to be young, the right to know about Jesus, but you need help in finding the answer in fulfilling the emptiness you feel without losing your young dreams, without craving lustful sex which last about a minutes of instance gratification without love.

For true love is a blessed union between a man and a woman that each is willing to give all of themselves to the other till death do they part. Stand up, he said for Jesus he died for each of you, because he loves each one of you, then quoted, no better love is there than to lay down your life for a friend, and for all of you here tonight that friend who died for you, his name is Jesus.

So powerful was his preaching that at the close of his bible shows he ask all in the hall if you believe in Jesus, then come forward, show your witness. I walk forward proud with the huge crowd that I too wanted to be counted in the believer numbers. It was the first time in my life that I consciously made my own validation of yes when tested about my Christian belief, am I prepared to walk with others or alone in witness that Jesus is the son of God, aloud I said yes.

As a young Irish Guardsman station in Chelsea Barracks London I had great access to all the Irish clubs and dancehalls which thrive where you saw the best of Irish artist and great showbands that came to London made you feel back home in Ireland for one night. The bands that tour in England especially my new home town London acted as local postmen from back home and brought from their village and home town news to the dance halls family the local news on their different stop on their British band tours that folk in Ireland knew the band would be visiting in the UK. Great places like the Blarney dancehall at the top of Tottenham court road was for me my favourite, with visit to the Galtimore ballroom in Cricklewood, the Town and Country, the Garryowen in Hammersmith and the infamous Hammersmith Palley was a must in listening and seeing the great Joe Loss and his orchestra that thrive as one of the best dancing nights out in London.

I really loved the Café De Paree in Leicester square known to many young Micks and locals in London as grab a granny hang out joint. I was first introduce to life in Café De Paris as a washer upper by another infamous Mick of my day who was in the Irish Guards regimental band, and who play in a trio piece for the club four night a week, courtesy of another old great Mick the Chelsea postie Johnno who knew every Mick of his day and was my introductory contact with the trio bandsmen.

Café De Paree was a fantastic and expensive night club that combine eating and dancing in a most romantic setting with low subdue lighting, soft music, that in the sixties was one of the most exclusive places in London to be seen in, if you were someone importance and wanted the press to write about you in the gossip column.

You had to book in advance if you wanted dinner and dance as its popularity for fine dining was second to none and reservation for both had a long waiting list, there was a lounge area for those that wish only to dance and drink that was limited to a safety number. It was a two tier place with dining on the upper floor. The upper level was very popular and you could request a balcony seating so to look down and see the people dancing below, the beautiful décor of the walls carpeted in velvet red fabric gave it a royal palace look as everywhere was dress in gold and red velvet, with twisted gold and red ropes holder in cordoning off table setting letting the diner have that intimate dining and dance experience, the chairs were gold colour and the seat cushion soft were woven in the same velvet red base cloth, and the dining tables braided in a gold laced band set of by an immaculate snow white table cloth.

The Café De Paree was opulence at its best and a night club for the rich and famous to enjoy without be photograph or annoyances if you could afford without worry of the menu and drink list. Staff off duty could stay on as long as they wore a suit and tie for casual dress was not allow and you knew you must behave as a member of staff. Staff were restricted to one drink that itself would swallow up your night earnings as staying behind to be part of the scene was well outside a guardsman pocket. It was a treat to watch how the other half live once in a while, and reward yourself in thinking that for a hour you could mingle with money and the top set of the day appreciating the close contact with the hoi poloi and the chance maybe to meet a rich woman to take care of you if lucky enough to be her prize.

She chose to enjoy.

The Café De Paree traded on its reputation and was one of the best value for a night out experience that London of the sixties had to offer with it late closing time. It cared about it appearance and to that end maintain a very high standard as the place to be seen if you were anyone of class and money. If you were on the up and wanted to be seen and talk about then it was important to be seen especially visiting London as an up and coming star of film and music, and to be read about in the papers the next day as in the who's who of who is in town.

I have many good memories of that nightclub it was the only place where I could dance have a drink on a guardsman pauper wage, a discount drink as an employee of the kitchen team. Café De Paree was an expensive club the regimental bands lads played as a professional trio set, a side-line to their day job as top musician in the Irish Guard's regimental band.

They were in a good position as the bandsmen of the household division live in London and always it was safe for them having a second job that on leaving the army they could fall right back on. Café De Paree was great place in meeting the opposite sex, and I have to admit my weakness as I loved holding women close smooching in the low lit light the close touching of ear nibbling and neck kissing on the floor, while holding tight in warm closeness that sent everything racing and out of Catholic control. It was as far as I was prepared to go without getting myself into deep trouble yet stopping myself making a sexual conquest that often was on offer and not easy to say no. For my Catholic head would not allow me to go the whole way as an unmarried and because of the gravity of the sin my Catholic guilt kept my sexual urges in check.

Keeping the faith and been true to my Catholic roots wasn't always easy as London in the hay-day of this fast sexual revolutionary change was very temping, and it was a tide so strong that it carry all with it at speed of a fast moving train.

Had it not been my promise to be faithful to myself, my church, my friend Father Kavanagh, my godmother Dorothy, I could easily have went down the road of no return fallen and broken the sixth commandment most nights of the year. I honestly believe it was my daily prayers especially the rosaries and the help of my heavenly mother powerful grace that kept me in the practice of my faith, and protected me in those heady days of my youth that love of sin for the flesh was as strong as my love for God that each day was a fight to remain true and faithful.

I only had to go to Victoria a stone's throw away from Chelsea Barracks and call into Westminster cathedral the seat of the Catholic head of England and Wales, who at that time was his Eminence Cardinal John Carmel Heenan a very holy man that I saw on many an occasion as I attended mass over my two years stationed at Chelsea Barracks London. Mass in those early years of the sixties was still in the great tradition of our universal church Latin with sung Gregorian chant that made listening to a feeling of being in heaven as the cathedral choir led the hymnal that were beautifully sung. Westminster cathedral was one of my private haunts in going to monthly confession and other devotion that cathedral are great centre for true Catholic practices in devotion and piety to keep you truly centre in your faith as a lot goes on in a city cathedral that not seen happening in provincial parishes due to their being open for tours and dioceses visit.

London was a major hub for new Irish arriving in it capital as there was plenty of work going on, and a great need of Irish and other labourers for the building trade wanted with the new motorways project that were opening up new opportunity for thousands of people to work in the city and from around the home counties if they wanted to earn a better wage package. All this I knew after a few years of seeing the Irish at play and close up and could tell how they came to England as opposed to my own arrival two years before destitute with no idea of how thing would work out.

Now here am I in London at the centre of the Irish scene and the clubs, pubs, dance hall the Irish cling to as if they are back home in Ireland. North London was as Irish as any place in Ireland and the Irish who had come over in droves because of work and poverty especially from the west of Ireland like Galway, Mayo, Sligo, and southwest Cork and Kerry, but the dominant Dubliner held their own as the biggest number from the Leinster province, gathered in great numbers that you even had a lot Irish place and hearing the Irish tell their tale of how they came to cross the water through family and friends for work and where to stay as I learned in hindsight.

I thought to myself how different if I had as much as one friend when I started out on my adventure two years ago living on the other side of the Irish Sea how different my life would have turn out. Now I'm an observer now of the new Irish coming over in droves due to shortage of work in the sixties that I was able on my return to give first-hand information to the priest of my success and the number of Irish that leave to earn a living in England working on building sites and the new motorway that were opening more corridors so that commercial vehicle and produce could move about quicker and more efficiently, and making it easier for people from the north to move south in finding work were before was not really possible but by long hour on a crammed trains.

It was by any measure an Irish miracle for the Irish unemployed who came in boatload to England, and were eager to get work on the roads and new motorways bringing much needed cash reward for those who read the work chart right and saw the future being shaped and wanted to be at the forefront of this great innovation of change.

New companies were being created overnight, and joining the establish big names in being part of this new project of British building companies that Wimpey, Murphy's, Fitzpatrick's, the forerunner of other great names to be up against the new like O Rourke, O Brian and many more that tomorrow would be the names that fly of the tongue as names synonymous with the who's who of Irish builders in the United Kingdom as if they had always been there.

My time in Chelsea was passing fast and I was at this time more knowledgeable in getting about London than I ever was in my own birth place of Dublin, although born in Dublin I was thrown into the state care abandoned by my mother and her family. I really knew no Irish life other than one who went to the infamous Artane Industrial School. I was not a free Dubliner who was brought up on the street natural and feral that ran around Dublin as a rite of passage.

I knew Dublin only from the odd day out to my God mother and the school trips organise by the brothers in the summer to the seaside at Portmarnock or Laytown in county Louth if the weather was fine during the summer break. The brothers took the boys that had no home or relative and stayed in school and not of working age on day trip to the seaside carrying swimming togs, sandwiches, and a carton of red lemonade.

Without those outing days with my godparent once a month my knowing anything of Dublin experience would have been nil for the Dublin I knew was within the high walls of Artane Boy's Industrial School and of course Sunday if not being punish you were taken to Croke Park football stadium known to all as the home of Ireland Gaelic athletic association the GAA, because the famous Artane Boys band played at all the games, and the school were given complimentary ticket to bring boys from the school free. The brother who volunteer to go to Croke Park often it was his county team that was playing and to that end the school chose boys to see their county play I was born in Dublin and supported and adopted them as my own team.

The school hid from the country and it people the tears of cruelty and physical abuse that was meted out night and day with no mercy that most people in Ireland thought were getting the best treatment on seeing the Artane Boys' Band Play in Croke Park every Sunday during the GAA season. The Artane Boys' Band great reputation hid the cruelty and punishment meted out on children eight to sixteen years old as some brothers used to vent their anger in beating for what maybe going wrong in their own personal life that us innocent children were made to suffer in making them feel better in taking their vengeance out on us.

PHILIP ANTHONY McDONNELL

Dublin was not a city I knew well or work in much before leaving Ireland that I would have been confident to walk about in or able as I am of walking this beautiful city of London that being a guardsman in Chelsea of my youth was open wide to me. Living in Barracks as a young Irish Guardsman now on eighteen months enjoying all that this fantastic city of London has to offer on it doorstep, its beautiful parks, the great cathedral of Saint Paul design by Christopher Wren, and having close by the beautiful byzantine Catholic cathedral of Westminster with many other churches, palaces, theatres, museums like the V&A the portrait gallery within a few miles that walking or busing was easy to visit.

Battersea fun fair in Battersea Park was a magnet for young and old including the great number of visitor to London that found it alive and a must see with it colourful light that brought the Christmas feel whatever the time of year. Its many different type of merry-go-round and the swinging musical high chairs and the famous fair's wheel gave you a view in a time when it was the London eye of it day, and the wooden rollercoaster, the spinning tea cups, the shooting gallery was fun that as young infantry men we should not miss but the fair guns are fixed for the shooter not to win and at truppence for six shot to win a cuddly toy it would be lady luck if you won.

I think for most the best price and the most real fun was the bumper cars, while the rotor spin for me was the best as a bystander to watch as it was like a used gas tank sunk in the ground that held about ten person and as it spun around you notice as it went faster you no longer were standing on its floor but pinned like a magnet to it metal wall. As it spun round and it gain speed it held all on the ride in some awkward position especially for the ladies that wore skirts, and the laughter and screams heard inside the spinning drum of delight and fear added to the rides trill. The rotor spun for about ten minutes drawing big crowds because of the centrifugal force being made of gravity holding them tight that those getting spun did not spin out into the air but were stuck like magnets to it metal wall and with gurning faces and contortionists position it was great fun to watch.

Did I give it a go you bet I did it was scary but very enjoyable and worse was the horrible dizzy experience your head felt when it stop that I thought this really would be good for astronauts training for outer space that was being talk about. For President John Fitzgerald Kennedy said in an early address of his presidency that our space programme would land a man on the moon and in 1969 it happened and the world look on in amazement as Neill Armstrong set foot on the moon, making that now famous quote one small step for man one giant leap for mankind.

For me in those early days of being a tourist albeit an Irish Guardsman living in this fantastic city of London and taking full advantage of being in one of the world's greatest city having all it had to offer at my fingertips, and at no great cost to my pocket for a guardsman working and living in Chelsea Barracks. I had an evening job washing up at the Café De Paree in the West End and my life all in all was wonderful for a boy/man who had no family, no real fun growing up, no Christmases or birthdays celebrated in my past life, that as a Irish Guardsman a real Mick I can ticked all the boxes making my boyhood dream of adventure and travel a reality.

It wasn't long after the trooping of the colours in 1966 I believed that the commanding officer Lieutenant Colonel J. A. Aylmer informed the battalion on it upcoming tour of Aden. With the news of the tour and the troop behind us the battalion went on summer leave and as with all leave I made a bee line for the boat to Dublin now familiar with travelling to and fro on military warren and no longer was Dublin or other part of Ireland strange to me as each leave I met up with other Micks at home and I explore different part of Ireland because of my London Irish connection that won me over and it was living in England and being part of the Irish scene that I became more Irish in myself and getting to know places I heard sung about and its people from those counties.

I always made my first stop on arriving in Ireland to visit my godmother and the priest at Glenart College, especial my good friends Mick Bracken in Killcarra, the Maher Brothers by the seminary gate and my Artane School friend Danny O Keefe whose mum/ dad look after me many a night in Arklow they being Molly and Tom O Keefe.

Tom was a fisherman that went out to sea on trawlers a hard life for a man to feed twenty children that they had then with another on the way in 1966, while Molly was a fantastic mother look after her large family, whenever I visit her she was always cheerful and appreciated all the gifts God had bestowed on her, Molly wasn't about money or having the next modern gismo of the day but thankful to be able to feed and keep her children warm and safe.

Back off summer leave in 1966 and the battalion less its regimental band went for a few weeks to Sennybridge training camp in Wales where the battalion carried out mocked fighting situation in the Brecon Beacon under the shadow of the Penny Fan that is an old friend to all that trained in Wales especially the SAS, for it a tuft terrain in testing any unit ability outside of their comfort zone. The training in the Brecon Beacon was more to get us fit and into the mind-set of what lay ahead for the battalion nine-month tour of duty in Aden. The battalion training for Aden was about fitness and being battle fit as in London with only doing public duty the battalion did not have any proper testing ground for outright army field training other than drill fitness and indoor circuit training, weapon handling and cleaning.

This bombshell information on the Chelsea Barrack Square had everyone asking where Aden was and what was it that is happening out there for us to be going out there on an active service role.

Excitement about Aden was at pitch fever point especially for a guardsman like me who had been nowhere except on public duties in London and the cold training area of Sennybridge and the flat plains of Salisbury where the ancient monolith stone circle stand in the middle of a wide open treeless landscape, and come into their own on the yearly equinoxes. The news of our battalion going on active service in October had come out of the blue and was an opportunity for the regiment to soldier and put into practice all they know and are trained for in their dual role of soldiering.

What was the nature of our going there was on everybody mind and of course the fact that we are heading there in October on a posting without families, and will be over there at Christmas away from loved ones and families. Our company commander Major Peter Verney spoke to the whole company about Aden and what our roll would be in that we would be there in the interest of the government protecting British interest as in British Petroleum oil, its workers, families, in general a peace keeping role. In my guards' depot and Chelsea days' we wore blue-black beret that shortly after we were told Aden was on the cards we exchanged our blue-black beret for the new beige sandy type that Irish Guardsmen still wear today.

Our company commander Major Peter Verney gave the company an update on it upcoming posting, and how hot it is throughout the year that we were issue with our Aden uniform of khaki short and shirts, hose top, and a per of desert boots sandy in colour. Most of the lad hearing how hot it would be and the nature of our employment were over the moon and looking forward to be away over the winter months doing something different than standing guard in grey-coat order on Buck house, or St James's Palace and that favourite duty of mine the Tower of London freezing our hands, toes, noses and other unmentionables off.

I told my godmother Dorothy of our impending tour and how long we would be going there for, and a lot of what I told her I believe just went over her head. As what the British Army does in any part of the world never mind the Middle East meant nothing to her. Her interest was what happen in and about Dublin, and her family and with that she wished me the best saying I hope it not to dangerous and bidding me a sad goodbye.

I also had to tell my girlfriend who I have been stepping out with since August of 1965 having met her holidaying with her family on a caravan site in Arklow a year before. Her name was Annette O Connor she came from Goat-town in county Dublin. She was seventeen years old, and for me the prettiest girl in Dublin who I was head over heels in love with. It was in my head to ask her sometime soon if all keep going well as it had over the last year the big question, but for now it was not the right time with my leaving for a faraway place in the Middle East that I knew little about and what our job there would really entail.

My living in London and only seeing her while on leave and the odd long weekend was not the best way in keeping our relationship alive as it was often weeks before I could afford to go to Dublin and with having to pay bed and breakfast with the odd night at Dorothy house for free. Going to Dublin was a feat that needed planning in order for us to have an ongoing relationship otherwise she was more of a pen-pal come girlfriend. When we were together we held hands, kiss passionately, other than intimate feel around in learning about our bodies by touch which was the most sex she was prepare to chance. For no heavy sex ever took place in our two years of seeing each other as she was very church devoted and like myself knew the punishment of that sin which the Catholic Church in Ireland found a very hot topic to preach about and reminded the faithful often it must be avoided at all cost in order to live a holy and Catholic life and keep a faithfully preserve that pleasurable act for the sacramentally wedded night.

The main reason we never yield to our weakness in testing the marital love with each other was maybe because we only saw each other on and off and weeks apart. Second the consequences if something horribly went wrong if our weakness produce new life then there would be hell to pay with her father and I never be allowed inside her house or ever to see her again.

Courtship in my teen days could last four to six years before asking the parent for a girl's hand and then it was not always a yes. As getting married was about more than our saying yes to each other and telling the family we are in love it was weather a man could afford to keep his wife in the manner she was accustomed to as was provided by her own parent. A real plus was if they like you and were prepared to chip in when a date for taking her off their hands was announce by the bands throughout both parishes in order that any objection could be raised heard and iron out saving last minute embarrassment of someone contesting your marrying at the exchange of rings.

Going out with Annette in those early days of August 1965 had strict rules attach in that I always had to collect her at her house and was expected to join in the family rosary before taking her out to the pictures or a dance with an expected time of return that was always mention which they waited up to ensure was met. They were caring and that was no bad fault and in a way was to be admired for them who love her and were good parents.

It was sad saying goodbye to Dorothy and of course Annette who knew I was a British soldier that in 1965/6 was not yet an I R A, issues that a few years down the road was to raise its ugly head. It only became an issue about 1969 when the papers and the rhetoric of the opposing sides started firing harsh words and threats both ways that till then was under the carpet control. This made serving in the British Army especially those from the south of Ireland and came from nationalist family a question which bother-some and led them to talk about the Irish situation.

Those from the north that were active lodge members in the Micks took a grudge against the Catholic stance. For me it was a different matter having been brought up by the state institute I had no loyalty to an Ireland or a family that had abandon me when a child. I was a nobody to anyone to want and pretend that as an Irishman I would fight for a cause that I cared nothing for or knew no good enough reason for me to take a side. Having escape from Ireland and made a better life for myself in that most welcome land of England I was not going to take sides in a political football match that I had no personal interest in. To be honest Ireland as my country did nothing for me or ever knew me that I should put myself out for her, least of all died for. To take sides in an Ireland question that for hundreds of years could not be found that my taking side one way or another would make any great different to the big picture of an all-Ireland.

I was very grateful for my Mick family and my life in England that not one day did I feel afraid since being here as I did in the hands of the Irish state and church when quite small. My life in the Irish Guards and the excitement of everyday laugh and challenges made the experience of being my own man unafraid of the approach that a few Micks had in those early days of been warned off by members of the IRA, who wish to make you aware that they knew you're in the British Army, and who you serve and are loyal to, what rank you are, informing you that your every move while visiting your family on army leave is being watched. In those days that are known by all now as the troubles a few Micks on leave were whispered to by strangers in a quiet threat that the boys wanted you to know their power and for you to take heed of their threats if you knew what was good for you.

Most took the warning seriously and in order that their family were kept safe took the warning very serious and for their family kept away. I did go over under the radar while in the Micks and had a great time seeing the Ireland of my dreams, a country I was born to without really knowing it as my home when a child, but now a grown man I saw the Ireland that the London Irish sang often of their special counties that I visited and saw for myself why they felt the way they did, and missed home.

I only got to really know my Ireland from songs sang and lived in those Irish dancehalls of north London that the craic was more Irish in them than any place I holiday as a visitor when over in Ireland. All in all without any family or home to stay in I travel as a free-lance Irishman that was living in

England with no loyalty to any misguided idea that this Ireland was my home and a country I would put my life on the line for that was never going to happen.

Me with girlfriend Annette O Connor
by bus stop on O Connell St Dublin 1965.

All I ever wanted was to say thank God for that recruiter Sergeant Smylie who change my life and set me on the road of the Irish Guards and the mean to be the Irish man I am proud to say I grew more Irish in heart and soul through the clubs and eyes of other like me who left for reason of supporting their family or just wanted to travel like me and be a true citizen of the world.

October 1966 the regiment said it farewell to London and to all that made our time in Chelsea Barracks a success that the battalion laid on a farewell dance which I remember was well attendant and went on into the early hours of the morning, and a week later we had the greatest of surprise in that the colonel of the regiment General Alexander of Tunis an Irish Guards war hero and a military legend came to bid all a safe journey, and God speed in wishing everyone a successful tour of duty in Aden and a safe return.

Leaving Chelsea and making our way by buses to Brize Norton in our new uniform and in tactical dress on our outward journey was done in Mick style laughing and joking as we were being taken to an Royal Air Force base where the boys in blue that we in the Micks and other guards regiment called the brill-cream boys because of their combe slick shiny hair who made our stay in Brize Norton for departure to Aden very comfortable. The food and overnight accommodation were first-class and their looking after us was up to any top hotel standard you find anywhere in the world.

Leaving the UK for Aden on that autumnal day in October 1966 was a great day full of real excitement in that here we all were making our first journey on a aeroplane and not knowing what it would feel like as many said nothing as they did not want to show any fear. Most like me had never flown before as this was for the majority their first flight in a flying machine ever in their life. To help all that had not been on an aircraft before the flying crew took you through the safety procedures of crash position, and the use of a sea jacket, it was still quite scary as in those days the noise play havoc with everyone ears that the aircraft crew gave out boiled sweets to suck on as they said it lesson the aggravation if you are distracted and it also eases the jaw stopping the build-up of pain behind the ears, and to this very day whenever I fly in the world I still sucked a sweet on take-off and landings, it was an RAF tip to compress air bubbles in the ears I believe still work.

Our first stop out to Aden from Brize Norton was at an air force base on the mediterrean island of Malta, and there again we were in the confident hands of the Royal Air Force and were treated to a lovely meal and a rest before we boarded our V C10 for our onward flight to Aden. Malta I was to learn was a British colony and in the sixties their laws and security was under the protection of the British government with an appointed governor to legislate on behalf of Her Majesty government, and implement her decrees. This small island of Malta I was not to know then would become my second home, in that I would marry a Maltese girl within two years from that stop coincidence or what maybe just faith.

Malta in October was another surprise on coming down those step of the V C 10 aeroplane you were met by a blast of warm air and for other like me on their first trip out of the United Kingdom the warm blast of heat felt really nice reminded all of beautiful summer days we have in Ireland and England in July/August months. After our refuelling and fed and rested we boarded again for our onward flight arriving in Aden at the Royal Air Force base of Khormaksar six hours later and coming down from the VC aeroplane we once again hit by hotter heat and even hotter air and into your lungs was the hottest intake of air I sucked in my life.

It was hell just getting used to the stifling heat and the fact it was late evening was a question many ask themselves as to how hot it would be at midday. We were transported to our new barrack/camp which was over the causeway in the best air condition buses the military could provide that is windows open and the whooshes of fast air that cool you a bit as the bus sped to our destination under the military police armed escort.

We were driven from the airport out of Aden City to our new home at Salerno Camp in little Aden, a wide flat space that was surrounded by high craggy hills called Jebles as if we ware fish in a square tank. The Nissan hut we would live in were very basic and the drill square for morning parade was an open piece of flatten earth that when the wind blew it cause minute sands and dust particle and everything else to swirl around in a hot dusty haze that you could not see anything as the dusty sands cut through you like a pebble dash blower. When it got very windy you had to use your face veil for protection as it felt you were being pitted by sand stones during those strong winds that swept the dry dust particle into your face that if not properly protected could leave you blind or with eye damage.

This Aden or hell as other have been heard to describe it was in army slang a punishment posting, hot as hell a dry God forsaken place with no real air conditioning but a few twirling roof fan that move the hot air from one place to another without cooling you down. Sleep was impossible at first and getting acclimatise took a bit of getting used to as the average temperature at night never dip below twenty-five degrees. The day temperature near forty plus most days leaving you sweaty uncomfortable as you just felt your energy drain from you leaving you to just want to lay on your thin mattress that you felt the spring of the bed come right through the flimsy mattress while wearing only your army issue green draws. It was so hot most of the lads in the billet lay naked as privacy is a by word in the army when you are living away from family and living back as a singleton in an all-male exclusive environment.

Living back as a single soldier was a real test of discipline for over-active men missing their wives and girlfriends who took sexual release when they believed no one was about or awake. Not long into our tour of Aden and getting acclimatise it was rumour about the camp and heard in the canteen that in order to help the men keep their mind on the job and their bodies in check the medic put bromide in the tea to subdue those natural urges that in an all-male environment will help in controlling those unwanted urges that otherwise it was said some might start acting out of character.

The navy, army and air force institutes, N, A, A, F, I, for short had local domestic workers run the shop and canteen that lived on site i.e. beneath the stars. The NAAFI was the only place one could relax and hang out when not on duty. Salerno Camp because of no walking out made all believe they were back into a depot lifestyle as everyone was confined to camp due to there being nothing of interest close by and when not on duty been in camp was the safe place to relax as best to the situation allow for down time.

It was as hot in the evening as early morning never going below twenty-five degrees at night and reaching most days the high thirties and mid-forties with it being so hot day and night sitting outside in the open air soaking up a few cold cans of Tennent beer under a heavy star-lit sky that the girls on the beer tin that is the Tenants girls picture were for most their newfound pin up, and it became a competition when not required or not on duty to challenge others in how many Tennent girls you could sink in a evening working on the fact that a case of Tennents was twenty-four cans a number one might drink if it was a company smoker or more for a serious money bet.

The picture I remember most clear of my time in Aden beside the craic and comrades we had sitting around the NAAFI tables looking into the night heavenly canopy that was its beautiful night sky and how clear and inky black the deep black curtain with trillions of shining eyes not since I was a young boy in Ireland of the fifties saw peep through and a trip to the Uluru in Australia on our fortieth wedding anniversary in 2008 had I seen a matching night sky. Those Aden night in the outdoor canteen were beautiful and because of no light pollution the natural phenomenon of the night heavens is seen in its full glory. Such night sky today is denied to many in our overpopulated towns and cities because of excessive artificial light.

A night sky with no light pollution if seen in all its beauty is awesome and give you a glimpse of a wonder of gods night eyes now only visible in an uninhabitable area of our world that to see a clear night sky shine it trillions stars is a true wonder lost too many in our over-lit world.

A posting like Aden was a big test on active service duty meaning everyone was on twenty-four hours alert and with nowhere to go when not out on duty all one could do between called out was take advantage of rest, sleep, and NAAFI canteen. I was over the moon when it was said there would be a film shown by the canteen in the open air. This was another puzzle to me as how we were going to watch a film under the night sky and it was done so simple by hanging up large white sheet on prefix poles that you brought your own NAAFI chair along with your drink, and hey presto there under the stars was the open air picture house. What a great idea this outside picture house was under the stars and the casual way we smoke, laugh, and drank beer while the film was shown.

A great success all in all for without the NAAFI canteen, and it restaurant style food our life in Salerno Camp, and the chips and sausage Walla who operated a barbecue like take away as an alternative to a N A A F I snack, life would have been boring as hell for there was nowhere to go when not on duty to get you through down time other than swap books we brought out ourselves. If volunteers were asked to go on escort to the other unit up the road in Falaise Camp where

British married soldiers have quarters it was an opportunity to see a bit of skirt the request was oversubscribed a principle against the norm of never in the army should you volunteer, exception to the rule seeing women.

The married had a lovely lifestyle in Falaise Camp with all the usual facilities and a little more freedom to use the British Petroleum complex with its swimming pool, shops and restaurants, great facilities of an all-inclusive holiday resort years away that the military families had use of including the private beach inside a protected zone with access only to BP personnel, accommodation, shops, restaurants, and B Ps private beech sealed and screen so as not to break the country modesty laws of a woman be seen in bikini or undress by unwanted eyes. The military like all other walk of life has its own class system in that officer and senior warrant officer were able to enjoy BP facilities when invited that other rank were out of bounds to.

Aden City was a culture shock the first time I went out and about doing internal security on mobile and foot patrol on the streets in big Aden. Seeing all the local women with their whole bodies cover leaving a small window for their eyes to see out from black clothes generally worn head to toe was a shock, and a question came to my mind how did men and women interact in getting to know each other in fining love if the men could not see the women/girls full face and know if she a real beauty or just an average run of the mill that women most in life really fit in.

Stupid as I was in those early days of foot patrol on the Mala main in Aden City Main Street that tourist from the ships came in to browse and buy gifts. The Mala main thorough fair was Aden City busy street and on par with London Oxford Street for shopping especially jewellery that was the big draw in any Middle East country where gold worn on the body is worth more than money in the bank.

Out on foot patrol duty on the Mala main seeing so many females wearing these long black peeping dresses I thought at first were some order of Middle Eastern nuns that modesty forbade them to show any flesh part. I knew nothing of this Arab culture, their faith, what they believed, nothing about the Muslim religion, and if there was a different between being a Muslim and an Arab, and if not could you be one and not the other.

The call to prayers by an Iman from the mosque minaret made a lot of repetitive noise that was heard across the city, and was not something I ever got use to as it was loud and a bit annoying not sweet as the bells that call the Christian faithful to pray. When you have not a clue what is being screamed out but saw men and women answer the call that in their faith I had learn prayed five time a day facing east where the sun rises. When they hear the Iman call to pray whether they are inside a mosque or not I saw them use a prayer mat to kneel and pray even on the street that it matter not who's watching as they said their prayers.

Patrols on the Mala main through Aden City commerce and business centre with it shops and stores crowded with many of these nun like women whose deep muddy brown eyes look far away so as not to make contact with any male or people of foreign race mainly us military from the UK They saw us as un-invited guest that stopped and checked their bags and them from going about their business. At first I thought they were all sisters-clones of each other because of the identical black dress they all conform to wearing and each look alike when out and about in public, faceless people.

If I'm honest I was fascinated by this culture and what the women look like when not wearing the long black head to toe garment of how attracted a race of women are they as the men I saw did not greatly impress, brown in coloured and all seemed to have moustaches and blackish beards not clean shaven like us soldier that being clean shaven is part of our daily grooming and military dress.

When out on foot patrol you saw how the city of Aden was a real mixture of rich and how the poor beg on the street, the disable, the old, all begging for handout, the worst being the street cripple children I saw under ten years old strapped onto make shift type skate board in a kneeling position as they beg using their hands wearing rag gloves as they propelled themselves along on the ground it being the only protection for their knuckles-hands they use to move themselves around begging. I ask my platoon sergeant about the cripple boys and girls the poor beggars and how any family could let this happen to their small children that seemed so cruel in earning a living. Sgt McDermot said they maybe the family only lifeline and only income for food to live on that some are made cripple by their family as the only means of them getting by.

Our accommodation in camp did not compare to what we were used to in London but we had the basic and good food, with no night life to spend money it was great place to save your credit, and when the tour is finish to have lots saved to spend on disembarkation leave when we return from Aden to London and for me onward to Dublin into the arms of my lovely Annette O Connor for the missed hugs and kisses I long for.

Our nearest neighbour to Salerno Camp was Falaise Camp occupied by royal ordnance and logistic units of the army that supply all the units ration and fuel. It was a permanent base for married military and was out of bounds unless by chance you were volunteered by your platoon sergeant on fatigues in assisting the ration sergeant whose job it was to collect the compo and fresh produce weekly then it was eyes front and not crumpet watching when on the ration run detail.

The battalion in just a short time of operating in it new role and now about acclimatise to the winter heat that was hotter than a British summer with the weather in around seventy degrees for their winter made one think what it would be like when Aden summer comes. We were informed by the medical officer that temperature hear on the Arabian peninsula can reach up to one hundred and twenty Fahrenheit, and in that heat you can believe is hot that one could fry an egg on the ground or bonnet of their Land Rover. Not long after we arrived and just getting used to our new role on internal security duty when the battalion was paraded and informed by our commanding officer Lieutenant Colonel Tony Aylmer that it would be going on a naval exercise for a week or so and your company commanders will fill you all in with more information about the exercise in the next few days.

In the short time of being in Aden all were happy in getting our teeth stuck into our new roll of internal security which involve carrying out foot and mobile patrols, looking out for suspicious packages left in shop doorways or suspicious person loitering about with intent on causing injury and death, in itself it was not an easy task to spot a dissenter that was hell bent on showing the government of Aden they disagreed with bringing foreign troops onto their street to police their streets with powers to stop and search, and arrest anyone they found to be of interest to the government official. Picking out an individual from everyday people on the street going about their business is not in a second of quick reaction easy to carry out and stop when in your head all look and act the same. Aden at that time was a country under some form of martial law that the British government was given the authority to be a force for peace, security of its own interest and stability.

Like most situation the army is put into when it comes to stop and search, male soldiers can only stop males and do a physical check while women are a no hands on except to ask may I look in your bag or other packages that they may be carrying. Having no female searchers out on patrol to do the women body check I think left security back door well and truly unlocked and our job much harder to police, for of course the government enemies would never consider using a woman to carry out or plant any such devices to cause harm and killed or hurt the occupying force of the day, right pull the other one as the saying goes.

Another roll undertaken in Aden was as guards in their main city prison where conditions for both prisoner and the staff were terrible that come the summer the heat would be insufferable hot, sticky with no real air condition and the food horrible fit only for the other residents the cockroaches, ants, that were numerous and had a free run of the place.

Government house was a security priority in that no one was allow in unless thoroughly check then escorted over to house security for them to take over and escort. On patrol one day feeling great I am thinking this is amazing in a bit of daydream time that here am I a fully trained guardsman soldiering in South Arabia less than two years out of Ireland three thousand miles or more away in the Middle East where the temperature is so hot and I'm loving it. It hadn't dawn on me that I could be shot and killed out here as this thought was the furthest away from my mind that death never enter my head and to that end I wasn't frighten and just carry on. It only when you hear the platoon officer tell everyone that we are all to be on our guard when out on patrol be very vigilant and watch for persons acting suspicious particularly a sniper type that made shoot or throw an explosive devices especially when patrolling in a crowded place causing havoc and untold harm. You soon take notice as it sink home that you could actually die if your luck ran out.

As with the army it always cover your own backside in that we are on active service duty and all are issue the green card as to the do's and don'ts and if you do have to shoot then it better be within the rule of the green card engagement otherwise it a court martial and if wrong you're on the way to Colchester military geol. Because the battalion is on active service the commanding officer ask all platoon officer to ensure everyone under their command had wrote their letter of goodbye to their family or next of kin. For should the worst happen then your love ones back home would have your hand letter written in your own words what hopefully would comfort them if faith went against you.

Your letter would be something they could hold reread knowing your last thoughts were of love for them and that the career you sign up to was your own choice and one you enjoyed and if you are reading this letter then I have died doing the job I loved with no regret, and hope you will understand it was my life and my choice, ending with, all my love yours forever xxxxx.

There was great excitement about the battalion going on the HMS Fearless ship and it taking part in a sea exercise as the rumour machine had gone into overdrive on its own about what we are going to do and were we are going. Nothing concrete comes from rumours as they are a way of passing time and keeping people busy yet hoping for someone to let slip what is really on the cards. The one thing that was true in that there was a war ship in the Aden port and it was HMS Fearless and that is the ship our battalion would be going on a sea exercise in. What the battalion role was to be on this ship no one had a clue other than we would be taking part in a sea trial of sort in what role the battalion and the navy together would act out was still unclear.

Well the waiting was over and the reality of the exercise was about to begin as the battalion boarded HMS Fearless Battle ship for it first naval exercise with the Royal Navy and a first for the regiment in its short history. The excitement among the lads on being part of this new adventure working hand in hand with our senior service was not something any Mick in his wildest dream would ever believe, but here we are on the open sea sailing about to where is as yet our unknown destination. Because of our numbers we are billeted on the deck floor which incidentally is also our training area when we put away our sleeping bags with use of the upper deck for runabout and fresh air.

The Micks to be involve with the Royal Navy on a joint exercise on the sea instead of land was a first as we trained naturally for land and not the ocean and seas like the boys of Her Majesty Royal Navy. After a few days training and learning our way around on the ship rumour are heard that something is about to change as in the close confinement of the ship walls are skin thin. It's not till we are near our target that we are told the reason for this trip and the training we have been doing on the deck is call to a halt, and a voice come over the ship tanoy informing all on board that the training you have been preparing for is no longer class as an exercise but from this moment on what we are about to undertake come under the heading of live, active and real.

It was then said that the Fearless is about to make history as an assault ship going into action the first to do so as an

23 YEARS IN THE IRISH GUARDS

assault landing since World War Two. The game had change from exercise to real in a second and once again there was a buzz as to what it is all about, and what this new role of active to real meant in respect of what it is we are about to undertake and where are we going and what our objective in this game changer was. This change meant the battalion officer would have a briefing by the commanding officer and we at platoon level would be told of our role in the upcoming operation, and the important of carrying out our mission as instructed if it to be successful by our platoon commanders.

The exercise part was easy in the sense that the on-board training was limited as to what a battalion can do other than brushing up on weapon training and circuit training we were shown a map of the area and the place where we would be landing, and the in and out of the operation and the enemy that were causing untold damage terrorising the small out post of the local sheik authority, and if successful the culprits would be detain and imprisoned. The whole emphasis was being stress on the element of surprise and use of the least amount of force apprehending the targets and locking them up.

There are many facet to military exercise that on being upgraded to real and the issue of live ammunition, preparing for an assault landing and how it will be done bearing in mind this will be the first ever assault landing carry out by any British military since World War Two making what we were about to do more serious than what we knew from our section briefing and a first test of the Fearless in her roll on active service. HMS Fearless stopped out in the deep water and the battalion in brake down of platoon fully webbed up and ready for whatever awaited boarded their landing assault craft, our platoon sergeant Harvey McDermott instructed us his boys to listen out for his words of command as when to run and jump off the assault craft after the landing door touches ground.

We were dropped by our assault craft on shore early morning in order to carried out our surprise dawn attack in apprehending our target that in all honesty would rather not come away with us. Everything when according to plan and we were all in and out inside of a few hours and heading back to Aden proper after a successful raid and hostages captured we confiscated many old and still used antique weapon that on leaving Aden I brought one back and gave it to my godmother husband George as a souvenir of my first oversea military deployment on active service.

It was a French rifle an M80 render unfit to use by the brigade armoury for me to travel with, and a signed certificate of proof that it was beyond use and not theft. It has been a treasure and looked after by George and yet I regret one thing not asking George after I married in 1968 if he minded given it back to me as it would be a magnificence heirloom to hand onto my own son as a family earned momento from my first and only campaign of active service duty in the Irish Guards that I was part of in my twenty-three years of service.

It was in twenty-eighteen my godmother sister Carmel told me George pass the rifle to his youngest son Dermot who now own the M80 souvenir with the copy of the military letter stating the weapon was render unfit for use in order that it could be carried when I travel to Dublin and gave it to George my godmother husband as a proud keep sake in September of 1967 when it was the only safe place I could have it look after in my godmother husband hands to take care of.

The laugh heard on our return to HMS Fearless of an incident about big John Graham of number two company and little George Toner that when their assault craft door was lower it hit what was thought rock beech for big John Graham a six foot five jump off and found himself standing in ankle deep water calling little George Toner five-foot nothing and the rest to jump to the right and left side of him. Little George ran and jump landing in six feet of warm water and big John catching George by his webbing and lifted him to safety as everyone was wearing full combat kit no doubt young George on this landing was not laughing and a very unhappy wet bunny not just with the navy but the other laughing wet hyenas on that assault craft.

It was later said that the landing door of the assault craft rested on a boulder-rock UN-be knowing to big John and George including the rest on disembarking who got the bath end when they jump off, it was only afterwards back on HMS Fearless when everyone was relax that they saw the funny side and could laugh out loud, and how successful the capture of the hostages went. All in all our time on HMS Fearless was great with an eye witness view of our navy boys life and their day to day routine of life at sea in that their food was first-class and the rum issue a big yes with all the Micks. I was glad all went well and that little trip was one to tell my sea merchant friend Paddy Maher in Glenart Cottage on my return of my short time on Her Majesty's battle ship the Fearless and the tightness one lives in that the accommodation and ablution on the ship are a tight squeeze while our own accommodation on board was on the belly floor of the Fearless ship because of our battalion numbers. We return to Aden and back on internal security settling into our new life and daily routine in Salerno Camp.

Church on a Sunday in Aden was another great craic in that our priest Father Michael Holman knew how to get his audience to attend and want to be at mass. It was the first time I had a beer drink offer by a priest after mass when he asked all who had come to mass that first Sunday in Salerno Camp to enjoy a cold beer with tea and coffee offered to those that could not drink for reason of going on duty later in the day. I remember it well as it was excessively hot and the sweat was rolling down the father face right through the mass and no amount of handkerchief or wind up fan could keep him cool and dry. Keeping cool in the metal bin of a makeshift church was not easy with metal doors and metal windows open and a twirling old fan with no coolant just spinning to no real effect.

Those Sunday masses started off with about twenty to thirty attending and grew nicely by word of mouth that many lapse Catholic and protestant came to the surprise of Father Michael. With the numbers growing each week that the father had to get another fridge and more beer for the Sundays masses had grown, and of course it was the only pub open out of hours and operated by a Catholic priest who also nourish the body and the souls making a great different in many a young Mick life, that many started a proper return to fulfil their Sunday duty in keeping the lord day holy. It wasn't long for the secret of why so many were at mass and the after drink that made the Catholic mass last a whole day if not on duty.

Chapter 9

Now three month in Aden and life was going well until as they say in book and films I got myself unknowingly into hot water when on check point duty at the little Aden causeway manning check point which was part of our security duty as instructed by our platoon officer that as guardsman on duty to do random checks and send the vehicle you'd stopped over to the layby for the royal electrical mechanical engineer REME for short to do a thorough check over the vehicle.

These engineers would check vehicle for any suspicious or hidden item in the vehicle that might later cause grief to lives being lost in big Aden if not found on entry. It was as usual a scorching hot day when I see this gleaming big black limousine with four or five well dress men all in fine white robes and head dress of sort what you might call well to do Arabs of the rich kind. I'm only a thick Mick doing my job under instruction of my platoon officer to stop and search at random vehicle for a check with no waver of sort for anyone but to random check like every fourth or second maybe fifth vehicle that you felt needed checking.

My platoon officer in Aden on the check point was no other than an old training cadet recruit I met in the guard's depot whose now an officer in the Irish Guards Second Lieutenant Philip O Reilly, whose family hale from the county Kildare a well-known family in the Irish horse racing fraternity.

On check point and doing my duty that day when I stopped this vehicle and politely ask the occupant to exit the vehicle but was met with a flat refusal of don't you know who we are. To which I reply, No I ask the gentlemen again to get out of the vehicle at which they again refused spouting some rubbish that they don't have to do what I'm asking and to let them pass in their best of English that they learn in school.

Not to be put off and now not listening to them wine on about their right I allow the point of my gun to drop at their face level reminding them that I'm in control of this search and that I'm not prepared to budge until you all get out and allow me to complete my stop and search.

Sticking my heels in for I did not like their self-importance in that they thought themselves better than others in their attitude that we will not be searched and you cannot force us. Well I changed that and did force them out and had all the occupant of the limousine body search as well as their big black vehicle inspected.

My covering man on check point Charlie that day I believe was John Delvin who watched keeping me cover and said nothing letting me handle the situation that I started. I insisted again that they now get out of the vehicle and stand away while the engineer check the vehicle while they too would be frisked for any concealed weapons. They certainly did not appreciate the military position in keeping their country safe from terrorism and certainly did not like being physically check for they drove angrily away on a mission for revenge after being checked and cleared to proceed.

It was about thirty minutes later that my day turn sour and my worst army nightmare began when the military police arrive at the check point screeching their tyres and certain words were being shouted and directed towards the security sentries on the crossing that was me and John in asking which of us it was that stop the diplomatic car and had the VIP personnel and vehicle search. On being questioned of the incident I said it was I who carried out the check, and without further ado I'm arrested return to my base at Salerno Camp, and locked up without explanation and not seen until the next day when I am attending commanding officer orders to be hung drawn and quarter.

Major John Head second in command was standing in for the colonel in the chair, and said, on hearing the charge brought against me, I'm sorry McDonnell but they have higher friends in Whitehall than you and me, and as I know you were carrying out your duty to the best of Micks standards, polite and firm by all account in a good and military fashion, it of no use to you, for my hands are tied, your punishment too is out of my hands as this charge is class as most serious and is a 252 charge knocking on the head any chance of you ever receiving a long service and good conduct medal on completion of your service. You had the misfortune to encounter at the check point those dignitaris with diplomatic right for which you knew nothing about or ever heard about as persons that have immunity in their own or any country having embassy immunity that is reciprocal throughout the world.

Their class status gave them right above the law and wherever they are they have immunity to any country laws that they can walk away even if it is a murder charge being aimed at them as they can just laugh in your face for this is a diplomat right worldwide. They use and have for their protection that is worldwide agreed, honoured, reciprocated by whatever host country there in to enjoy all it perks and right and especially for them here in their own land.

They were certainly not impressed with you having stop them for a vehicle search that you also had them undergo a physical man handle check and it's to that end your punishment is coming from the top to do twenty-eight days in the guardroom and serve your daytime sentence in the cookhouse on permanent fatigues from 0600 to 2200hrs daily.

Master cook Pollock nickname Fatchop, was very pleased to have my service as he put me in charge of the few Somalian kitchen Walla's which done the general mess room cleaning. I remained in the cookhouse for the rest of my tour and was join by Burt Smith and others that all done short stint in the corner hotel for a few days and those who were on restriction including an ex RQMS Mc Coombe who was a senior Mick posted to Aden headquarters and for a misdemeanour which he would not speak about was court martial and busted to a guardsman and work with me for a few weeks before he was dishonourable discharge into civilian street.

Being confine to Salerno Camp on cookhouse duties and no longer part of number three company and number two platoon stranded without belonging to any company. A prisoner of the corner shop hotel sent to work in the cookhouse to serve out my twenty-eight day sentences and used as a dogsbodies on permanent fatigues as number one mess hand in the battalion mess room. By the second in command own word my punishment was out of his hands and my sentences unfair and an injustice to me that was never put right in my 23 years of service on leaving without my long service and good conduct medal as a full sergeant.

It's ironic but at the beginning of my career my platoon officers in the guards' depot of 1964 was Lieutenant Shaun O' Dwyer, and in my last year of service 1986/7 he was my commanding officer who ask me to write a mitigation that I may have the 252 charge overturn and be able to leave with a long service and good conduct medal he firmly believe I should have.

My letter in longhand stating my reason of why I should receive my long service and good conduct medal was never answer or my 252 charge overturned. I was never allowed to go back to my platoon after serving my sentence that became a five months sentence and no longer able to do my job as a trained infantry guardsman but use as a cookhouse skiffy.

My new role in the battalion kept me away from doing my infantry role and for now I am a dogsbody no longer a three company man as informed by the master cook Fatchops on completing my sentence that I will remain as a member of the cookhouse staff until the battalion return to London and back on queen guard's duties.

Now a new member of headquarter company cookhouse staff on finishing my time in the corner shop hotel I've had to move my kit into the cookhouse Nissan hut that was worst for peace and quiet for the cooks work all hours night and day and my hours from 0600 hrs daily finishing most night about 2000 hrs or later if required.

Leaving the platoon I joined in March 1965 was very hard I had got used to working as a full accepted member of number two platoon these last two years. We all knew how each other ticked besides the strong trust that was built up knowing that if you were in trouble you could rely on each other especially if it was a situation in saving one life.

Working in the cookhouse was not a job I enjoyed it was humiliating a punishment detail that all in my Mick family were aware of my sin and the unjust way I was used as a cookhouse Walla. I missed very much my infantry roll I had been trained for and was really annoyed and most upset having serve my sentence for those angry white sheeted high official Arabs that my infantry soldiering days should abruptly end. After four months into the battalion tour that I was no longer part of two platoon of number three company and no more would I be with my platoon on Aden streets carrying out stop and searches and other roles we undertook as prison guards in Aden main prison, and sentry box duty at the entrance of government house as if we were guarding Her Majesty the queen. For the governor is the queen represented and is accorded by all the greatest of respect in the holding of his office.

When on prison duties it was like being a prisoner yourself as the prison was old and very run down with little investment as to the comfort of the detainee and staff, and in such bad condition you felt for them in that the heat of the day made you feel sweaty and wrenched forever hoping to have a shower to feel clean when your shift was done. Now a fatigue man extraordinaire in the cookhouse of Salerno Camp for the remainder of my tour and a new member of headquarter company, and the cookhouse staff. It was a real shock to see first-hand the hard work done by the regimental cooks behind the scene and the intense heat they work under making ready each meals for so many at different times in different location and at all hours of the day and night.

The regimental cook earn my full respect that as a three company member who before my transfer to the cookhouse staff I was like the rest in the battalion who just turn up for their meals and filled their plates, their bellies, scoffing down their food then walking away full without ever a word of thanks with the usual jibe to the cooks that you might learn to cook as the banter between squaddies is more for a laugh than what made sound to a unmilitary person as sarcasm or criticism. I was seeing first-hand how the regimental cooks clean and wash down and made ready the next meal that all would rolled in and eat again without a thought that these regimental cooks work their backsides off in such heat that was made worst from the hot pressure environment they work day and night in.

I have to say the boys in the kitchen were very good to me as in my punishment days I got to know all of them very well and while they are guardsmen first and battalion regimental cooks second they deserve more credit than they get in the variety of culinary dishes that like true magician make the meals happen. Names I still remember and their rank in Aden days were Guardsman Taggert, L/Cpl John Clavin known to all as J.C. L/Cpl Ray Kidd, battalion boxer and cook comedian, the infamous L/sergeant Paddy Shannahan, and guardsman Gerry Harmon from Liverpool, Fatchop the master cook and his 2 I/C a big well fed cook from Belfast L/Sgt Billy Boal a few others whose names escape me after fifty odd years.

Working alongside the cookhouse staff were many Somalian workers the army employ and accommodated in their own hut that most night because of the Aden heat I saw bed down under the stars on make shift beds behind the cookhouse and washroom. They were very good workers especially in the heat that as they came from a neighbouring hot country Somalia working in the heat was not a big problem for them. I never saw any of them ever without a big wide smile as they greeted each other and the cook staff with a customary God greeting Salam Alekum which we learn to mean, God be with you and you in return reply the same words in reversed Alekum Salam.

They all had a chewing habit that they fed themselves from small pouches held around their waste that after working with them for a few weeks they began to trust that I would do them no harm and when I ask could I have some of what I thought was chewing tobacco I learned as time passed how addicted it was, and my reliance on it that while chewing this tobacco like substance it kept you alert awake and generally calm. It was known to all in the Middle East and the India sub-continent as kaki and in the do and don'ts of military drug takings this chewing stuff the Somalians had was not on the army ban list as far as substance not to be taking.

I got to like it and found it kept you going when you should be resting it was no doubt a magic tobacco that kept you alert, full of energy. It took a while after Aden to get used to not having it as the withdrawal feeling was thirst, restlessness as opposed to never being tired that it took a few months after Aden to be on an even keel again.

A big part of my cookhouse duties after meals was in cleaning down and washing the stone floor and doing pan diving and spuds bashing with company fatigue men that the master cook Fatchop requested and company rotated in supplying a task no one volunteer to do. Another job of mine was to make sure the hay-boxes were clean and ready for collection and label correctly for the company's CQMS to take out of Selerno camp to their men on security patrols and check point duty. With so much going on for the battalion in Aden our main role was of course peace keeping and the security of British interest like the BP oil refinery, their dependants, families are quarter.

One company from the battalion went up country to the Red Fan this stretch the battalion as another company was task to work on the dock due to an all-out dock strike unloading ship's cargo in order to keep the local businesses and stores supplied with their goods. It was all too much

Myself and Gerry Harmon showing of our Muscles Aden 1966/67.

Myself and guardsman Taggert having a break Aden 1966/67.

Cookhouse staff Aden 1967.

really in the task ask by Her Majesty government that besides our other duties as infantry soldiers we must be equally Jack of all trade in every situation ask. There was little time in Aden for rest and recuperation although a lucky few from the battalion when the docks strike was over were able to have a break in Kenya for a few weeks while most carry on soldiering, and other selected to do a corporal course which would be a six weeks' hot and gruelling course in the Aden heat.

This was a real test of soldiering at its best as the heat on the square was a killer and the corporal course started each day at six in the morning and again 1700hrs in the evening supposedly the coolest times of the day but in a hell hole like Aden the heat was twenty-four hours and without trees to shade and the rocky nature of the camp setting surrounded by high Jebels that deflected heat it was a rock fish bowl that the heat bounce off the ground making it horrendous for those doing the corporal drill course.

I do believe it was not a course anyone volunteer to be on remembering the army first rule never volunteer. But the army is an ever-moving part always moving forward and making ready those that will lead it in the future never letting a rolling stone gather moss as an army has to be ready for anything, terrain, and temperature in doing its job that when you are sent you just do and get on with.

There were sad and bad days in Aden when news reach the battalion of fatality in the like the anti-tank weapon that blew up killing four when practising their drill procedure in it firing. Other in the ambush up country by FLA the freedom liberation army when four Micks died and other wounded fighting their way out of an ambush.

I learned first-hand from guardsman George Doyle who was on that patrol in the Wadi who told of the bravery of all the lads especially guardsman Bell who was one of the four killed and high praise for the quick thinking L/Sgt Ken Lewis, now MM (Military Medal) who saved the day and more lives from being lost. The sad death and accident in which Sergeant Fitzpatrick's died was avoidable if the stud of the 9mm holster had not unfasten itself when he bent down to lift the lunch hay-box the 9mm gun hit the ground and fired a discharge bullet killing him.

We had funny days too when the likes of some scruffy undercover soldiers visit our camp for a few hours and I honestly laugh at the incident in which they line up in the cookhouse for food to eat when Fat chop Pollock the master cook seeing them pounces on them given it the big I am in how dare you come into my cookhouse unshaven and scruffily dress that he order them to leave and return when they have cleaned up. The senior of the three individuals lined up pulled Fat chop aside and quietly but for all in the queue to hear ask who are you, and in a no un-Mick manner told Fatchops to keep his big fat nose out of their business, he was heard to blurt out you cannot talk to me like that because I am a senior warrant officer and you should have more respect. When he whisper in Fat chop's shell like ear I'm a major in rank and I'm not asking you for an effing salute.

Nothing more was said as Fat chop return behind the hotplate for safety and talk away to himself, saying he should have been told of their calling in for lunch that would have save looking the big eejit he made of himself in front of what every guardsman in the cookhouse queue knew them to be member of the S. A. S, special air service, who give no information of what they're about or information to those who don't need to know, and are only answerable to their own project leader.

St Patrick's Day Aden 1967 went down very well with our number one soldier presented the regiment with the shamrock. Having the top-man of the Irish Guards Field marshal General Alexander of Tunis a World War Two legend and an Irish Guardsman to boot our colonel in chief to celebrate the regiment St Patricks day was the biggest morale booster the regiment could ask for. Not only did he present the shamrocks to all rank but deserving members with their long service and good conduct medals to those having completed eighteen years outstanding service and any other awards such as colonel's own accommodation on a good report.

The Micks soldiered on with all the duties thrown at them for the next few months having now got use to the extremely hot days and night that it became no bother to member of the battalion in doing their duty patrolling on the Mala main or other hot-spot and places of trouble where the enemy live and thought untouchable that we enter and flush out and apprehended if need be. Maintaining security on government house, including twenty-four-hour manning of check point between big and little Aden kept the battalion very busy. The docks and it cargo strike ended after a few weeks and life at Aden port return to normal and the daily routine of preparation for hand over was loud and clear that we in the August would be returning and Aden would become self-governing thereafter.

It sounds silly that now we are ready to go home to the UK the general feeling about our tour be that it was without families the regiment had become close in the months away from their home base of Chelsea London. All know when back in London and doing public duty our time spent together in Aden will never again be as rich as it was in our getting to know each other that those months gave us as the close family we know ourselves to be the true meaning of our

Mick family. The tears we shed for guardsmen friends left behind in Silent Valley that forever sleep name I include so they're forever remember, and my remembrance poem. Roll call of our dead.

Guardsman E Bell 30/1/1967
Guardsman WJ Coleman 30/1/1967
Guardsman P J Corry 30/1/1967
Guardsman A S Cornett 30/1/1967
L/Sgt P Reilly 20/4/1967
Sgt T P Thunder 20/4/1967
L/Cpl M J Frear 20/4/1967
Guardsman T Bell 20/4/1967
Sgt E J Fitzpatrick 06/6/1967

My remembrance

It five a.m. this November morning
As I recollect this is a special day,
I am making my way to work, this being
Sunday I know others will go to church.
Standing near the railway bridge in the dim
Artificial light I notice the quiet of this new
Day, and that those asleep may have never
Seen their village at this ghostly hour. I look
Down at it emptiness and watched shadows
Move from under a swinging light and see the
Wind sweep the dry crisp leaves golden and russet
Brown, loudly along as they find shelter against
Doorways and gutters, clogging the rain drains.
All this rushed through my mind as I waited for
My lift, the thought of age old men and women
Who themselves have no reason to be out of bed

But will because they're still alive and kicking,
They, last night would have met fellow hero's at the
Albert Hall who done their duty like them when they
Were called. Again this weekend live for their
Friends who never came home by remembering them.
Recalling the days when they were young and answered
To their name
For them we have live never forgetting the pain of war
That forever haunts us who have grown old in peacetime
While the vision of our comrade's dead, lie forever young.
The turnout of veterans in Whitehall by the cenotaph is
Enormous and the watching crowd too, is huge.
The colours of the ribbons and battalion berets worn are
Complimented by the high standard of spit and polished
Shoes,
Shining and gleaming medals that are worn with pride by
Soldiers who stand ramrod straight, letting their battle
Wounds and missed limbs take second place, in honour
Of those who gave their lives should be remember first.
The camaraderie that bond soldiers is special in that they
Give selflessly of themselves no matter the years of being
Apart, when they do see each other on parade. At reunion
They behave as if no years have past and the memories of
Yesterday come flooding back reliving the war stories told.
The great two minutes silence is led by Her Majesty and
Her government, and in that eerie silence can be heard the Mind
Play-back of a million memories, each caught up in his or
Her
Own war that s personal to them. The remembered fallen
Faces,
The loud scream of get up and the emptiness felt in going On
And leaving them to be counted and found later. The noise
That

Disoriented you and your deafness in not hearing the Command.
The question asked in the years since, "why me", and the Guilt it carries,
In the faces of those families whose sons, husbands, fathers, Never return.
My two minutes of remembrance is over as my lift pulled
Up beside me, the leaves that lay about my feet have become
For me this Sunday morning my own remembrance poppies
To the fallen. As I too remember all since the 1914 /18 & 1939/45 war and
Reflect silently on my own service in the Irish Guards, our fallen
Men who lie buried in Silent valley, Aden. 1966/67, and the
Sacrifices made by young Irish Guardsmen of today.

The regiment tour of duty was coming to an end and all could say with hand on heart we did what was ask with honesty and fairness to the best of one military trained ability. The argyle and Sutherland highland station in big Aden around the crater area when they were hit and loss several men that their colonel known as Mad Mitch live up to his name for as a soldier-soldier he went in search of the perpetrator to avenge their cowardly attack that hit the news that in the modern annals of post-war history he will always be remembered as a man who looked after and care for the men that he commanded.

We came home to public duty better men than went to Aden as living and working together for near on a year made us stronger and closer having tested our reliance on our mucker that each and every Mick is and under the most trying condition prove what Sgt Smylie told me in that Liverpool recruitment office on joining three years before I know now to be true.

The battalion first orders on return to Elizabeth Barracks in Surrey was to send all rank on block leave for a well-deserved three weeks' rest and recuperation. Having been away in Aden and not seeing my girlfriend Annette O Connor for a year somehow or other our relationship had taken a knock when we did meet up again. Although she wanted and was keen to start again I realise it was time to be honest and I told her let see how we get on over the next few weeks. I knew both of us over the last year had changed weather we wanted to accept it or not we were wanting different things and to travel different roads in life. I knew the relationship I had before without pushing was not what I wanted. I was now twenty and wanted to have a proper girlfriend that was nearby and not across the sea in Ireland and one who wanted to be my wife and support my army career.

Annette was a Dublin home bird and she knew I was not coming back to live in Ireland as in some way we both knew our relationship had change and was not working and maybe we should just remain friends, it was puppy love that was going nowhere that both of us knew had run its course, and unless I stayed in Dublin it was best to finish. During my nine months away in Aden her letters were great to receive from Dublin and her family news, and if honest it was hard for us both to say we love each other and really mean it when all what we ever had was odd weekends and army leave over the last three years to be proper boyfriend and girlfriend.

Annette wanted me to come back to Dublin as she had no thought ever of leaving her home and family to live in England. What she wanted could only happen if I left the Micks and returned to Dublin and restart a full and meaningful relationship with her in the hope of us settling down and of course my finding a good job in the guarda sicohana/police or security industry to support our family to be.

I told her it was no good my returning to Ireland as it was not on my cards at this time for I was very happy in the Irish Guards and I was hoping she would make the jump across the sea to be with me to which she did not want to do, and so on that embarkation leave we parted as good friends with decision to where our relationship was.

I left sad and told her I would think about what she wanted as I did not want to hurt her by stringing her along as our lives must move on and find whatever plan the lord has for us, and with that I said I write as to how I'm getting on and if I be coming back. I brought back a rifle from Aden as a souvenir which I gave to my godmother's husband George and the army citation that this gun was made safe and not for use in any way. I acquire the rifle on that exercise Operation Fate we carried out from HMS Fearless when we search the village to apprehend the dissenter the Micks surprise in capturing and detained. The souvenir weapon I brought back was part of the confiscated arms we collected up the coast of Aden on that surprise dawn raid and as there were many find of this kind it was a beautiful present to bring home as a real military souvenir of my first campaign in a conflict zone that I thank God I came home safe from and the rifle was a relic made safe by the artificer for me to take home.

On our return to Elizabeth barracks after leave I began to settle into my new home in the Surrey countryside unlike London where all the amenity were close to hand by tube or bus. To go anywhere worthwhile it was the local bus that took you to the two nearby towns of Woking and Guildford. Woking was an old friend of mine as that were I attended Sunday mass three years ago when I was a recruit in sixty-four at the guards' depot when I was a past parishioner of St Dustan's in Woking. Like ducks to water the battalion was back on London and Windsor guard duty and life as a guardsman become the norm again as if we the Micks had never left.

The local bus travel through Deep-cut and our new accommodation lines at Elizabeth barracks on route to Woking and Guildford our escape to civilian life outside of the military routine, it took the bus about thirty minutes to Woking and an hour to Guildford, and forty minutes to London by train from Brookwood station. The last bus was just after ten past midnight not good if you went to the Atlantic ballroom or invited to a party from the pub, and it was quite common that many a night we got back to barrack by Shanks's pony on foot.

On the battalion return off leave I was put into number two company under company sergeant Major Billy Cook who had a croke voice that I found hard to understand although a very fair and a real gentleman. His son Billy Cook junior was stocky build and talk like his dad and like his dad a very kind Mick who work in the MT platoon as a driver/mechanic.

I got to know many Micks during my time in Aden from other company as they passed through the cookhouse inasmuch that many became exceptionally good friends, like Jimmy McInerney, Andy Doogue, William Murphy known to all as Spud, and my predecessor of the Hoffman press, Bernie Boylan a smart and clever Dubliner. It was through my friendship with Bernie the battalion presser and hanging around the tailors' department that I learned how to to use the Hoffman press while keeping him company as Bernie was an officer in a guardsman head he was a very clever lad and always well dress as he loved wearing suit and tie no matter the occasion to a dance or to church. Every occasion outside of barracks Bernie was as a guardsman should be immaculately dress that his civilian shoes were also highly spit and polish as if going on Her Majesty the queen's guard.

In keeping up with my faith I was back at St Dunstan in Woking that a few years before when training in the guard's depot I landed myself in hot water for wanting to do my Catholic duty that I still hear the whisper in my ear if McDonnell does not go to mass on Sundays I want to know so said the company commander Major RTP Hume.

Father Seamus Hester the parish priest mentioned that the legion of Mary would be meeting after mass tonight in the parish hall, and it got me thinking remembering my own time being in the legion and prayers from the school, and decided I would re-join the legion of Mary again. I when along when I notice a beautiful dark hair and attracted dark eyes petite girl who caught my attention and I was hook like the proverbial fish that this must be what they call love at first sight she was wearing a black and white thin stripe dress that had a black piping to it border and she was small but nicely shaped. If I'm really honest she was the image of those beautiful Arab ladies without the sheet covering, and her eyes spoke a lot to me. I was mesmerised by them and have never look back I was in love.

I suppose one could say she had hot eyes and I was burned that the heat of my desire would not cool down and I was hopping around as if running on hot coals. My future wife I believe, so sure was I, that I told Andy and Bernie of the girl I saw at the legion that I will one day married, and they both thought maybe my celibate life was getting the better of me, and I should wait after all we all been out of action in the women department for near on a year, and maybe you should wait and see as you don't need to rush in where fools fear to tread. Getting serious with a girl can cause you a lot of trouble that right now you don't need as there is plenty of time and you have just turn an army twenty-one.

It wasn't long after my leave in Ireland that I was smitten and I wrote to Annette to explain I would no longer be stepping out or writing with her as I have found a new girl to go steady with from the legion of Mary where I go to church. I wished Annette all the best in her quest for the future and as we had been more pen-pal than girl/boyfriend it was sad but easy for me to let her go. And as we talk last when I was home that somehow or other we have both change and my saying goodbye to her in Dublin I believe Annette knew it was over. For both of us had whether we like it or not grown apart I thank her again for all her letters while in Aden and her Dublin news reporting in her frank way. I was sad we drifted and I did not want to use that old cliché lets be friends for it never works as I was letting her go and it was only a matter of time when she would have done the same to me.

Chapter 10

I started dating Miriam shortly after our introduction and going out together as legionnaires we visited and pray with those that would let us into their homes. For in Ireland knocking on door and saying you're from the legion of Mary you got a good response whereas here in England knocking on door and saying you're from St Dunstan's church on behalf of the legions of Mary you got nine out of ten the same result as if you just told them you're a Mormon, a Jehovah witness, or in the foreign legion it was a polite no and please do not call again.

About three months into our relationship I asked Miriam would she marry me and she laugh saying she would think about it. There were many obstacle and voices against her marrying or going out with me, not least St Dunstan parish priest Fr Seamus Hester an Irishman himself. One he's in the army and away a lot on posting and exercises which might not be what you want in your marriage and two he's Irish, and you know how they like a drink and enjoy the craic. My reputation destroy without knowing the persons that fed her this tripe as if all army and Irish men are no good.

To marry in the army in the 1960s you had to go on orders and ask for permission from your commanding officer and get his permission also to wear your public duty uniform and to inform the families' office in order to get a married quarter. Permission was needed in those days to get married and the wedding date we settle on after Miriam said yes was for the tenth of October 1968 a year away. My best man would be Bernie Boylan with other Micks and nurses friend from Victoria hospital where Miriam was a trainee nurse to invite and have as our family.

Miriam like me had no family in the UK, and I had none anywhere but for my new family of brothers Micks that Bernie Boylan was going to be my best man.

It November 1967 I getting on well in number two company although there is a little bit of excitement in that big John Graham has lost the plot in that there is a guardsman by the name of Flowers from South Africa, tan-brown in colour. Although a good Mick he fell under the hatred eye of big John who had acquire several rounds of 7.62 rifle ammunition by theft of the shooting range, and started shooting across the barracks square indiscrimialy on seeing guardsman Flowers return from a night out. Graham is heard shouting obscenities to get down and crawl on the ground like the snake you are weather he is drunk or sober is not known as he shout at young guardsman Flowers taking pot shot and frightening all and sundry of his stupid intent that was in no way funny though he thought a great laugh.

Never mind the chaos he cause and the drama for everyone else been search and the end of all guardsmen being responsible for their personal weapon that now we all have to hand our weapons in to the company armoury on completion of any training, public duty, weapon cleaning, that never again would this stupid act be repeated.

In future all weapons will be kept under lock and key when not been used it was written into battalion and company standing orders, and will require a signature when signing in or out no longer will any weapon be kept in personal locker as was the trusted practice. The conclusion of big John rampage came to an end when the piquet officer of the day call out the barrack guard and big John escapade was brought to a control end with him put into the guardroom known to all as been thrown in the hole. and for reason not know to any of us he ended up on commanding officer order and was given some form of punishment that some weeks later he was a member of the regimental headquarters staff in London never to return to the battalion for the remainder of his time in the Irish Guards.

This was not the punishment expected by all of us as member of two company at the time in firing live ammunition at another with intent and escaping proper punishment for the hurt he inflicted on poor guardsman Flowers. It was an insult and a mockery of punishment been serve that left a sour taste as to why. It was thought by all that a fitting place for him was eider in Netley the army own mental hospital or the military correction prison in Colchester at Her Majesty pleasure for a year or two. But like most thing in the army rumour control had it reported that his career was save and that he was being protected by someone in a very senior position of power who intervene for him how true the rumour was no one can really say but big John Graham was very lucky and finish his service as an guardsman orderly runner for regimental headquarters London district at the twenty-two year point rather than what should have been a prison sentence and on completion a dishonourable discharge.

Just out of Sandhurst academy of nineteen sixty-eight saw a new commission officer join our company he was a prince from Brunei now a new Mick officer. He was small by guards standard that the bearskin did not make him look any taller it was great having a celebrity to have on guard and he could rub shoulders with the best and the riches, for his wealth put some other guards officer income to shame for it was reckon most guards officers were of old money and landed gentry a nice way of saying of the aristocracy.

The prince of Brunei could afford to splash the cash as he was reputed to be one of the riches person in the world, and his buying of fast cars and clubbing the night away in the best of what London had to offer in restaurants and London night clubs was no obstacle to his bank account in Mick language his lifestyle was small change as to how rich he was.

Life in Elizabeth barracks went on with little change from nineteen sixty-seven seamlessly into sixty-eight and my looking forward to getting married to my girlfriend was becoming a reality the more we saw each other the more I knew we were right for each other. I have been going steady with my Maltese girlfriend Miriam a trainee nurse at Victoria hospital Woking just over six months, and was looking forward to being a married man on the tenth of October 1968.

As was the norm in those days of the sixties and for many more years a guardsman wishing to marry had to get his commanding officer permission to marry and his permission to wear home service clothing as most guardsmen took the opportunity to stand out on their wedding day by wearing their Irish Guards uniform in red tunic with shiny brass button to stand beautifully beside the snow white wedding dress of their bride which makes for a great photograph and one to treasure when old and grey.

With all the wedding plans made it was just a matter of being a good guardsman and keeping myself out of trouble and getting by without being pulled up for being in bad order on any type of parade or any breach of military rules as that would land me on company order being disciplined and if I ended up on restriction of privileges then I could not leave barrack for possibly seven days unable to see my Miriam who as yet did not understand confinement to barracks when undergoing restrictions.

Life on the whole was grand and if I were not on any duty then I was free to sign in and out to meet my girlfriend in Woking at Victoria hospital until require for my next day duty on muster parade. Over the Christmas leave I went to Ireland for a week returning to spend the remainder of battalion leave with Miriam. London duty kept the battalion busy and as March arrive the Micks saw in St Patricks day and once again the battalion is honoured with the queen mum presented her gift of shamrock to the regiment, with more spring drill, and shooting classification which took the battalion up to the month of May for the commanding officer and the major general inspection in full tunic order. Both inspection make for the battalion high standard and readiness which is key in their mind for Her Majesty birthday parade in June when the seven guards regiment together honour their commander in chief on her official celebrated birthday parade.

I believe all rank think the queen birthday parade is the highlight of the London ceremonial season that whatever battalion turn it is to troop it colours will as if it is a competition go out of their way to making it the best troop she seen and win over Her Majesty's approval for the expert eye she is well noted to have that the regiment doing the troop wait to receive Her Majesty's warmest thank and her signed letter to all those that had taken part in her birthday parade and making it a wonderful success.

A few weeks after the trooping of the colours the commanding officer informed the battalion of an upcoming adventuring training period in Cyprus for six weeks, away from public duty and an opportunity to do something different than staging on and off on Buck house, St James's, Tower of London and the beautiful Windsor Castle duties that has been our daily diet since our return from Aden and with little time for anything else this going to Cyprus was a real battalion pick us up.

There was in the battalion many ex-Irish Army boys that had serve with the unite nation in the Congo of 1960, and infamous among these ex-Irish Army men was Congo Joe Connelly, Snag Sean Kelly a good friend of mine from Dublin and Andy Doogue from county Kildare and other not familiar to me, it was suggested to me with the Irish Army on tour in Cyprus we should try and arrange a Gaelic football or a hurling match. Snag Kelly contacted some old friends as did the other Micks that serve and got the ball rolling of the possibility of a game as a mean of a welcome and an extended hand of friendship between Irishmen serving in both armies and the fact that we were first and foremost born Irishmen.

Our time in Cyprus was to make a big change from marching and soldiering and take on an adventurous attitude in rock climbing, boating, and swimming. This was seen as another form of military fitness and one all enjoy in learning new skills that would come in handy on other exercises in the future. There were a few Micks who had serve in the Irish Army and wore United Nation medal from serving in the Belgium Congo when in the Irish Army. Because the British Army is part of the United Nation force an agreement was made that any of the Irish Guardsmen who serve first in the Irish Army and received their United Nation medals were allowed to wear their earned UN medal with the British medals for the ribbon colour and medal is the same for all

Battalion Hurling team Cyprus 1968. Back row, left to right.
Tex Egan, Dixie Dean, Jimmy Fitzsimmons, Sean Duffy, Pat Dwyer, ?,
Willie Wilson, Patsy Fahy, Kennedy, Cunningham, Joe Quinn,
front row left to right, John Galvin, Jack McDonnell, aka Philip, ?,
Wally Welsh, Paddy McGowan, Flowery Lynch, Fergie Hall,
L/Sgt Guiron, Name ? Escapes me.

10th October 1968 wedding day with friends and best man
Jimmy McInerney, and maid of honour Doreen Shanley.

Miriam & I cutting the wedding cake.

Wedding couple & 3 Priest, Father Seamus Hester in black soutane, army Chaplain and Maltese priest as witness for the Malta government.

United Nation countries that do peace keeping service which the British Army is a signature to.

When Ireland first joined the United Nation in 1960 its troop were sent on it first peaceful mission to the Belgian Congo I was a boy of thirteen working on the school farm, and four years later here am I in the Irish Guards and able to speak with person that first serve outside of Ireland as part of that international force. It was through Sean Kelly contact that we were able prior to our Cyprus training that had made contact with some Irish high command officer that he served with and he offered the challenge at the Curragh for a game of hurling against their boys serving while we the Micks are in Cyprus on adventure training.

Though not part of the United Nations but as a training battalion on out of bound course for six weeks guest of the British sovereign base in Cyprus while the Irish Army company is up the road in Nicosia serving with the United Nations peace keeping force in Cyprus. This would be good for Irish morale on both side of the divide to see that there is no fight with fellow Irish men in both our countries army that we represent, and to have Telefis Eireann come along and film a historic meet of two opposing sides that Irishmen who serve in both armies can play a friendly game. The Irish Guards regiment was form by Her Majesty Queen Victoria in honour of Irish men over the centuries having fought for Great Britain and it empire long before there was a Free State that came to be after the Easter rising of 1921. This meeting on the field in Cyprus of Irish men playing a hurling match would go down in the regiment history as it would for the Irish Army that in July 1968 before the trouble showed itself what friends and good sportsmanship both armies made happen and was a great success.

The great day came and our team was up for the kill, and with gusto both side play as if in Croke Park a sunny Sunday afternoon our corps of drum and some Irish pipers done both team proud in leading both sides out for the game. I believe we won the hurling match but lost the return in Gaelic football two weeks later. The Irish Guards hurling team on the field that day I remember are, Tex Egan, Joe Quinn, myself – Philip/Jack McDonnell, John Galvin, Willy Wilson, Patsy Fahy, Dixie Dean, Flowery lynch, Willy Walsh, Paddy McGowan, Fergie Hall, McCarthy, J Kennedy, Foxy Cunningham, Jimmy Fitzsimmons, Ginger Duffy Sean Kelly C/Sergeant Mick Guerin? Names not remembered.

It was during this six week of adventure training that I really got to know a few more good Micks that became great friends the like of Bullets Fitzpatrick's, Richard Coe, and Johnathan Coe a Mick cadet from rugby school on a visit that a year later was a young officer in number one company, Dicey Reilly and George Doyle three of whom I knew in Artane Christian Brothers school and were ex Artane Boys as was Willy Wilson who played on the Irish Guards Hurley team.

Flowery lynch from the cookhouse was another good friend and told me and the boys when having a jar in the make shift NAAFI that we ought to think about the situation in Ireland changing, and I must confess my stupidity as I had not a clue what he was talking about in that there was trouble brewing in the north of Ireland and we might be needed if our country call.

I was at a loss to what he was on about as I had no real interest in anything about Ireland for as a boy brought up behind walls I knew nothing of that patriotism he talk about. For the Ireland I remember was one of daily beating when young and being called many names and a good for nothing.

Like Richard and Dicey we just shrugged what Flowery said as talking spoof and it was only after Cyprus leave that we found out Flowery had done a runner and never came back. It was rumour in the Mick grape vine that he did wrote a letter explaining that he could no longer serve two masters as his country needed him how true that was is anyone guest. Many a night local transport took those that wanted to go into Famagusta the biggest town in 1968 before the division that came in the Turkish invasion of 1974 putting an end to the best clubs and night life on what was then Cyprus and my favourite haunt the blue angel a great place to enjoy the Greek craic.

Cyprus sixty-eight was a great break and it was for all a real change of pace to London duties but like all good things we return and went on block leave for two weeks. I stay in Elizabeth barrack and got to see Miriam most evening when she was not on duty and to be honest I could not wait for when we would live together as man and wife in our own home that the army would help provide for it would be the first real place I could call home and I wanted it so bad.

My best friend and best man to be at our wedding Bernie Boylan the battalion presser and my instructor in using the Hoffman press where I use to hang out a lot after duty and had done cover when he was on sick-leave. Bernie went home to Dublin on leave and as one of those street Dubliner that pulled himself up from the corporation flat and always dress smartly walking around with that air of having made good as an Irish Guardsman secretly wishing he was well to do and an officer because of the way he showed off.

After the battalion return of leave and the company's muster parade was taken it was found that Bernie was missing and an investigation was made with the British embassy to ask the garda in Dublin to check on him at home and see if all is well. They reported back to regimental headquarters that Guardsman Bernie Boylan was killed in a hit and run and the driver failed to stop or call the emergency services. The only information the family was given by the gardai was their son was involved in a hit and run and found dead on the road other than that the family were left very heartbroken.

Bernie's death was local news for a day or so with no one ever brought forward or charged for his death just another statistic in the reported death that devastate family, and the government promises it will act that really nothing ever changes. It was then that I was called to work as the battalion full-time presser as I was the only one outside of the tailoring staff that was trained in it used.

October came and my new best man Jimmy Mc Inerney another Dublin man from Balbriggan came to my rescue and done a great job also with the best man speech. The wedding went off without a hitch, and all round it was a lovely day once the obligatory photographs were finished we all headed to the Cotteridge hotel in Woking and got stuck into the wedding proper. The reception and the Hooley went on into the night and the Liffey Guinness water freely flowed.

Our piper Frank Stanley another great Dubliner played beautiful and in true Mick style let his hair down a bit too much in he was found passed out on a settee chair late in the evening not as an Irish piper but more as a Scot piper with all the world viewing his crown of jewels. Many years later we learn that Frank on leaving the Micks move back to Dublin and his weakness for the drink got the better of him that within a few years Frank sadly died on the street of his beloved Dublin, was found in the gutter as a down and out so the Mick rumour machine from Dublin reported some time later.

A very sad end to a fantastic Mick who was a great piper that live life in the regiment to the full should end his days in his own home town alone and lost.

With the wedding having gone down well we were off to having a fantastic time in Malta and my getting to know Miriam family as our married life got off to a good start. We spent two weeks in Gozo/Malta and their custom on greeting a visitor into their home was to offer a martini, a whiskey, a beer, it was for me very hard to say please no after the second house for she had many family in the village I would be on my chin strap if I did not say an emphatic no because a drink at each house would be too much when we are calling just to say hello.

It seemed to me that everybody we saw was a relative to my wife as we walk about Miriam would say what number cousin that man or woman who say hello keeping count was useless it was easier to ask is he or she a relative for even the local priest was a cousin three remove and another her uncle, and many women of the family were nuns including her sister who was a Dominican nun. Miriam spent a few years as a nun in the Malta order of the Sister of Charity. When an orphan baby I was put into the churches hands and it was the Irish Sister of Charity at Rathdrum Convent in county Wicklow that took care of me till I was eight years old when I was handed over to the Christian Brothers the Irish church gestapo at Artane Industrial School till the age of sixteen.

Being married I found out it did not entitle us automatically to getting a married quarter as we had no point as newlywed and I was of the lowest rank a guardsman. Advised by the family's officers Capt. Byrne and families C/Sgt Freddy Brown our best option was to go out and find a hiring that the army would contribute rent towards as there is a great shortage of army quarters right now and this we did before our wedding and found a flat that on our return we could walk straight into and begin our married life.

We did find a private hiring by Ascot Heather wood hospital where Miriam found work as a newly qualified nurse from Victoria training hospital Woking. The hiring we found was on Burleigh road a stone throw from the renowned Royal Ascot race course where Her Majesty the queen open Royal Ascot each year in her carriage procession that on each day of Royal Ascot racing is a highlight of whom the queen has chosen to escort her as she see out her special week watching the classic royal races that proper code dress is the order of the week, and the fashionista look to see what colour Her Majesty chose to wear and type of hat to match.

You could see the best of money men and women splashed out on fashion, hats especially in the sixties like the infamous Mrs Shilling whose hat each year was the talk of Ascot.

You also see the best of horse flesh that on show and the great numbers that attend and enjoy the craic, betting, drinking, wining, laughter, tears, and the raucous cheers that goes up at the race finish line, and at the end of each Ascot day they gather around the Ascot grand bandstand to rousing singing and the swilling of much varied drinks from beer, gin and tonic, and copious champagne.

I and Miriam settled down well and are getting to know each other better in the small thing like the food we eat and the household jobs we'll do. Miriam job as a qualified nurse working at Heatherwood hospital help to pay the rent on our hiring in Burleigh Road Ascot in what may have been the servant quarters now converted into a flat inside this huge big house that was owned by a Mrs Hanna who during our time there I believed was widowed.

There was an elderly man in his late sixties with a good tuff of grey hair and a reddish face that occupy a mobile home in the big house rear garden. He was such a nice man and he introduce himself to us by saying I am Mr Pink noting his colour he looked pink and wore expensive looking clothes and worth a few bob. He lived on his own and for us was an original colonel blimp type ever so nice and gave good advice if we ask any question about the area and the best place to shop, where the nearest Catholic Church he recommended Bracknell as our best choice for shopping and the Catholic Church you want in Bracknell is called St Joseph.

Burleigh road was the second left turn after the roundabout well situated for going to town and seeing the races for free as you could walk and picnic in the centre of the course when there was no horse racing, as then it becomes a nine or eighteen-hole golf course. Our hiring was well place with Windsor just up the road and the Ascot race course on our front door which was great to walk about and relax and go straight into the great park as in those days there was no barrier between the two and it was known you could walk to Windsor without ever walking on any roads.

Christmas sixty-eight came quickly and it was our first Christmas as husband and a wife with expectation of a new arrival in the spring boy or girl we waited to see what gift the lord chose for us. Miriam was saying her choice of names if it were a boy would be Francis in honour of her late father Francis, and if a girl Margaret because of her grandmother and the patron saint of her village Sannat in Gozo Malta.

To feel a real part of what it mean to belong for the second time in my life was making me crazy not only were the Irish Guards my first family on leaving Ireland but hear am I four years out and for the first time in my life I would have Christmas with a person I love who would never leave me. In my institutional life of sixteen years I have never known any Christmas with a family that now a married man with a wife and best friend making this Christmas the greatest gift I've ever known as a boy/man.

Life was on the up for sure as hear I was now the battalion presser making a few bob on the side pressing civilian suit and shirt that the handsome reward of my labour was paying off in that I was able with the tips side-line to buy my first car a green Austin 1600 for four hundred pounds.

Having no licence to drive I ask Sergeant Terry McGill of the MT platoon to help me out with driving lesson after working hours and with a few runs in and out of Windsor to Ascot mainly straight roads through with two roundabout I manage to do quite well other than the odd grazes from road high curbs. I manage to take my driving test with the help of my examiner sergeant Dolly/Billy Grey like Terry great Micks who got me through and passed me with these sound words of advice just because you got a driving certificate does not mean you can drive everybody else of the road for good driving is a practice skill that you will master the more you keep driving and in time you're driving skills will become second to none and you will do us both proud as your instructors.

1969 was a fantastic year in that I became a father for the first time I had responsibility that outweighed anything I had ever known before. To hear I was a dad and looking forward to seeing my son, and thinking how my life in six years had change from having nothing to the happiness I felt in being a family man and knowing I will never again be alone for there were two people now who loved and depended upon me. And I was never going to let them down as my own family did to me when my desperate mother who had no one when she gave birth found herself with child and unmarried was forced by her mother and step-father to give me to the state/church to be look after.

In the days leading up to my son being born Miriam was in Wrexham Park Hospital in Slough I asked to be excused guard duty so I could be there waiting as my wife was down for a caesarean birth due to her size and the bigness of the child she was carrying. Well my asking was to no avail so I went to see the regimental sergeant Major Patrick Duffy to have myself excused from guard duty and he said McDonnell women have been given birth for thousands of years without their men present so its soldier on and wait for the hospital to call you and when baby arrived then you can have a few days off.

Francis made his entry into the world on the 18 March 1969 between the feast of St Patricks and St Joseph on the 19th had Miriam not insisted on his first name I would have named our boy Patrick Joseph, but still very happy with Francis Joseph and George added at his baptism at his grandmother's request.

1969 is the year man landed on the moon and the world was hook onto every bit of news coming from NASA space centre in Houston that President John Fitzgerald Kennedy back in 1962 promised the American people would happen, and before all our eyes it was achieve with those remember words of astronaut Greg Armstrong one giant step for man one giant leap for humanity. The investiture of Prince Charles at Canavan castle had the world as we saw on our hire television looked in on what can only be describe as a Hollywood epic as the pageantry of history unfolds in front of the nation that is being seen live across the world as it happen making the occasion a memorable one recorded in time the moment the Welsh kingdom had long wanted of the queen crowning her son the Prince of Wales a gift to her Welsh subject within the United Kingdom four part union.

That year the battalion went to Batus in Canada for live field battle training I stayed behind on battalion rear party keeping the Hoffman presser working for those on rear party duties including turning out smartly our regimental band. I was glad in myself that I did not go to Canada for when I was not on barrack guard duty I be at home with my family as my wife needed my help with the baby for one so small take a lot of looking after.

1969 was also the year Miriam mother and two sister came over from Malta for Francis baptism at St Edwards's church in Windsor which gave us all a fantastic two week doing with them the tourist thing and I getting to know them much better. For the rest of that year the battalion kept busy with Windsor and London duty and a spot of leave for Christmas and New Year.

There was tremendous joy in being young as our time was full of excitement saying goodbye to the 1960s and more excited about what the 1970s new decade would bring and its wonders that may even tip man having gone to the moon.

I had not been over to Ireland since I married and my godparents had not seen or met my wife Maria Anna, Evangelista Publius, Miriam for short yet asking to see her and especially our new son Francis. It goes without saying they were invited to our wedding, and Francis' baptism, for reason not told no one answer any of our invite. We were planning a trip to Dublin at the Easter as Francis was now nearly one year old and a little more manageable and we were looking forward to showing our Francis to my godparent that Miriam would also meet for the first time. Dorothy's sister Carmel my favourite Irish aunt was living in Luton and unable to go anywhere for looking after her husband dad, a promise she made before her Tom died, and only been married five years with no children a sadness

Carmel spoke often to us about as one of her big regret as she would have been a terrific mother.

By the year end we had completed many public duties and Her Majesty birthday parade the state opening of Parliament and other special occasion like the Earls Court show and the beating of the retreat on horse guards, beside keeping all on duty well pressed my little side-line of pressing civvies' it had been a good year for the McDonnell's all round. The time was passing so quick that here again another Christmas with our new baby making real our own Christmas scene, like Mary and Joseph with their newborn baby Jesus in that stable on that first Christmas night celebrated their joy as we do now in our two room bedsit of a big house that as a family it matter not where we live as long as we are together.

So many good things have come my way it wrong to be so happy that there is no other to thank but the lord and his holy mother for the blessing shower upon us as a family as we end this bounteous and fruitful year of 1969 looking forward to the 1970s to what they may bring and hold.

I manage a few days in Ireland on my own in the September as Miriam felt it would be too much expense taking our son to Ireland and to cover hotel bills that because I have no direct family and nowhere proper in Ireland I can say is home. My godmother Dorothy apologised because of her own family of four like Jesus family in Bethlehem in my case no room in their Dublin inn.

Chapter 11

It was not long after Christmas leave in early January 1970 when the battalion heard that Hong Kong is on the cards and would be the battalion next posting and an accompanied one at that which was fantastic as it is said that this will be another first for the Micks a posting in the Far East, and going out there in the November for two years. For now the battalion routine of public duty, St Patrick's Day which Her Majesty Queen Elizabeth the Queen Mother has consented to distribute the shamrock that all in the regiment love for that classis smile of her that is so infectious and her own love of the Micks.

No guardsman ever forget the battalion spring drill season that for a few weeks each year remind all of their guards' depot days when we go back to basic, preparing for the commanding officer, and major general annual inspection in May and in preparation for Her Majesty birthday parade on horse guards.

In June.

About July/August which the military and the country calls the silly season start where nothing of great important is pen in, to allow for military leave that by September the battalion had a few weeks of field training joining the sheep on the Brecon Beacon tabbing and exercising our military skills. Annual field training, and shooting classification recorded, and each solider ability in his handling his personal weapon.

We headed over to Ireland during the Easter block of 1970 and I introduce my wife and son to my godparent, especially my friends in Glenart College and the O'Keefe family in Arklow, and then we motor to Athlone onto Toughmcconnell where my own mother family came from and who rejected her when she was in most need, i.e. pregnant with me. We called up at the Blackwire/McDonnell family home as my grandmother married Henry Blackwire a short time after my grandfather Patrick McDonnell died and I believe my mother their daughter was only nine years old when her father passed away.

I called to introduce myself in those early days of the Irish Troubles and I in the British Army had to tread carefully not putting my wife and son in the firing line be that my wife wanted me to find my blood family and ask them questions. Miriam was interested in my family health that could affect her children future, for as a nurse she was aware of hereditary illnesses she wanted to know might be in my family that could be down the line that her children should know off.

At the house we met Henry Blackwire Junior's wife Margaret she welcomed us first mistaking me for her husband and asking who is the woman and child with you, I said my wife and son, she drew a long breath having thought I was her husband because of my strong resemblance to her husband that it spooked her. I told her my mother came from here and her name was Brigid Theresa McDonnell and I come to find her and ask her a few question why she left me in the hands of the church and state when I was a baby.

Margaret was very nice in offering us tea and she told me her husband Henry is with his dad below in the field near the old family house now used for storage.

She showed me the way to the old house and I found them resting. I asked if I could have a word as I needed to know the whereabouts of my mother who is Brigid Theresa McDonnell. Henry junior was startle by my looks and watch his father go into a fiery rage as if I had accuse him of something when all I ask if Brigid who I believe is my mother is about, and if not here where may I find her. Without any provocation he went into a tirade of abuse that she's not bloody here and said he wanted nothing ever to do with her or any bastards she may ever have had. Because I was in the British Army I kept stump as the IRA were becoming very active in the Republic of Ireland and the safety of my family came first. I left with him shouting she lives in St Helen/Liverpool, and that where you'll find the bloody whore.

Thankfully Margaret gave me Brigid's address as I collected Miriam and Francis I saw sadness in her eyes knowing my visit to her in-laws did not go well. I was to find out many years after finding another like myself my sister Maura McDonnell/Tully who got on well with them and was warmly accepted into the family that they regretted the welcome I and my family received back in 1970 as my mother's shame outside of marriage that is accepted and looked upon different today, was not the true account of his action as I was to learn from my mother of his part in my being here.

We return to life in Ascot after our Easter holiday in Ireland and while all did not go well we did enjoy our visit to Dorothy my godmother in Dublin, and Arklow town in Wicklow visiting the O Keefe family and the priest/student, and friends in Glenart College. It would be a few years more before I returned for another visit as I would be away on a two-year tour in Hong Kong.

I found out as did many that the married quarter's situation was not good and many married men will have to do the tour unaccompanied which is not going down well with the wives, and we are on the list of no quarters available at this time. Miriam would have to return home to Malta on our embarkation leave in October of 1970 as we could not stay in our Ascot hiring. Miriam and Francis would remain with her mother in Malta until the army called her forward. I return alone from Malta after my leave having check before taking my wife and son to Malta of my chance in getting a married quarter, and was told we did not qualify as the army through years of moving people about has a well tried and tested though not always fair system of points in which to qualify for a married quarter.

How long of service you done, number of children, if they're in school, how long you have been married, are you presently living in a married quarter, what rank you are carry the biggest punch. The battalion made its move to Hong Kong in November 1970 I was put into the officer mess as a mess hand and as orderly to Father Robson who had become the battalion new padre. After about a month living in Hong Kong and doing my best to change my situation I could see as long as my family were with her parent in Malta nothing was going to happen as in all things if you do nothing then the power to be will also do nothing.

Christmas came and was not great as I missed my family so much and seeing others making inroads in jumping the queue I knew it was up to me to get my family out as letters from me to Miriam were pressing in what is happening. I wrote Miriam for Christmas and ask Miriam to make her way from Malta to London in early January of 1971 and wait at the door of our regimental headquarters on birds cage walk London, letting them know you are guardsman McDonnell spouse carrying our one and half year old child and you have just flown in direct from Malta after staying with your mother for the last two month, and you want to be with your husband who is in Hong Kong.

With a few tears and sign of stress because you have nowhere to stay, no family here, no friend in the UK to put you up as my husband is out in Hong Kong, we are homeless until we can join him emphasising the fact that you are not going back to Malta, and will wait hear as their responsibility to do with you what they can as with no family in the UK we become the military responsibility to look after and for them to find accommodation till we can be reunited with my husband in Hong Kong.

The situation was as if a fox got into the hen house and feathers went flying about as I was call into the family's office about my wife's predicament that she arrive at regimental headquarter doorstep as homeless and I was told by the families C/Sgt Freddy Brown to get busy and find a hiring as my wife and child will be en route very shortly. I was allow time to go in search of a place and did find a flat in a high rise building in Hong Kong central near the Catholic cathedral on Arbuthnot road not too far from the Governor Murray Maclehose resident, and within walking distance of a beautiful park that every morning I saw the local go and do their exercise which is called Tai Chi, and done in what I thought was their pyjamas.

Miriam arrived ten days after her visit to London and had a week stopover in Singapore all at the army expense or should I say complimentary digs in a beautiful hotel of the Royal Air Force choosing.

All was great and life in Hong Kong though good only got better with my family on hand and we settle into our high rise flat in central overlooking Victoria Harbour.

Within a few weeks Miriam saw we had a problem as Francis broke out in a serious rash. Miriam being a nurse was sure it was rat related as she took what looked like rat dropping from our son cot and saw the rubber teat of our baby bottle had been chewed on. She went to the British military hospital and the medic doctor seeing our son agree the family should be moved ASAP as the rash was from rat in his cot was worrying. It was a fastball move authorise by the family officers on the doctor report to have us moved to a rat free flat.

We were moved to a new high rise building in North Point and the new views unlike central that overlook Victoria Harbour overlook Aberdeen floating city of a half million boat living people, and the colour lights of the beautiful decorated floating restaurants and floating homes made it a sort of a wonderland, with floating pathways that weaved in and out of a tight floating city within Hong Kong that was magically lit all year round like a Christmas tree that it was said a half a million people live on that floating city.

Getting in and out from North Point on public transport wasn't too bad once you got to know the buses route and if push came to shove a taxi. Knowing your way about on the local transport was important in getting about for shopping and seeing the sites especially visiting the China fleet club that was great for good meals and easy access to Kowloon ferry and Chung Chow, and Lantau Island. The China fleet was in the busy commercial area of Wan Chai that during the day was respectable and low key on its massage parlours, bars and nightclubs that come the evening into the night the Wan Chai awoke becoming another face of hidden pleasure the neon light invited all to enter and enjoy their offering as their ladies of the club made a easy living by working for the management in enticing you to buy a drink that cost double when in or using their company.

With the Vietnam War sadly costing many American lives the United States Army used Hong Kong for their soldiers to have R&R rest and recuperation as opposed to returning them to the states to be with their families. They were instead dropped off in Hong Kong to let off steam and by did the girl in the Wan Chai welcome these big spenders that left the old British squaddie unable to match what the American soldier was prepare to spend that the British soldiers was taken of their menu while the American soldiers bought up and pay more for everything, they live the moment for many knew on return to the war may never see their home or family again.

There was army transport toing and froing picking up the children for school and they had security on board and often if you ask there was room you could get a lift as an extra security escort.

Many families employ Amah's as they were reasonable in their hourly rate and as we got seven Hong Kong dollars to the pound for fifty dollars a week many senior rank employed them to do their washing, ironing, and cleaning, leaving their wives to live as ladies of leisure.

Miriam would not use an Amah for domestic use as she felt that it was wrong to lord it over others what you should do yourself she was a fantastic housewife. Looking after Father Frank Robson was a real pleasure in that he always made contact with other Christian and Catholic community as was the case when we went up to the new territories and we met the nuns near Sha-Tin a border village that waited for re-entry after been kicked out of China twenty odd years before remaining close to China proper in the hope of been allowed to return. They had a little church hut that was in need of attention and we were able with a bit of Mick muscles to replace the corrugated roof and give a little long lasting food of tin compo in helping them out.

On another day there was great excitement and pandemonium in Hong Kong when a Land Rover with a few Micks by the names of Tommy Myler, Kieron Gillen, Danny Cullen, and two others who names escaped me went visiting Mau See Tung without having an appointment or a visa. I believe a map reading course was their first stopped after their embarrassing return and political release for which all enjoy their fifteen minutes of fame. Everyone is entitle to basked in their fifteen minutes of fame and those Micks certainly did as battalion celebrities for a day or two living up to the catch phrase coined by that great American who made famous himself for his tin of beans painting, new Yorker Andy Warhol.

In those early day of Hong Kong before my wife came out the laugher and the tears at breakfast of fish eggs and there fishy taste that the piquet officer who see out the meals and hear the guardsmen complaint was at his wit end in understanding how this could be, and ask for it to be investigated.

The egg saga was investigated by the quartermaster and it was found that the army supplier was feeding the hen crush fish and you get the end product to what you feed your hens. That egg supplier contract was cancelled and free range eggs from the United Kingdom were back on the menu, I suppose in hindsight if you grew up eating fish fed hens eggs you probably feel the same if you were given English hen eggs fed on their corn seed diet.

Early December 1970 we heard great news that the Holy Father Pope Paul the sixth was doing a stopover for a few hours on his way back from the Philippians, and would be greeting the Catholic of Hong Kong with a mass and

Irish guardsmen on a catholic retreat course Chung Chou Island Hong Kong 1971, At the front Sgt Liam Mills, & Father Frank Robson the Micks Padre.

Myself & Jimmy Hagan sitting with our retreat master Father Ty on Chung Chou island 1971.

Myself in Officer Mess dress British Honduras now Belize 1973.

blessing, this opportunity was too good to miss that Father Frank Robson arrange transport for those that wanted to be part of this history in the making and see the Holy Father, as he himself would join the other priest of Hong Kong concelebrating at the papal mass on the Happy Valley racecourse. For the first time in most of our Catholic lives here was an opportunity to see the man appointed by the Holy Spirit and the head of our church on earth in the flesh. The direct successor of the fisherman Peter in an unbroken line of nearly two thousand years.

We set off for the big event at Happy Valley to the government stadium and were very fortunate to get a good position on the entrance isle we could see the Holy Father as he was driven in and on his leaving, Jimmy Hagan was taking a photograph of the Holy Father leaving with his new bought camera, and got such a fright that he drop the camera. He told us afterward that he look through the camera eye and because of it magnification he thought the Holy Father was in his face as appose to a few hundred feet away we all laugh and thankfully he got his treasure photograph and no real damage to the camera.

Life was good and after three happy months in North Point high rise building we were moved to Stanley fort into the barracks married quarters making life for us much better as now I did not have to travel an hour on local buses to my job looking after the padre and working early and late in the officers' mess. As duty waiter on breakfast or on dinner nights was very demanding especially regimental night which were many for the officer mess was more a club house as was the high life of the sergeant mess. Living in barracks on site was a bonus all round for the family I was able to be on hand for daily mass and my wife took charge of the church linen keeping it in pristine white. So convenient was life in Stanley fort and only a stone throw from our own local beech called St Stephen that the regiment in Stanley fort made its their own and it was within a ten minutes-walk from Stanley village and Hong Kong's best street market.

By March 1971 three months after Miriam came out she was overjoy in saying I'm pregnant and it will be good for Francis to have a sister or brother. Francis was now two years and nine months old when Margaret was born 3 December 1971, a little storey we now laugh back on was when Miriam was pregnant with Margaret she had a funny incident or so I thought at the time but not Miriam, we were in central for a Chinese festival on the harbour waterfront watching the colourful display of colourful dragons dance when Miriam felt a hand slide between her legs and being accosted, and at about seven months pregnant, and as quick thinking goes she grabbed the offending hand and not letting go confronted the terrified little Chinese weasel red handed as she landed an unmerciful clout and words of sound advice don't do not do that again or I castrate you, you little pervert creep. She was given a big applause by those nearby and the said offender received the odd boot up his backside and some Chinese curses from within the crowd for good measure.

You know all about rain coming from Ireland but nothing on the scales of the water that drops from a typhoon and especially Typhoon Rose that hit Hong Kong as an angry woman with a vicious bite causing so much damage that it will last in memory as the worst typhoon for many a year. When the storm of 1972 hit in June it was mention by the geologist expert after assessing the ground and the horrendous destruction cause by the hill landslide which cause the Kotewall disaster on the Po Sham road which left many dead and injure, that the Governor Sir Murray MacLehose declare a national emergency, calling on all services including the army engineer and the resident battalion on Kowloon side and Hong Kong main to help as both area had major damages.

The 1972 storm disasters it was said on assessment had been first weakened from Typhoon Rose battering an eleven months earlier that the ground was ill prepare to take another weight of water so soon. The battalion was thanked by the governor for their effort in saving lives and assisting in clearing away dangerous rubble.

A very sad incident occurred in Hong Kong when one of our battalion and a good member of our church made Father Frank Robson very sad and quietly shed a tear or two as he himself could not believe that the killing of the

Chinese taxi driver murdered allegedly by guardsman Willy Wilson. He was accused of stabbing the taxi driver to death and is being held in police custody at Hong Kong central police station. Willy was a quiet man and here I have to confess was one who I had known in my old school at Artane run by the Christian Brothers twelve years before we were good friends because of our past association in Dublin and our friendship within the church and the regiment.

The evidence against Willy Wilson was that he was drunk and found asleep in the back of the taxi with the said knife in his hand, and blood on his clothes, it was just too obvious he done the dastardly deed and the police wanted the crime solve and were very happy in getting a quick conviction. The consequences weather he was guilty or innocence was incidental they were happy to look no further and as Willy who normally was not a serious drinker was found drunk as a skunk and totally unaware of his movement on how he ended up in that taxi blood stain with a knife in his hand was compelling enough for the police to look no further.

Father Frank Robson believe in his heart he was set up by persons unknown as it was out of character that he would do such a terrible thing. Father was so concerned after he was convicted and sentence to life imprisonment on Stone Cutter Island prison as to the treatment he would receive, that father Frank ask me to visit him every week which I did to ascertain his health and cheer him up by keeping him updated on battalion news and more to see how he was being treated. This I did until the battalion left Hong Kong at the close of 1972. It was on the cards before I left Hong Kong in December that a transfer of his prison sentence to a United Kingdom prison would shortly take place. If it ever did happen that he was handed over to the British prison service we in the regiment never got to know. Over the years I have thought about Willy Wilson if he had served his time and if he ever did get free and where he might be today.

After a few month in our new quarter in Stanley fort I was inform by the family C/Sgt Freddy Browne our family would be one of the guardsmen family that the queen mother's brother General Bowes Lyon who was on an overseas visit to Hong Kong would be visiting the Irish Guards and he would like to meet some Irish Guards families. My wife was over the moon to be ask would she accept a visit from the queen mother brother General Bowes Lyon on his visit to Hong Kong as she is from Malta and loves the royal family after all his niece princess Elizabeth now Her Majesty the queen spent two wonderful years with her Husband Prince Philip as a service wife at the villa Granamounga in Malta from 1949 to 1951, and of course Miriam remember when princess Elisabeth come and unveil a plaque in her village of Sannat/Gozo in 1948 on the wall outside Mario bar.

The queen mother brother coming to our quarter's cause a lot of fuss that Miriam was ask is there anything she needed and she hinted a new oven and a front room carpet would be nice before you could say abracadabra she had them in and fitted. The army cookbook that came with her new oven has been her greatest cooking companion to this day. The general visit went off very well and he was very relax and showed a lot of real interest about my wife being a service wife and about her life in Hong Kong and did she like being here. He was more down to earth than the fuss that was made about him nit-picking I don't think he care for our new carpet or oven, he talked happily and freely to us, asking how we both met and about our son who just played. He asked Miriam if she missed her life in Malta as he too said it was a place he loved, and that his niece Her Majesty the queen always says her first and real home with her husband Philip that she loved and the simple life of a service wife she still misses.

Christmas 1971 we are a family of four our daughter Margaret was born three week before Christmas day, and I must thank the China fleet club for being on hand in feeding myself and Francis during our daily trip to the British military hospital on Kowloon side where Miriam had a hard time because of her being anaemic and having a second caesarean birth. Hong Kong was memorising, a place of traffic, noise, smells and colour, street market, with many small islands to get away and visit like Chung Chou, Lantau, Portuguese Macau, all in all beautiful places.

The officer's core had beautiful quarters and a lovely beech close to Repulse Bay and one of the best places to swim that was very scenic and expensive because the rich bought up the hillside overlooking the bay making it their Hong Kong bel air. Families living in Stanley fort had all the facilities with an onsite nurseries with easy access to St Stephen beech, and Stanley market that was very popular for military, locals, and tourist which crowded it for it was the market that had the reputation for the best prices of textile, bedding, lace, jewellery, paintings, food, every kind of souvenir especially the beautiful jade, silver, gold, and wood carving. There was nothing in Hong Kong that was not for sale as it was the place a genie wish was granted and made true.

Father Robson in one of his many jobs as battalion Chaplin took time out to Chung Chou Island a nearby island that he with a local Chinese priest named Father Ty gave military retreat making it very interesting and stimulating emphasis the key point of the retreat in thinking out your faith and why it is you believe. The afternoon were free to go boating, swimming, and sightseeing especially to see the Po-ling temple that is renowned Buddha temple in Hong Kong. In the evening after our meal we sit around a few table with drink and generally everybody talk over the day points while Father Frank Robson sat close by and enjoyed being drawn into questions that the group threw at him, this I knew he like most felt a lot was gained in much the same way he believe Jesus did similar answer and questions when with his apostle while teaching and relaxing with them.

In the two years I look after Father Frank Robson we visited many places about Hong Kong and the new territories that was on loan for the growing of food to feed the people of Hong Kong Island in them days of the opium trade when commerce was good and no friction with mainland China emperor.

It gave me a big insight into his pastoral work as he never tired in his effort to do good in that he always on call be they military, families problems, hospital and prison visit if needed night and day. Father Frank Robson conducted baptism, marriages, communion and confirmation, visited the schools, especially enjoy visiting the British military and the Chinese hospital in central where Irish Columban's nuns nursed the sick in the Rutigee sanatorium hospital that became a favourite tea-stop and an opportunity for him to visit other sick and elderly that live on the island, and tourist that fell ill while visiting Hong Kong from cruises or flight stopover or just passengers travelling through.

When the Kotewall disaster happen in 1972 the Micks were asked to supply manpower, and Father Frank Robson was on hand in case of found fatality and to console the injure. When all that we could do was done in assisting the Hong Kong emergency services in their work which took a few days the governor Sir Murray McLehose thanked the Irish Guards for their efficiencies and sterling work. Loss of life was said to be over a hundred and twenty in all with many more injured, putting right the damage would take many years and new thinking in how to build in such tight and overcrowded hilly places was again being looked at seriously by the geologist and city planners.

Our time in Hong Kong was nearly through and our next posting to Caterham was now drawing near and everyone was making busy again with packing the MFO boxes for going home to our new quarter for Christmas and disembarkation leave. We moved to Caterham leaving and feeling quite sad as Hong Kong was a fantastic place where we had experience a rich culture and saw life from another side not as a tourist but day to day local living. Seeing a people who make every type of what they work with whether it be stone wood, iron, cloth, they let nothing go to waste, they are an industrious people and in the recycling world of art and innovation none I believe can match.

Hong Kong will forever be an unforgettable memory and I leave with sadness and a wish to return for it magic and vibrancy is what I will miss most, and our special gift we bring away our daughter Margaret the best reminder of our stay in Hong Kong.

Christmas 1972 and one once again the battalion is back in its world of public duties but first the battalion has been granted Christmas block leave until the middle of January 1973. We took the opportunity on that leave to spend Christmas in Gozo taking our new daughter Margaret to see her grandmother and all of Miriam sisters and brothers a total of seven, and her extended family as Gozo is a small island not un-similar to my own Ireland, it was as if everyone on the island is family. We when too for Miriam brother

Salvo Azzopardi wedding to a beautiful red head that when I first saw his bride to be I could not believe as I though all the Maltese have black hair but because Malta had been occupied by so many nationality in its history, the Phoenician, Arabs, French, and the English, it really is a melting pot of people from many different lands, that Salvo wife to be Antonia Sicluna look so Irish and very young. Our three-year-old son Francis was made a page boy at his Uncle Salvo wedding and was loved by everyone for being so cute, happy and go lucky.

Chapter 12

Back from Malta and from block leave January 1973 the battalion was strait into it old routine as we settle into our new married quarter on a brand new estate in Uckfield a few miles away from our army barrack in Caterham, once again I take up my old position of battalion presser and my side kick duties of looking after Father Frank Robson who has come back with the battalion and is staying on as the Micks chaplain.

Within a few days of the battalion having settled into their old routine we are all inform by the commanding officer Lieutenant Colonel G A Allen that in mid-February the battalion would be heading to British Honduras in central American on a six months tour this by all account was a fast ball as the battalion had just got settle into their quarters and the single lads into barrack life to be heading off without our feet touching the ground on an unaccompanied posting on a six-month tour in British Honduras a totally new experience of jungle and third world living as appose to the crowded and busy industrial life we had live with the people of Hong Kong just over two month ago.

My dream of seeing the world was being answer big time since joining the Irish Guards and those early days of hunger in Scotland and my ending up in Liverpool as my last chance saloon as is said of cowboys on their knees, well that advert in that shop window started my changed of luck and the door to my seeing the world began, for Sergeant Smylie was my genie who granted me my wish and allow me to go forward, and what had happen before I join the Irish Guards is pass and consign to the trash bin. My fairy godmother/father in the guise of Sergeant Smylie who took me under his wing from that first offer of a cup of tea on that beautiful August day in 1964 when everything change and my becoming an Irish Guardsman paid off, for from that day my being an orphan and alone came to an absolute end, and all my Micks brother from Eddie King have been my family.

Having left Ireland eight years ago with nothing and not a clue as to how I would achieve my travel ambition, here am I on my way to another part of the world I don't think my old mariner friend Paddy Maher in his days on the ocean waves had got to Central America, and the British colony of British Honduras, I had been back to see the Mather brother and the priest at Glenart College four years ago I told them of my life in the Irish Guards to date, and that I had serve in South Arabia, been on adventure training in Cyprus for six week where we climb and abseil, mastered swimming and was taught basis in boating skills, all to the good if in bad situation where emergency survival may come in handy. I remember my platoon officer Lieutenant Bingham in 1966 Chelsea Barracks London hire the guard's sailing boat the Gladeye and we had a five day sailing training, learning the ropes as we sailed around the Solent and the Channel that any proficient sailing officer could booked the guards yacht for recreational training, I never did catch the boating bug and that really was my first and last trip on a guards yacht. Being in Hong Kong for two years and now on the move again for a six-month tour to Central America I feel with my kids so young it will be a lot of work for Miriam and I hope with the battalion back up machine that is the families office they do their best for our wives and children's in keeping all updated on battalion news.

We arrived in Airport camp and it looked like a throwback of years pass to a barrack the army forgot they own, a Second World War relic in the back of beyond no longer use that the Ministry of Defence purposely forgot. The run down Nissan hut had little comfort and British Honduras being hot adding to your discomfort when the sun dance off the hot metal, cooking bucket of sweat. Inside the Nissan hut was metal side lockers, metal beds with a mattress so thin it made no difference if you just lay on the beds bare spring.

After a few days of settling in, one of the battalion companies went up country to a place call San Ignacio, as did a detachment of person from the signal platoon who maned a hill station gathering information. Both sites were on the edge of the jungle in fact much of British Honduras was third world in that the city of Belize had poorly built houses show stress and neglect with the paint long dried and peeling. No real high building was there in Belize City as most houses were made of wood and stood two story tall or look higher if up on stilt as were many in the poor quarters. The few sturdy building made of stone were owned by the church and the government with a few off limit places such as the Fort George hotel and other posh places to attract the rich American and millionaire that visit for fishing and who sailed around the Keys in the Caribbean warm waters on route to other islands or onwards to resorts in Mexico. The Hondurans people are a mixture of Africa slaves that never felt they belong, and Spanish decedent of the conquering conquisodor that pillage and killed having rape their way through these lands having interbred with the Mayan women folk to establish home grown root.

Both races had little time for each other that you could feel the tension between them one of the reasons that each kept to their side of the bridge as the African chose to remain in an area call Mesopotamian, and the Spanish in the centre doing the money jobs including hiring of boats to the keys it biggest money earner from selling boat ride to the reef and keys. If you visited the night club that was mainly by the bridge in the centre of town called the Crossroads it was built on wooden stilt along the river it was an unwise hang out and not safe place to go if on your own.

The Crossroads hotel come nightclub was very much a place you did not want to have casual sex with a one-night pick up. The local trade was risky and was not worth contacting an unwanted friend that could not be explain to your other half if you caught an infection as the timeline in some cases took months to clear.

Being a monk for the six months is the best way to be safe rather than sorry as was brought up in the personal hygiene by the army doctor that to avoid sex in this country would be best for your health as there are sexual disease that kill if left untreated and the picture shown of what male genitals look like if unfortunate to catch look horrible, ugly and the best visual warning the medical officer could offer in warning all especially the married to stay safe. The Anglican vicar who had been living in Belize City for over ten years and told Father Frank Robson that while it alright in the day time there are some nice restaurants and hotels that are not in the bridge area where the clubs and pubs with their easy on the eye sort of night attraction are best avoided by all rank if you want to return home to your wives and love one from this tour safely.

Father Robson made contact with an order of American nuns on the outskirt of Belize City that had a beautiful set up, and they care for their convent as if it was on American soil so clean and fresh. These sisters of the Pauline order had a beautiful convent and taught the local children. This community was well established and the convent was one of the most beautiful building in Belize City a great watering hole to those visiting and working in it for they kept it very cool with the latest modern gadget that you could move unlike the old twirling fan in Airport camp Nissan huts. Mosquitoes and flies found it hard to live with the sister as they used flynet over beds and burn incense that may them go elsewhere to find others' sweet blood to suck.

I had a good laugh once when Father Robson not long in Airport camp went to have a bath or should I say he had an uneasy experience as a half hour had gone by since he told me his intention to taking a bath. I went to the officer bath/toilet Nissan hut and I called out are you alright father as I was worry about him taking so long. He was frozen petrified and would not move after he sank himself into the tub and notice a long dark snake resting on the pipe above and him in the bath naked and very disadvantage. He called quietly Jack, there's a snake in my bathroom which I shouldn't do but did and laugh while he talked softly in the hope of not arousing the snake to his present that if he stood up he would be eye to eye with the snake. It's not every day you see your boss in the buff and laugh while I tell father I will hold a brush with a towel hanging over the brush bristle part for a screen in front of the resting snake while you father calmly get out of the bath no sooner had I said you can get up and out of the bath father like an Olympian was up and gone in seconds. Father learned to inspect the ablution on all occasion thereafter before and after use.

British Honduras was a fantastic place in that the wildlife seen was like a glimpse of paradise to the huge amount of colourful birds large and small, especially the common green parakeets that were as common in Central America as robins and blackbirds are in northern Europe. The main battalion lived in Airport camp that having Ma's Blake come style pub/bar situated just two hundred yards outside the main gate was obviously an ex-squaddie operation who married a local girl having left the military and settle down in British Honduras to a great lucrative business. It was well sited and a good money spinner knowing squaddies needs on their short tours as a place to relax and feel as if you are at home in a English pub that Ma's provided with local female interest to make the place viable for a one stop drink before hitting Belize City and again on return for a nightcap as is said in Ireland one for the road before heading back into camp for the night to sleep.

It was a common site at night also on coming back from town to see snakes lying out on the road keeping themselves warm on the gravel as this was their living room after the sun when down to enjoy the natural heat that the open road absorbed and retained. The lizard like iguana a prehistoric looking miniature of a crocodile or alligators stroll around day and night and were not afraid to stand their ground as it was their country often on seeing them you gave them a wide berth avoiding any contact, just letting them be.

There was recreational training at a beautiful resort not far outside Belize City that was the playground of the rich and platoon on leave went there to enjoy all the water sport and a week of rest and recuperation after being up country in the jungle or base at San Ignacio or signal hill that chose a rewarding break on San Pedro Island.

I was very lucky to be able with another five guardsman to be led by our own intrepid Indiana Jones of the day, Lieutenant M J V Warrender to the Mayan ruin of Tikal in Guatemala to see the wonderful sights of Mayan life and climb their monument that are in some way equal to another advance culture, of the Egyptian build pyramid on the continent of north Africa. We had lodging in a basis type hotel for a bob a night on an island Flores Petén, a most beautiful place and the nearest place that resemble my picture of what it would be like to live in the real garden of Eden so peaceful, and heavenly-heavenly beautiful.

This fantastic trip was organised and lead by Second Lieutenant M J V Warrender, now the Lord Bruntisfield who had done his homework and in another life could well be a tourist guide. Tikal Mayan ruins in Guatemala is a place that has lived with me and its memory has never faded as like my going to mass on that first Sunday in Guatemala on Flores Petén I was amazed at the poorness of its people, and the richness of the church interior and it beautiful décor. The casualness of the people attending and their relax attitude when animals just walk in and lay down as did domestic dogs to keep cool, that just walk in and out without turning a head of anyone in making a comment. Because the church door were left open due to the heat and having no fan it was the breeze off the lake that kept the church cool, this Sunday mass was one fantastic and raw experience that often I think back on, and how the animal in some way were better behave at keeping still in the present of our dear lord than a few who attendant.

That Guatemala trip was just one highlights of our visit in our six-month tour in British Honduras with many a night in Holdfast and the craic near the local town of San Ignacio. Sgt Liam Mill's another great Dubliner and long-time Irish

Guardsman who ran the medical unit up in Holdfast camp in San Ignacio, and we found to our surprise that the local people also knew Sgt Mills nickname when asking to see the medical sergeant at the entrance gate they say can we see Sergeant Tabs his nickname due to the size of his feet.

Tabs was an experience medic and often it was to him most casualty went for treatment as he was a very caring person that never wore his rank in ordering anyone about as he asked in everything he wanted done in a father-like way that he was hard to refuse. Sgt Liam Mills/Tabs was our daughter godfather and a great family friend now passed on to his heavenly reward that I'm sure he richly deserved.

Father Robson on his trip to Holdfast camp in San Ignacio would often spend quiet time with Tabs as he was as much the eyes and ears that when the padre was not about many call on Tab's great experience and age for all sort of advice another door if you will to the confessional that help Father Frank Robson on his weekly visit in helping guardsmen that would not ask for it directly.

The officer commanding Holdfast Camp was Major Ra Wilson who bought an old small six-seater plane that as a newbie pilot was able to enjoy in his free time a bit of jet set life and for convenience able to fly down to Airport camp for a visit to go to the Keys or take off duty officers on flight jollies.

Pine Ridge lodge was another favourite place for platoon rest and recuperation where you could believe you were back in Ireland as it was a beautiful valley unlike the jungle this was manicure by heaven, it was a place where waterfall and river work seamlessly with nature and the log cabins that we used were for tourist that wanted to be one with nature. We acted out our youth as if we were all ten years old and all acting as in the story of Huckleberry Finn that we became Huckleberry Micks. It was mentioned by the medic as with all things on health that the rivers in Honduras have tiny insect that can travel through your manhood especially if you are passing urine as this is to be avoided when in the river and if this happen it can be fatal if not seen early.

There is sometimes on posting and battalion exercise fatalities and injuries, and on our tour in British Honduras this unfortunately was so in that we sadly lost Sergeant Cunningham, a very experience soldier and it was not fully understood why he went alone into the jungle, and what occurred. For his body was found many days later not far from where he left his platoon to do a little recce. It is thought that he may have missed his footing banging his head that left him seriously injured and unconscious in a storm dyke and the ground insect and other creature dispose of his flesh leaving little to identify him when found.

There also was a very serious injury to guardsman/regimental cook McIntyre from the cookhouse who on his first day off went happily on a keys trip. So excited was he that on nearing the keys he dived into the clear blue sea misreading the waters depth as it was not deep as he though. His head embedded itself into the seabed and his body flipped backward cracking his neck and damaging his spine. He was quickly taken to an America ship that was lucky for him was on exercise and close by that he was given the best medical attention inside the golden hour but sadly was left paralyse from the neck down.

While I've highlighted the best of a soldier free time there is a military field role in maintaining good security and that no argument with our Guatemala neighbour should cause them to disrupt the peaceful coexistence that has to date kept both countries from escalating to the next level. Thankfully with the new name of Belize replacing British Honduras you can feel a calm in that the Hondurans people can now feel good with their new name of Belizean people.

Often when the army are on oversea tour in war or in peacetime celebrities of the day volunteer or are ask if they will go and give the troops abroad a show to remind them that they are not forgotten and are value. That special job was given to me while working in the officer mess to look after Cannon and Ball and to be honest I had not a clue in 1973 who they were or what sort of show they would put on.

They came out to British Honduras as part of the entertainment national service association or ENSA. for short. They sign a willing contract to do a few live performances that all military personal could attend and the show would be held in Airport camp as it was easier to bring the out-line troops to the main British base of British Honduras for this extravaganza.

Cannon and Ball were very easy to look after and they told me this was their first time doing a gig for the army and how did I think they would be received. Well to be honest I said, you'll should go down a treat as any performer that gives their time to the military are always well appreciated. It really all went well even though I hadn't a clue what they did though some guardsmen from the north of England on seeing them about camp knew them and before they said a word you could hear them shouting in their direction Rock on Tommy. They put on two great show and were so funny and were well rewarded with a few days at the keys and big fish fishing before happily returning to the UK. Having done a great job for ENSA, and on our return I saw them become big on British television in the years ahead.

Many a time with Father Frank Robson on our drive to San Ignacio or into Belize City we saw the Amish people farmed their land using horses and hand-controlled machinery. Their fields were neatly farmed and the crop grown healthy looking, without any modern ways they manage as their forefathers had in the old country of Germany, to produce the best of their labour and were rewarded for their work. The Amish were a tight knit people that keep themselves to themselves, and as a religious communities they all dress the same the women and girls wore long dresses and head bonnet, while the men heavy boot, jeans, and a stripe shirts with braces to hold up their trousers, all the men and boys wore the same wide straw hats. What was nice was their mode of transport that reminded me when I was eight years old on a pony and trap ride to the Rathdrum railway station on route to an eight years nightmare in Artane Industrial School Dublin unprepared.

Here am I in British Honduras watching these Amish drive their horse and trap with family on board to church and shopping, they home school their children, operate a farm shop that sell their produce that in return bring needed income to keep the community self-sufficient. In my mind eye I see a people living another style to another age that want nothing to do with the fast space race, and changing world. They are folk who wish to live their lives without new fashion in and ever changing world that their only modern gadget is the telephone for outside community use when in need of doctors, police, and fire and ambulance services.

Looking back over our time in British Honduras having celebrated St Patrick's Day I believe not a hundred percent the governor of the day presented the shamrock on behalf of our wonderful patron Queen Elizabeth the queen mother. We did our last parade in Airport camp in our jungle green on the hand over name ceremony of British Honduras to what is now renamed Belize. The battalion witnessed the birth of a new country that would still need Britain support and money as it goes forward finding its own way in the world. To celebrate the name change from British Honduras to Belize the Belizean government also named Belmopan as their new country capital.

A few days later the battalion said it goodbye and once again we are on our way home to the great joy of seeing our children and wives having not seen them for six months. The letter wrote while away are letter of true feeling and I would love if today I could reread her and my own letters of the closeness we shared in our love for each other apart. But the storage company we place all our content for safe keeping while serving in Germany burned down wiping out all we owned in a suppose fire at Skinner storage in Croydon 1975, destroying seven years of personal item bought especially many nice things bought while in Hong Kong, Cyprus and other bought souvenir, my early stamp collection of Malta and coins, household item too big to carried and wedding present unopen, personal letters, new Britannic encyclopaedia and my religious encyclopaedia on the lives of saints with other prize book and house appliances.

We return to Caterham in the August of 1973 and as with all things Micks we went on embarkation leave and on return carry out our role as Irish Guardsmen on public duties like ducks to water and visited those welcome hills and mountain of Wales our new playground for the next year and a quarter. I settle down into my usual roll as battalion presser making a little money on the side and keeping my head down looking after the padre when I could and Miriam took to doing all the church vestment and linen and keeping Father Robson immaculate in his personal laundry and as a nurse in the local mental hospital.

Because of my job within the tailoring department we got a move into Caterham barracks residing at number eight besides FF Taylor who live in house no 2 and Sammy Connors our next door neighbour in number 9 on my return from Belize we move from Uckfield into the quarter in Caterham barrack a neat row of lovely terrace houses that border the battalion square to be on hand in keeping the battalion uniform for public duty nicely press. While living in barracks at number 8 Miriam was visited by an excited FF Taylor before St Patrick's Day 1974 not knowing Miriam well bladder enthusiastic having knock on our door that she was going to meet the effing queen mother, my wife asked me who that was and I told her that FF Taylor harmless but can't string a sentence without using two effs hence his nickname. FF Taylor was also a member of the quarter master department and at heart a generous and loyal Mick who do anything for anyone.

Life for the married man in barracks at home was fantastic but as with all good things the next move of the regiment was looming and the battalion moved just before Christmas 1974 to Buller barracks in Germany on an accompanied three year posting. As with all move my job as battalion goes to sleep and I take up my new secondary role as a storeman in headquarters company stores under company quarters master sergeant Robert Kelly a perfect gentleman and the most patient Mick I ever knew always calm no matter what storm or crisis is brewing or taking place.

That first Christmas in Munster Germany was a most blessed time as to see the way the German celebrate this festive time and their Christmas market was an eye opener to us all. We settle into our house on Billerbeck Strasa and it was in a military enclave where the wives could meet up in each other houses for coffee morning when their husbands are away on exercises. The coupons for petrol and the new cars most of us bought made all look as millionaires overnight.

There was competition between the Jones as there will always be as to who has the biggest and best and on that one I will leave it to the wives to vote on. My memory of 1974 was the corporal course and my getting through the torturous drill course that having been made a real skiver hidden away for the last seven years in the cookhouse, Hoffman presser, officer mess and/padre orderly, now as headquarters company storeman I was found wanting in having to brush up on what I left behind in the guards' depot ten years before and now not the fun I thought then as I shouted one two three one. I passed my corporal course and found I had just climb one step of the military ladder that in the past I laughed at other and now wanted to do better myself for my family.

1975 saw many exercises and family weekend trips around northern Germany, annual leave we took off for Lourdes in France and San Sabastian in Spain. battalion quartermaster was a genius having bought a holiday coach that wives could use to go back home when their husbands are away on exercises in taking advantage to see their own families back home, as could single soldiers if free and not on duty or on exercise. Mosel Mick was another great idea and a fantastic success for families on an army run summer camp well organise with all family amenities, that you could do as you wish as all meals were cooked, and proper beds to sleep in, with a well-run restaurant and bar type canteen. Leaving you free to go sightseeing and vineyards wine tasting and see first-hand the treasure growing white wine that we on one of our wine tasting visits were told that their most expensive white wine is the ice vine so call for it is the picking of the grapes after the first frost.

When it came to winter sport those that wanted a skiing adventure were encourage to go on snow queen in Sonthofen in southern Germany and tried it out many caught the bug and still ski today with their family. Life in Germany was great and I certainly took the opportunity to see other country's as I expect most did too on company leave and over weekends, especially to the Holland border town of Enscheda to enjoy it fantastic open air market that fresh meat and Dutch cheeses were half the price of the same buys in the German stores. In October of 1975 I got the trip of a lifetime as did four other Micks lead by Lieutenant D H O. De Stacpoole to represent the army of the Rheine at the British military pilgrimage in Rome. It was at breakfast on our second day in Rome that I was informed I would be having a private audience with his holiness the Holy Father Pope Paul VI and the opportunity to received Holy Communion from him as well. To say I was excited would be an understatement as this man who is God represented on earth and of an unbroken line from the successor of St Peter whom the lord first chose and ordain I would meet.

Three people were chosen from the military contingent for a private audience inside the pope palace I a corporal for the army, a female commanding officer for the air force and nursing services, and a naval commander for the senior service Her Majesty Royal Navy. After the papal mass and having received communion we were directed into a special reception room and there we stood and waited, as a secretary to the Vatican household brief us all as to how to address his holiness as he meet and greet us. All that you are told goes out the window as his holiness stood right in front of me and taking my hand ask how are you in the tenderness of touch as I reply great father and you as a whoosh of breath by those accompanied him when the Holy Father said smiling to me, you are quite right I am but a priest and chatted a little more about my visit to Rome and what it offer then thank me for coming moving slowly to the woman officer and the naval commander given them both the same personal one to one that in meeting him is really his personal gift, and the captured photograph memento of our handshake that is now part of our family photo and a treasure procession.

It was told to me later by an insider of the Chaplin department that a general thought it wrong for a low rank to be given that honour but the voices that spoke the strongest were the Catholic padres, Fathers Robson, Poole, Beatty, and bishop Walmsley the Chaplin bishop to the forces, and not forgetting the Micks machine in the form of a very strong Catholic commanding officer Lieutenant Colonel R T P Hume who must have had an idea of the bigness of this occasion for the regiment and of course for me on behalf of the Irish Guards.

Poem written on my return from Rome

Touched
Having shook the hand of Pope Paul the Sixth
At his home in nineteen seventy-five
I had a fusion of all popes past
Since the death of our lord crucified,
The church at the beginning was Jesus Christ,
The son of the one most high
Who chose his mother Mary

And the way he was going to die,
At the age of thirty and in his prime

PHILIP ANTHONY McDONNELL

To his mother he did say,
I must be about my father's business
The reason of why I came,
At the river Jordan sat three men
Peter and his brothers James and John
A quiet voice was heard by them
Put away those nets and follow me,
I'll make you fishers of men,
Not knowing what he meant, they thought
What the hell, curiosity got the better of them,
Man fishing they did not really comprehend
But in time, he would teach them their trade
Peter you will be my rock
The foundation on which his church was made,
Making Peter the key holder of heaven on earth,
Whatever Peter you decree on earth, by my Father
Will, will also be decreed in heaven,
When three years had passed, and his work on earth was done
Jesus shared his last meal with his disciples
A physical present, at which he had consecrated
With all present the union of their priesthood,
And yet two thousand year on, the hand that first
Touched Peter, is unbroken to the present holder of
The keys, that is, the hand I touched today, Pope
Paul the Sixth, I had really been touched by our lord.

Chapter 13

Since the military pilgrimage of 1975 I and my family have visited Rome many times it's a city I love best in all the world.

Father Robson had been with the Micks for near on five years when he was asked by his diocesan bishop to take up another post and obedient to his calling left the military and took up his new role as parish priest in his native diocese of Washington Tyne and Weir near Durham his birthplace. Father Frank Robson remain a great friend and after many years of myself having left the Micks I was sadly told by another good friend of Father Frank Robson captain Richard Dorman on return from our family holidays in Malta that Father Frank Robson was called home by the lord who he now at rest with, 2017 RIP.

A few weeks after my Rome visit a good old Mick approach me by the name of Vinnie Brennan company sergeant major one company asking me for a favour that as his mother was coming out to stay for a few weeks would I make sure to let her know if she enquired that he always went to church. This I could not believe when I met his mother a small five-foot lady in her late sixties that would not hurt a fly and her son a big six foot two inch man of senior rank towing the mum line singing loudly to the surprise of the regular church goers that I thanked God for mums everywhere for without them strong tough men are truly loss.

The army is quiet about a lot of good work i.e. of charities it support as one Sunday morning after mass in York Barracks Munster 1975 we were privileged when ask to view a new vehicle that the army had made a generous contribution too, called a Jumbulance. It was the first time I saw a portable hospital on wheels and it would be staff by volunteers doctors and nurses in taking the worst medical cases with state of the art equipment for pilgrimages to Lourdes and other places of interest that otherwise paralyse or bed ridden persons now could be taken and visit with the love and care this new vehicle built makes possible. We had a new chaplain for a short while who was an ex cook in the catering corps who was very shy and found leaving his squaddies days behind him that now as a military chaplain with the rank of captain he found too much to ware. Well his pedigree as an ex cook did him no favour as he preferred to socialise with the lower rank as he felt more at home with them when not on duty which was poor Father Paul Lenenhan down fall for once a squaddie always a squaddie. And so it was on one occasion that we were all in York barrack church waiting for father to arrive to say evening mass that I was tapped on the shoulder by my commanding officer RTP Hume also my old depot commander in 1964 who was attending church and said you're on for father is detained by the police for being over the limit, and so I conducted the liturgy of the word without doing a sermon.

It was in Germany between the year seventy-five and seventy-six that the first round of what become the army biggest curse word redundancy and a great loss to the army of good men who chose to leave with none better than my old and very good friend of ten years now sergeant Jimmy Kearns who to all intense and purposes was known

23 YEARS IN THE IRISH GUARDS

Some members of the battalion chess team Munster Germany 1974/77 Captain B E Bellew, myself with pipe, & Davy Allen.

Captain B E Bellew receiving a winner shield.

Military pilgrimage Rome October 1975 selected on behalf of the Army to have a private audience with his holiness Pope Paul VI.

to all as mister Mick, my guardian angel in Chelsea Barracks back in March of 1965.

This redundancy lark gave an golden opportunity to the Colonel R T P Hume a sharp knife in which to culled a few soldiers he saw upsetting the battalion way of life because of the trouble that was bordering us in the battalion when the trouble heighten in Ireland in the mid-seventies that it was take the offer voluntary, or you're on the way anyway.

1976 was the hottest year on record that it must have had an effect on everyone especially Miriam who rang our neighbours Joan and Andy Doogue both from county Kildare to tell them of her lottery win. Andy was an ex-Irish Army soldier that received his United Nations medal as one of Ireland's first troop into action in the Belgium Congo of 1960 that the Irish Army saw action and loss ten soldiers on that peace keeping tour only to learn the hard truth that peace come at a high price.

It was Easter Saturday of that year when my wife Miriam done the German lottery for the first time, telling Andy and Joan Doogue the great news of her big win and not to let it go any further. Are you sure Miriam they ask many times to which she reply yes do you think I'm stupid in not knowing if I've won or not. With that the celebration got under way and they call around to our house and party widely until the dawn.

It was at Easter Sunday mass the following day that it was noticeable something was up with the McDonnell's and the Doogue's families it was as if they had a secret, as none of the two families could stop their happy sniggering that the excitement of Miriam lottery win was getting the better of us all that Bill Murphy who was at church suspected some mischief going on with our sly laughter that he approached in his usual Cork-manner forthright and asked what are you eejits about and what was that shenanigan at mass today as if you were pre-school-children up to no good.

We let Bill Murphy in on our story and he ask Miriam to let him do a double check just to make sure we don't make right old eejits of ourselves when we come to making our claim. She showed Bill the ticket and he took a long time checking when he told us that we had not won a penny because the permutation required to win is not right. Having promise Andy my car and television and anything else he wanted from our possession while we were drunk millionaires it was a fact that we were good friends that he did not take us up on our offer. Needless to say Miriam never played the German lottery again, and of course Andy & Joan Doogue saw how generous we were and in hindsight we thought it better we never won as there is an old saying an eejit is easily parted from his money and that Easter weekend that was us.

I was coming up to my twelfth year in the Mick and having been a corporal now a few years in jobs like the battalion presser when U K based and as headquarters company stores corporal or officer mess hand when abroad that my opportunity of going higher were looking pretty slim. With so much going on and the army downsizing though the Ministry of Defence won't say it straight out I watched others in different platoon sent on courses and promoted. I knew it was up to me to grasp the bull by the horn in putting myself forward for a battalion transfer and see what my chances were in transferring to the ordinance corps for they are the army biggest corps and issue the whole army their supplies from depots stores in all military garrison.

In itself it would be a great opportunity for a person like me that love the army but not drill sergeant material to make my last few years count and get promotion. Seeking to put his corporal days behind him and move forward as a sergeant in the ordinance corps if successful and permission granted from my commanding officer to approach the corps and act on my request.

I was inspired by L/sergeant Denis Adams who was going nowhere in the battalion orderly room and had applied for his transfer earlier that year as opposed to redundancy. He was successful in his transfer and on finishing his entrance course was promoted and posted to his new job also station in Germany. Denis told me on one of his visits back in Buller barrack that promotion in the guards is to stand in dead man shoes while the ordinance corps has a thousand outlet for promotion whereas guards regiment have vacancy when one become available. He broke the mould and got his transfer and within two year of his transfer was on route for further promotion. I did hear through the old association grapevine that he reached the rank of regimental sergeant major before retiring to civilian life.

Weather it was the heat wave of 1976 I was becoming a bit restless in that I was now a corporal for a few years and there did not seem any opportunity towards my making it to the rank of sergeant, I worked out that ever since that nightmare day in Aden and the incident with those Arab diplomats in 1967 I have been left to do menial jobs within the battalion such as cookhouse mess hand, officer mess hand, battalion presser, padre orderly, storeman in headquarter company, all non-active role but important in turning the battalion wheel, that make me nothing more than a dogsbody for want of a better word without any further prospect in bettering myself or getting promoted. So I put myself forward for a regimental transfer and went on commanding officers order to make my request. The commanding officer Lieutentent Colonel R T P Hume granted my request to apply. I headed off two weeks later for my interview at Monchengladbach and to my surprise was told that I was just the sort of person the ordinance corps were looking for with good prospect of promotion in the future.

Obviously my acceptance preceded me back to the battalion and it was now down to the commanding officer to let me go or not. I was back on battalion orders in rapid fire when I was told by my commanding officer that no way was he going to give away a good Mick to the ordinance and that he was refusing my transfer, and in the next breath spoke that he was very impress with my gumption and initiative on wanting to better myself that he awarded me my lance sergeant rank, and before I could say thank you sir, and still in shock at hearing the sergeant Major Tommy Corcoran shout march out lance/sergeant to take up my new position as P R I sergeant in the quarters master department and let hear no more about this silly matter as you are a Mick and always will be as he riffed me out of orders door with his Dubliner smile.

I spent the rest of my tour in Germany working for the quartermaster Major J E Williams as a store man until I return to England about end of October on advance party 1977 prior to the battalion return in December to take over the home service clothing and run the battalion PRI shop. Which mean President regimental institute, an in-house shop that sell military and regimental item to old comrade, officer, and guardsmen of the regiment.

By Christmas the battalion was back in England in Victoria barracks Windsor for all it was an instance shock to be back as if we never left doing what guardsmen do best. for our time away had given the spit and polish side of cleaning our boots and kit a rest during our mechanise roll while serving as part of the North Atlantic Treaty Organisation in Germany, NATO, but like ducks to water we switched into our London duties role as if second nature.

January 1978 battalion back of disembarkation leave with time to settle in as we would be station in Windsor for the next two years. It was a funny year as it seemed when not on public duties or visiting Sennybridge in Wales galloping over the hills you found yourself working for Bill Murphy in Mars factory or working for the ration sergeant Alan McLean who was hiring carpet cleaner for office work on the Slough trading estate. Then there was the Blazer night club run by a very suave person called Mr Savage a tall slim and very smart manager, and a fair employer who had great time for Mick bouncers and table wine waiter server that acted as back up to the doormen if undesirable needed sorting out another fitness workout for Micks who like to party and get paid with the added bonus of marching off pretty girls on dates.

St Patrick's Day 1978 I believe Major Philip O Reilly command company commander chose our family to meet the queen mother and as with her brother in Hong Kong six years before my wife being from Malta was mention, when introduced to Her Majesty the queen mother. The queen mother in her St Patrick's blue was very knowledgeable of the Maltese islands and the fact that her daughter served as a military wife much in the vein of my wife with the Micks. That family photograph of Her Majesty shaking hands and smiling with the four of us show how comfortable she is in greeting any persons of any station in life, and never in a put down way. What a marvellous woman she was and always happy to distribute the Micks their shamrock on St Patrick's Day. The battalion I believe received it new colours while station at Victoria barracks and the presentation was held on the east lawn of Windsor Castle as was the garden party for the regiment, and again our proud moment on horse guards doing the troop in front of Her Majesty Queen Elizabeth the second on her birthday parade, in the company of the other guards regiment and the vast number that turn out to watch this long held pageant of splendour and colour.

The long walk to the copper horse became a familiar place in Windsor for it three mile flat stretched that never seem to end when out on a company run that the companies used for their new battle for fitness test. A run up and down the long walk many soldier took to do long before that clown thought up the trend jogging that the army done most days as a mean of keeping fit.

In the July and August of 1978 most of the battalion went out to Canada for BATUS training over the period of the Calgary stampede while I remain with the rear party available for barracks guard and quartermaster stores duties.

On their return there was great talk about guardsman Muc Andrews a Dubliner from number two company who while in Canada went out on the town in Medicine Hat and fell in love with a Native Indian girl. So in love that he went back with her onto the Indian reservation and only by invite can you be there. The local Canadian police are not allowed to go onto the Indian reservation without special permission from the reservation police and cannot break protocol for any reason to enter. They however can ask the reservation police if they could check and see if a person is on the reservation and being held against his will. The answer came back in a note form from Guardsman Andrews that he is very happy and would not be returning to his old life in the Micks for the foreseeable future. We never saw Chief Muc Andrews again. No doubt there are some real Dublin Indians running about the reservation that as a child Andrews himself on the Dublin street of the fifties and sixties would have played cowboys and Indians that most did in those days, and he is doing for real today.

I knew Muc Andrew as a very street wise Dublin Mick in my time as a member of number two company he was like many a native of Irish blood, a fun character that like a good laugh, yet was very good at his job when put to the test. He loved his Guinness and no doubt on the Indian reservation their fire water will have to be plenty to quench his Irish thirst. How he came to be known as Muc I'll never know. It a funny thing in the Micks that for reason or a quirk of habit in doing something will end you up getting a nickname like my own nickname Jack the press. It made have something to do with his looks or his eating habit, as Muc in Irish mean pig. Another great word used a lot in the Micks was mucker which means friend or one who a great help that is a rich word that most Micks used as they look to each other by and large as great muckers.

1979 life in the battalion was fairly steady for me inasmuch my job in the quartermasters department kept me firmly in barracks as lance sergeant in charge of the home service clothing stores and the P R I shop that sold only Micks items, ties, belts, badges, sweat shirts, jogging suits, silver statutes, ashtrays, pewter mugs, and many other item with the Mick logo engraved on, and the profit made against any sale went straight into the regimental fund. The hassle I got when a guardsman of any rank returned their kit on leaving and my having to charged them for damage to Her Majesty property especially when it was obviously not wear and tear like trimming their bearskins with a scissor or having broken the inner cane frame, item missing as in shirts, collar studs, trousers, tunic, plume, curb chain, many a time when it came to the expensive item to be charge like bearskin damage it was the senior rank that went berserk and I had to said if you don't want to pay you are free to take your grievance to the quartermaster captain Pat Duffy and plead your case to him why you should not pay and if he wave your damage cost bring his sign excused chit form back.

In the four years as home services sergeant none ever went to see him or Major Frank Groves they took their medicine grudgingly and the name they called me was worse than Scrooge in Charles Dickins' Christmas Carol, it was more akin to the jump up corporal of the Second World War. Windsor Castle and the Tower of London guards became my two favourite duty when not doing barrack guard as often in the past headquarters personnel were kept back for last minute cover but those days are long gone since the cut across the army have now taken hold that no one can hide behind their job as battalion cooks, tailors, storemen, orderly room and pioneer staff all have to play their part as it all hands to the pump and as you are all guardsmen first when public duties requires you.

It was beginning to be seen in Whitehall by the big boys at the top of the military tree that the daily changing of the guards could no longer be with the numbers shorten by government cut that the Ministry of Defence had to introduce forty-eight hours public duty guards. This guard change did not go down well with the married soldiers as you still only got the afternoon off on the day you dismounted queen's guard and if unfortunate you could find yourself back on another forty-eight hours duty after a twenty-four hour rest.

With our children at boarding school Miriam was itching to buy her own house so that the children on holidays and weekend would now have a steady home with no more army moves. We took up the army offer of boarding school to give first and foremost our children a better opportunity of a stable education at one permanent school as opposing to moving every few years as and where your next posting might be. With seven years left in the army we bought our first house in the autumn of seventy-nine in Camberley, at 19 Brook road a small two bedroom house that while still serving was great, and with the army contribution it help towards our mortgage. It was then Miriam gave up her nursing position in Heatherwood hospital Ascot, and the Princess Margaret Hospital in Windsor as an agency nurse and applied for a job in Frimley Park Hospital where she spent 24 years caring for the elderly as a night nurse retiring to see her grandchildren more.

We had settled into our new house by Christmas 1979 and for any further barrack move I would drive from my own house as all guard unit if not posted abroad are within a thirty mile radius of London. My reputation in the home service and as the PRI lance sergeant in taking no prisoner of any crafty Mick trying to out flanked me in advoiding to paid up where it was due having misuse military property may well have been a big factor in my being chosen to be the acting police sergeant on the battalion upcoming adventure training in mid-November to the twenty of December in Cyprus of 1979.

The battalion had two locations one in the sovereign base in a tented camp called Radio Song and the other camp up in the Troodos Mountain. I would be base in Episcope garrison and Colour Sergeant John Smith would run the Troodos centre which the Ministry of Defence claimed is their highest working office.

Again I'm in Cyprus for a second time in the sovereign base and up the road are other British unit on attachment to NATO and because we are sovereign base position there no military silver earn that if you were in the American Military you get a medal for going to the Naffi. My role on this adventure exercise is to be police sergeant and ensure camp discipline and fire covered and that camp duties are all in place with standing orders carry out as to the camp officer command. The most important task in a tented camp to be undertaken daily was that the barrack guard patrol the tented camp as fire piquet while on twenty-four hour guard duty. It was my first priority that all guardsmen on guards or fire piquet knew how to handle the fire equipment, and have knowledge in the used of the stand pipe, hydrant key, and fire hoses if a fire shout is call.

Every morning and evening I had the guard and fire piquet practice their fire drill ensuring all on fire piquet knew what to do and their position in the fire team if the call to attend a fire is heard. I reminded all on fire piquet daily that no matter if someone is larking about and shout fire any alarm sounded no matter if false are to be treated as real, and to carry out the fire alarm drill in the manner what you have been taught.

Colour Sergeant John Smith known to all as Bushy and his sidekick Lance Sergeant Tommy Meyler ran the Troodos centre, and Sergeant Dennis Watson ran the transport between both camp for mail and change over as different platoon swapped so all got the opportunity to do the adventures courses on offered. Base camp Micks were split into different groups one doing water sport and the second doing abseiling and rock climbing, while those up in Troodos Mountain learn to ski and other to hike in the snowy mountain. Many of the Micks found that they took to some of the courses like skiing and abseiling like duck to water that it became additive and for them a lifetime sport that without the army having introduce them would never have had a go.

I had the opportunity to spend a weekend up in the Troodos with Bushy Smith and Tommy Meyler and Dennis Watson, finding them walking about and sitting on the white stuff laughing and shouting it not wet. It was a fantastic weekend walking in the Troodos and inhaling the pure mountain and pine trees scented air that made the lung feel rejuvenated and the spirit of newness in God wonderland of natural beauty that uplift your soul, and although it was fifteen degrees and snowing it was magically warm and the white stuff fell as white sand. I was taken on a mini tour through the Troodos Mountain and Brought to the renowned archbishop Markarious grave/tomb that is guarded night and day by the Greek Army cream le cream that are vigilance and smartly dress as Irish Guardsmen are when on royal public duty in London. On the Saturday night Bushy Smith and Dennis Watson took me to a traditional Greek restaurant in the Troodos Mountain that they check out so that the food and drink was fit for a king as they laid on the red carpet for me and as a Mick it should have been green.

As with all good things time flies and so it was a great night in their chosen restaurant that it was early morning about two thirty and I thought it Sunday and I got to find myself a church for mass, having just said I must find a church my good protestant friend Bushy from county Tyrone before you could say up the Micks was asking the Greek restaurant owner where the nearest Catholic Church was and he recommended the monastery about a half an hour away and that their mass started at 0500 because of the time we had one more for the road and then we took a taxi to the monastery arriving there at about half past four. We rang the bell to the monastery and after a few minutes the door open and a bearded monk in a long black habit and a Tommy cooper type black hat ask can I help you when Bushy Smith said he like to go to mass, when he understood I wanted to attend their church the monk put his arm over my shoulder and said come with me to the snigger and sarcastic remark of your all right Jack laughing their Northern Ireland heads off as they jumped back into their taxi and sped off to the Troodos centre and into their welcome bed promising my lift would be here to collect me at 10am.

In I went with the monk and was sat in a choir like stall that you only saw the monk in front on the other side and not the monk on your left or right side. It was the weirdest mass I ever attended in the Greek orthodox style that had a lot of the Latin of the Roman Catholic style in my understanding of my childhood that was familiar, and I must have said a few thousands Kyrie Eleison, Christe, Eleison. Kyrie, Eleison, when I saw the vail like curtain being drawn back and the people of God coming in and taking their place for the service to begin that I thought what an eejit I really am that I had to laugh as I got the full monk treatment and would never have this insight again that was in itself a truly holy experience. My time with the monks was five hours and I was pleased on my saying goodbye to see my lift had arrive and thank the lord that Denis had been true to his word and I returned to the Troodos centre for a well earn breakfast and a few hours in the land of nod before going back down to base camp.

A week later about the twenty of December we all arrived home to Windsor and the battalion split leave over the Christmas and the new year that it was all hands back to normal in the January that again like the year gone 1980 promises to be a very busy one from the off for the regiment.

The battalion new posting to Chelsea Barracks in London would be straight after St Patrick's Day 18 March it will be a very sad departure from Windsor for it was a lovely posting living under the shadow of Windsor Castle and the side-line jobs many Micks like myself enjoyed on the Slough trading estate, the freebie bags of chocolate received as a line operator in Mars factory that at the end of each night shift I will missed the most. Seamlessly we left 1979 and rolled into the new year of 1980 when the Micks would be saying their farewell to Windsor on moving to Chelsea Barracks on its new posting come March.

The early months of 1980 saw no let-up in queens guards duty or slacking off from the spring drills on the battalion square as it was known that before we leave Victoria barrack Windsor the Micks would be given the honour of the freedom of the town and marched as freemen accepting the grateful applause and cheers of the town people with a proper goodbye.

It was a battalion treat to have both their majesty visit together on St Patricks day the queen mum our patron and on this special occasion her daughter Queen Elizabeth the second to celebrate St Patricks day with the Irish Guards. I believe in the history of the Irish Guards forming 1 April 1900 that having both their majesties attending a St Patrick's Day to be a battalion first. The queen mum in her usual smiling way presented the regimented its shamrock including a sprig to her daughter the queen. With the usual three cheers screamed loudly for their majesty hip-hip hara. Then the Irish Guards march past seeing both their majesty on the saluting dais and the sovereign flag blowing in full that never in the regiment history will ever be repeated or forgotten because of Her Majesty love of Malta our family was introduce to her by my company commander Major Philip

O Reilly, Her Majesty wore black on that St Patricks day in Victoria barracks in respect of some member of her family that had recently died. Her majesty hearing my wife came from Malta smiled as if she for a moment remembered her own time there and ask, do you go home often, as for her Malta was a special place her only real home as a naval serving officer's wife. That that memorable meeting on St Patrick's Day in Victoria barracks Windsor in meeting Her Majesty that has left us only with a memory photograph picture of our being presented to her on that special of Micks history.

Chelsea Barracks London 1980 and its temptation for the young guardsmen are greater than the 1960s for the seedy night life, clubs, the ease of drugs as an everyday use the military warn against that will be hard to control and enforce for it easy supply and use. The male sex trade that was hidden until the law change in 1965 has made London attractive for it new clubs where the word gay has been adopted by the homosexual as a descriptive noun, and where they can meet other in a no longer taboo same sex relationship that young guardsmen to London should be on their guard and be aware male predators no longer hide but will use pubs and clubs offering free drinks to snare the weak.

1980 18 March and the battalion moved to Chelsea Barracks has went smoothly and the Micks expectation for our own queen mum who is the same age as the regiment that the P R I commission a commemorated crystal glass with the queen mother motif emblazon on. This large brandy glass became a must have item for many Irish Guardsmen past and present of all rank to own for Her Majesty eightieth birthday making it a special beautiful memento, for many Micks a family heirloom.

The Irish scene was still going strong in north London and the clubs were used by IRA sleeper hid among the honest and law-abiding Irish who wanted to enjoy the visiting bands and the Irish festivals that was open to all especially the renowned Willesden Green annual show that the best of Irelands twenty-six counties and the north sixth had stalls showing off their local produces and homemade goods. Dublin was well represented with it Arthur Guinness beer tent where the drink flowed and was smoothly drunk. The all-day celli bands and dancers competed with other Irish groups while the main stage you saw the big names of the day like Brendan Shine, the Fury, Foster and Alan, the Pouges, Philomena Bagley, Daniel O Donnell and his sister Margo with other big name and big bands, that each year it was the must show for the London Irish. While most Irish live peacefully and are not involve with the trouble it still meant as an Irish Guardsman being observant and not putting oneself and family in harm way. We went with two other families at the Irish festival the Davies and the Smiths when the boys wearing black berets rattle their bucket for fund Bushy John Smith reply sharply eff off and stop ruining a good day out.

Being back in London and Chelsea Barracks where I first started fifteen years earlier was a bit harder for me the second time round as I was a married man commuting from Camberley daily and found myself doing the road runner leaving earlier in the morning to avoid traffic but not so good at the end of day due to heavy traffic trying to escape west London before the evening rush hour became worst.

There was great variety and more going on in my earlier days when living in Chelsea Barracks London in the sixty we had a smart hang out like the Nuffield centre close to

Trafalgar square that was situated behind St Martins in the field church a stone throw from Leicester square and Haymarket. There were a few pubs I was told to be aware of like the Lemon tree a known place in my Chelsea days of 1965/66 of males seeking same sex love as told by some old sweat like Leo Tighe the Bat, and Kenneth Brown Hovis both Dubliners saying a good Catholic like you Jack should certainly avoid.

The best thing about the Nuffield trust centre was its location, and the place service men and women stayed when in London that did a first-class bed and breakfast. The Nuffield receptionist handed out unsold ticket to anyone that ask for them as the Nuffield received unsold ticket to give away free to veterans, and serving military as a thank you from theatre land for many business leaders had served in the military themselves, and in a span of only twenty years since World War Two ended many were at the top of their game, and fully appreciate those serving as voluntary as opposed to their conscription days that in the 1960 ended.

The Nuffield trust centre was a great place because of it convenience to the West End and a great place to eat a fantastic meals for much less than the city restaurant, it had game rooms, recreational and lounge area to relax if meeting up with friends before going out on the town or if you just wanted to meet up with friends and rest that you could do. The Nuffield centre now long gone and a new replacement home for visiting service and veteran called the Union Jack Club near Waterloo Station is convenient and a great place for a meal or to stay at a subsidised rate if staying in London.

Public duties was the order of the day and I must say I found myself doing a lot of Her Majesty's Tower of London, and felt that this particular duty was the bastion for

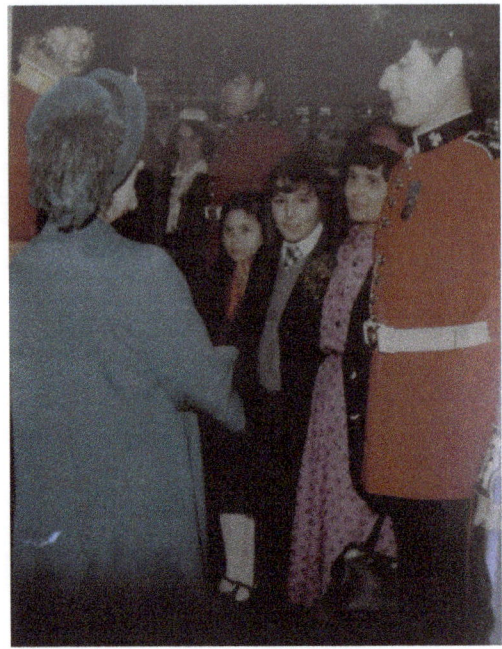

Windsor Victoria barrack family presented to her Majesty queen Elizabeth the queen mum on St Patrick's Day 1979. Myself, Miriam, Francis & Margaret.

Three Micks L/Sgt Tommy Meyler, Sgt Denis Watson, and myself spinning the bar outside the Ministry of defence highest Office top of Troodos mountain Nov/Dec 1979.

Photo taken by battalion photographer of myself on the second rehearsal of the Queen Birthday parade June 1981.

L/Sgt John McDonald, L/Sgt Tommy Meyler, & myself making ready to take up our street lining position on the Mall for Prince Charles and Lady Diana spencer wedding day 29th July 1981.

the second division of guardsmen that were not Buck house or St James' Palace standard. I did not mind commuting as it was lovely each morning especially in spring to pass by Richmond Park where the cherry trees lined both side of the road greeting you like a wedding folly.

I will always remember Victoria barracks with fondness as I think back to being on duty when my son was born in 1969 and 1970 when the regimental sergeant Major Pat Duffy called me into his office for an incident in which my wife a learner driver with guardsman John Duffin a full licence holder in the car beside her as she mistaken the accelerator for the foot-break and loss control driving the car into the guardroom Victorian veranda damaging military property. The regimental sergeant Major Pat Duffy informed me I would be paying for the veranda repairs and I should put my wife in house arrest until she can control a car and find a proper instructor said with the usual Mick humour. And another time when I ask for time out to be with my wife at Wrexham park hospital near the time of my son birth that I ask for time off barrack guards to be told women have had babies for millennia without their men present and you can carried on doing your guard duty till the hospital calls that your wife has completed her delivery.

Many of the married will have to commute from Windsor to Chelsea due to their children settle in school and also a shortage of married quarters in the London area. Miriam and I thankfully had moved into our own first home that we purchase for sixteen thousand pounds in Camberley on a twenty-five year endowment mortgage that on a lance/Sgt pay I struggle to afford but with Miriam's salary as a nurse and the army married quarters contribution we manage to keep our heads above water.

1980 everyone knew it was going to be a busy year with it being our queen mother's age and the regiment eightieth birthday, and with our new posting to Chelsea barrack the Irish Guards were back into the routine of public duty life and the ongoing preparation for the annual commanding officer and major general inspection as is the norm every spring to May.

The guard's depot like screams could be heard across the Chelsea square as rehearsal on military drill and marching was at full pace with officers too being beasted in their handling of sword drill as there was no place for second best in this special year of the battalion receiving its new colours at Buckingham Palace from Her Majesty the queen, and will proudly troop their colours on her birthday parade in which the nation celebrate drawing tourists from around the world and Londoners to flock and see this magnificent military display.

1980 is a special year in the life of the Micks and a milestone for our queen mother as she too will be eighty on 4 August and the sergeant mess had a painting commission by a well-known artist Terrence Cuneo who capture her wonderful smile that is our queen mum best trademark and has pride of place in our sergeant mess. As sergeant in charge of the presidential regimental fund known to all as the PRI, a special crystal glass had been commissioned by regimental headquarters as it was secretly believe it's a now or never moment in how long more Her Majesty maybe around. This year also mark the Micks' eighty and there was a buzz of excitement of the number eighty being a double birthday the queen mum and her regiment of the Irish Guards.

Life in London is a Mick world as you have all the theatre and what going on at your fingertips, I must confess I missed the Battersea funfair of the sixty in which we went and check out the local talent the Christmassy coloured lights, fair rides, and it holiday buzz of fun. There were ups and downs while stationed in Chelsea Barracks as our role in overseas duty was call upon from time to time as with those who went as monitors during the handover of Rhodesia power to its new leader of the now new name Zimbabwe. During the transfer of power the regiment lost Lance Sergeant Buckley in a road accident while out there on the monitoring team.

Chapter 14

Public duties and all that goes with the London scenes like the troop and our regiment getting it new colour was just part of the best year culminating this wonderful year that was getting better as each month pass. My role in the store and the important of my job did not allow for me to go on what is believed to be the biggest exercise in Germany called crusader eighty, again that number eighty. In those last two month of 1980 with a fire brigade strike looming we once again saw the green goddess arrive and line up on the battalion square that a few years earlier many still serving were able to show how they work and the art of driving a swirling vehicle full of water that needed careful and safety handling. Thankfully our fire cover was limited and the battalion after a very rewarding year of public duty, the troop, two state visit and a state opening of Parliament, and the nation remember at the cenotaph and at the Albert Hall in the services of remembrances. As a resident London unit the regiment had a small part in the royal tournament at Earls Court exhibition centre that draws thousands of visitors to it military venue and I would say London greatest military show. Of all the services taking part in the royal tournament each year for me it is the naval gun race that is the highlight, with the RAF queen squadron doing it silent drill movement with fantastic precision a close second.

As 1980 comes to a close I can say the regiment has met all it tasks with the usual Mick commitment and humour that at the end of a day the Micks and our most royal patron of the Irish Guards the queen mum both celebrated their eightieth birthday.

The battalion went on Christmas leave not sure if it was broken into company leave in order that everyone had Christmas or the New Year off. Whatever happen the battalion welcome in 1981 after a fantastic 1980 year that everyone was at ease and optimism that all was going well and hope this new year will be as good as the one we left behind, in that it already on the cards that there will be many small trips for company training and attachment with other regiment on foreign short joint service exercises.

For me it will be another year of mainly Tower of London duties that I love as I am now on first name with the chief warden and the tower special residents the Tower ravens. There is a folk tale about the ravens in the Tower of London that if they left England would fall, and to that end they are cared for by a special raven warder as to their important in the tower in keeping the folk tale alive for the tourist who cannot get enough of British history and its infamous Tower of London stories. Stories especially of the boy princes kill in the bloody tower, and the execution of Henry queens that die on tower green losing their heads, and about the ghosts that still walk and dwell within. To see the dungeon torture chambers the brutal relic of shackle and racks used in torturing the kings and queens' prisoners like our own Sir Rodger Caseman locked up for treason during the first world war and executed at Pentonville prison 1921 and was claimed by Ireland as one who die for its cause. And not least the must see crown of jewels that today are visible behind a state of the art bullet proof glass presentation display that any would be magpie be proud to own any of its beautiful bling.

Her Majesty Tower of London now on 1000 years old is itself it biggest story as to the different times line that it grew from when the white tower stood alone having been built by William the Conqueror in 1070 to defend and protect his royal power. The Tower of London I think was the main royal resident for near on seven hundred years of the royal kings and queens to James the first in 1601. Many ghosts are seen and talked about by the yeoman wardens and tower guardsmen one in particular Mary Queen of Scots whose ghost has often been seen walking with her head under her arm as she walks the tower battlement wall on the traitor's gate side. I loved the Tower of London its history and tradition it holds, especially the beautiful ceremony of the keys held each night at 2200 hours it never fails to impress or do. I have it on good authority from the chief yeoman warden even through the two world wars the ceremony it was nightly enacted.

I once had a guardsman on the ceremony of the keys freeze after he shouted halt, who comes there, when the key yeoman warden said "the keys" from the lowest voice I ever heard that the challenger froze frighten white, as if the voice came from a tower ghost, I shouted from within the ranks, pass Queen Elizabeth keys all is well, I earned a drink in the yeoman warden club that night. For me as tower guard sergeant it in the night when London is still and the quietness of the tower with it low lighted gas lamps castes its eerie shadows that the greyness of the Tower of London comes into its own and most atmospheric that you can well believe when walking on the smooth cobbles how time is unchanged, untouched, by the outside world, and that the ghost in the tower walk, never sleep, as if time for them has stood still and no one told them they are dead not alive but live suspended in their own time that every night is relived.

It had been a good year all in all up to the autumn when an Irish Guards coach on it return from the Tower of London was attack by the IRA on Ebury bridge road near our local boozer the Rising Sun when a nail bomb exploded leaving many injure and other seriously damage. I know Wally Wallace of the signal platoon lost an eye, and Tower guard Sgt Danny Cullen had a torn arm, and would be awarded a BEM for his quick thinking in saving life and looking after his guardsmen including guardsman John Radley who received the worst injury that it was thought he might not make it for his damages were so extensive and like the bionic man was put together and for all the seriousness of the incident that day no fatality we say a big thank you to God our almighty protector.

Although an Irish regiment that had done no active tour in Northern Ireland it showed that we were not immune or out of reach of the IRA grasped, and with a Germany posting in the new-year this would give the battalion time to regroup as the attack had shaken all. Early November 1981 I attended commanding officer order and promoted to full sergeant informed that with the battalion on route to Germany in February 1982 my new job would be as regimental police sergeant. I was sent to the royal military police barracks in Colchester for my six weeks police training course learning all about military law and the handling of prisoners especially in the receiving of a live body into the guardroom to undergo detention. The one emphasis that the instructor drum in throughout my police course was never received a military person for detention that has not been pass fit to undergo detention by a doctor if there being handed over into your care from outside your own unit.

My work as police sergeant in Cyprus of 1979 did not go unnoticed by the fish Victor McLean who is now taking over as the new regimental sergeant major of the Irish Guards with Swannie Lieutenant Colonel Robert J S Corbett as our new commanding officer for our posting to Oxford barracks Munster Germany. Christmas eighty-one at home in Frimley we packed a few small boxes for our move to Oxford Barrack Munster hoping Germany a second time round would be as good as seventh four to seventy-seven in Buller barrack. We arrive in Munster in early February 1982 as usual with everyone having bought a taxed free new car and we settle into our new quarters on Billebeck Strada and after a few days of arriving at Oxford Barrack I was introduce to my new guardroom by the outgoing regimental police sergeant of the grenadier guards Sergeant Jonny Swayne a six foot two inch queen company man who was looking forward to his new promotion to c/Sgt on arrival in London. As battalion police sergeant it would be for me to carry out the command and the discipline ask by the regimental sergeant Major Fish V McLean, and Swanie the commanding officer Lieutenant Colonel RJ S Corbett, to understand both nick name i.e. the Fish because of the amount of drinks he could sink, and our commanding officers for his love of recce and wandering of the beaten track hence, Swanie.

Settling into my new role did not take long when you are tested at every twist and turn by the shenanigan and bluff tactic quick and crafty Micks think up. The day I accepted the position as regimental police sergeant I had made a conscious decision to do this job in an honest and fair manner, I would make my presence seen at all times about the guardroom and about the barracks as my way of stopping would be chancers becoming inmate of the corner shop.

I knew it was not necessary to use bad language or name calling to achieve the tone for correction that would bring home my point of view as first experience seventeen years before when I was first introduce to the army at the guards' depot and met on my arrival by one who I now know personally in the Micks and is now long retired.

Being lock up in my guardroom was not going to be a picnic for I had the handle of the bumper cut to eight inches that would be going twenty-four seven and not in the swing action for polishing the floor, but as a punishment exercise you done while doing press up and shining the floor. This for those that did not have the pleasure of my hotel in Oxford barracks and would like to practice in their own time it is done by getting into the press up position take the eight inch handle bumper in eider hand you feel comfortable then lift your body up sweep bumper beneath your frame right to left and repeat ten or twenty times.

I must confess it became a competition with the old stalwart who challenge even member of the barrack guard as the bumper was great in making one sweat and very fit. Overall the three who achieved champion status were Davy McCullough whose uncle was a company sergeant major both from Northern Ireland and two from Liverpool Quinn a footballer and Murphy a good soldier and one of life lucky chancer all could do a hundred and fifty in one sitting while most got to twenty-five at a push. I also had a grass roller fixed with a harness attached for outdoor exercise that was a killer to pull and yes there were inmate of the corner shop who could pull it a hundred yards and again the punishment exercise was turn into a game. In the army of today I'm told such beastly exercise would not be allow it would be classed as cruel and wrong.

Having move to Germany on accompanied posting Miriam missed her house in Frimley and her job in Frimley Park Hospital, and missed more seeing her children that she no longer wanted to stay for it meant the children would not be able to come home on weekends from boarding school, and we would only see them on the school holidays. Miriam saw my job as regimental police sergeant very demanding and in truth she was not seeing much of me as Germany was a very busy posting with ongoing brigade and battalion exercises. That after two months she upped sticks and said her goodbye returning to her life in the u k and her job in Frimley Park Hospital bringing the children home for weekends break, that in hindsight was the right move, and one we should have talk more with our children about.

I became a live in single sergeant mess member and to all a pain in the backside as an onsite police sergeant which made your fellow sergeant wearied of giving you any information for fear I was the regimental sergeant major snitch.

I must say when it came to battalion exercises and the role of the police staff it was like we were the battalion outrider escorting the battalion convoy and directing traffic into it field location, and yet having to maned the barrack gate for the rear party. Not being top in my class for field manoeuvring my second in command Lance Sergeant Davy Stratton and Corporal Doyle and Kearney being a good map reader cover my backside in finding the battalion location especially on night exercises. I was more comfortable in my administration role than playing soldier that having been demoted in Aden from infantry to the quarter master staff doing supply and demand I was rusty in frontline map reading that I was struggling to be proficient under the beady eye of the battalion top echelon. To pass away time when not on duty or away on battalion exercises I got involved with the Munster players which was an amateur dramatic company setup and run by Colonel Newton of the medical corps that fill in dead time when not away on battalion duties rather than sit in my sgt mess bunk twirling my thumbs or that other past time that could lead you down the wrong path the demon drink.

After six months in Germany a new addition to the regimental police staff came out to Germany it was no other than guardsman John Radley who almost lost his life the year before and was still in need of weekly physio to help him in his full recovery. For the man that he was he did not let his injuries stop him doing his job and I can vouch that he pull his weigh that no one could say we were easy on him because of the injuries and pain he still went through, for he himself told me on day one of joining the regimental staff that he wanted to be treated as if he had no injuries and wanted no sympathy against what had happen to him on the tower guard bus. I admired guardsman John Radley as he was determined to prove he had what it took to be a guardsman and wanted no special treatment and to that end he was a number one regimental policeman. He impressed all in the regiment having gone through many operation and skin graph because of the extensive damage he received on that terrible day returning from the Tower of London when the Irish Guards coach was attack, and a nail bomb was exploded.

As much as it was my job to ensure military discipline is carried out about the barracks it was also to ensure that those undergoing detention would never want to return again. Prisoners doing time were allowed two cigarette a day not at their choosing but mine hence smoking for our guardsmen undergoing detention was done under supervision and by numbers with ashtray held in left hand for wasted ash. I found in kings regulation a very important fact that men undergoing detention who did not smoke were entitled to a square of chocolate so they too lined up with left hand out to received their chocolate break.

There is much that goes on each day with men in detention that those on minor charges can be sign out to carry on their company training during the day with their platoon going into open arrest and these soldier can then in the working hours do their infantry duty returning at the end of their working day to close arrest for the night. Others undergoing restriction of privileges a punishment handed out for military misdemeanour on company orders that usually three to seven days but can be longer if you are pick up for been in bad order when inspected by the piquet officers on the barrack guard mount and defaulters parade. The guard that mount daily becomes the battalion fire piquet from 1730 hrs to 0700hrs on guard dismount while those undergoing restriction of privileges undergo two hour fatigues, i.e. cleaning about the barrack, cookhouse, sergeant or officers mess fatigues with other duties the regimental sergeant major may want done.

Men undergoing restriction are confined to barracks unless married when they can go home after 2200hrs, but all person doing restrictions must attend the guardroom at the following times throughout the day 0600, 1330, 1730, and 2200 married not excuse. The bugler on calls duty plays the last post at 2200hrs each evening, of all military calls it is for me the one I love and find very moving when you remember those you served with are no longer about, for me it always the Micks we left behind in Aden during our tour of 66/67 that come to mind especially Digger bell who came through the depot with me.

While I may have earned a bad reputation for being overbearing it was to ensure that those who are doing time on restrictions are never idle for we all know the maxim of idle hands, they makes for devil work. As police sergeant I'm responsible for the battalion fire equipment and carrying out fire training drill properly ensuring the fire piquet know what to do should a fire break out anywhere in the barracks. The piquet sergeant of the day and the piquet officers becomes the first point of contact should any incidence happen in the day especially out of working hours, the fire piquet are situated in the guardroom and called out when needed. The piquet officer see up all meals time and listen to complaints if one has a gripe about the food then the piquet officer will take action. The piquet officer to all is the eyes and ears of the commanding officer out on the ground and auditor of the battalion stores especially ration and PRI shop to check that its book keeping is correct. Any discrepancy found would first be taken up with the quartermaster for him to do a thorough check against any issue to the cookhouse or the officer and sergeant messes in order that if an error was made it can be rectified the same with the PRI shop of item bought or sold.

Every day the fire practice take place after the half five parade to cover the night until 0700 hrs when the guardroom staff take back over the guardroom and fire cover during the working day. It was important that the fire drill is enacted for real and that all know where the fire cart and the water main point by any building are in order to run with the fire cart and connect the stand pipe and hose outside whatever building a fire is reported to be at. The most important thing I was taught on my own fire course at Camberley Fire Station was to practice often correct procedure in running out the hoses and the proper use of the fire stand pipe key, and that the person in charge of the nozzle hose holder shout the command for water on, and water off that is relayed back to the stand key-point man on bringing the fire under control.

Having done my fire course at Camberley Fire Station the one thing that was drum home was how serious any fire is and the action of the fire team knowing their job the equipment that daily practice is the only safe guard in saving lives and to that end I ensure each new guard coming on guard duty weather they know or not the fire drill training it will be done as per battalion fire order with no short cut of who has done this before being excused. I would test very often to the dislike of the fire piquet to see how long they took in answering a fire call from a hidden location in the barracks watching if the fire drill is being carried out correctly. If not more fire practice until done right as all fire drill must be as real time action.

I fought on behalf of guardsman against the royal military police in Munster who went around making it their business to lock up Micks they found inebriated coming out of the Tenner bar and the local night clubs. One night I happen to be in the guardroom at two in the morning when I observed the military police arrive with guardsman Murphy of number one company looking the worst for wear. I heard the military police corporal state that he would like this guardsman locked up for causing untold damage in town and that he had beaten up two or three members of the royal military police staff and that he would be reporting his arrest to his provost marshal at Winterbourne barracks in the morning.

Just as the sergeant of the guard was about to accept guardsman Murphy into his care I step in and ask the military police corporal if he had a medical certificate from a doctor which says Murphy is fit to undergo detention.

A bit put out by my asking that he ask who I was that I inform him I was the regimental police sergeant, I ask again if guardsman Murphy had been seen by a doctor and fit to undergo detention for I notice Murphy holding his side instinctively knowing the military police had enacted their own punishment in a rough way and not just one but the four of them.

That was when the police corporal said you can have him and mumble expletive to himself as he drove away without making a charge and guardsman Murphy having escape this one with a smile of satisfaction that I save his backside, after given him a cup of tea to see if he was good he amble off to his bed to recover from his interesting night out. During my time as police sergeant, Sergeant Brendan McCann of our corps of drums made up a little ditty for those doing correction time to sing the new guardroom song that he composed and it became the guardroom anthem.

Chorus only

Jack, Jack wherever you maybe
Jack is on the ball you see,
He loves us all, he loves us all,
Jack is always on the ball.

Sung to lord of the dance tune and when sung it always got deliver with great gusto especially the repeat chorus as they know I look after them and my staff are fair in their treatment. For Micks singing is recreational and all have a good laugh that made those undergoing detention feel good inside pardon the pun. Our commanding officer Lieutenant Colonel R J S Corbett having heard about the detention men song made it a point to hear it sung on his next guardroom inspection he was very impress as was the Regimental Sergeant Major Fish McLean on hearing the detention choir sing in good form that both walked away with a smile, and gave the guardroom inspection a well done.

As police sergeant I tried carrying out my job to the best of my ability but it became hard to please the regimental sergeant major who kept undermining any decision I made. It became clear to me that he wanted to pull my string and I be his puppet in my making enemies for his pleasure and amusement.

I did not feel it right to make up number for orders just for my staff to look good in justifying they are doing their job when we are stretched carrying out our own job, maintaining security of the main gate, signing in and out of all vehicle and personnel, escort duty of men undergoing corrective training. The regimental sergeant major unnecessary burden on me and my staff to find guardsmen for order on any excuse to prove we are doing our job was to make him happy in his evil scheme in him getting the police staff a bad name of vindictiveness toward good guardsmen who have done no wrong.

Because the regiment sergeant major office was opposite the guardroom at Oxford Barrack gate he did when he was board just to give him a laugh to shout police sergeant what is that guardsman name and why is he walking out at this time of the day it was as if he was the regimental police sergeant and I was his second in command that often we clash because of his unwanted attention and bad interferences.

Guarding and looking after detention men out on barrack fatigues put great pressure to achieve the impossible with a small staff of one lance sergeant Davy Stratton, two lance corporal John Doyle and Tony Kearney, and two police guardsmen John Radley and I think Kearney brother. the regimental sergeant major often turn on me if there was no one to do his bidding when he wanted a fast ball acted on, and because of my staff carrying out escort and other duty that there was no one to run-around as he wanted whenever he require a runner to do his bidden.

He never allow us to rest was continually on our back for this and that, and it became impossible to know what it was he wanted as he never let up and I was glad in my heart that Miriam saw the writing on the wall after a few months into our posting in Germany that as regimental police sergeant I would have no life to be happy under this type of unnecessary pressure that was created and not warranted.

I could not after one year meet the Regimental Sergeant Major Fish McLean demands he broke our relationship that should have been a happy and workable one, but his hounding the police staff and myself to do this and that was too much.

I could have handled a lot of what he wanted done if he increase the police staff by having a standby guardsman as his personal runner during office hours. I have known the regimental sergeant Major fish Mc Lean from his days as a lance corporal right through his career and as he rose in rank to become the regimental sergeant Major. He was a great Irish Guardsman from Waterford who when not under any pressure was fun and great company to be in especially on mess function night, and like us all he was always up for a good sing song and the craic. Climbing up the ranks he was very smart in his turnout and in his himself was easy going in everything he done. His asking me to be his police sergeant was an easy yes as I was pleased to accept for we always got on well and I believe he would look after me as I would in doing a good job for him as his choice for regimental police sergeant.

Germany was a demanding posting and as the regiment share Oxford barracks with other small unit like sixth field medic and others, the Micks as resident battalion it fell to the Irish Guards to maintain barracks security and share its facilities in being a good neighbour. As a guards regiment in Munster Garrison other unit in the garrison through request to our commanding officer to have their men undergo detention in the Irish Guards guardroom as it was felt a rigorous standard of correction, drill, fatigues, and guards discipline would be enough for them not to want a return.

As police sergeant you are privy to the confessional of those doing detention that I remember this young sixth field medic who was put into our guardroom for refusing to wear a uniform, and was wrapped in a blanket for modesty. I ask him if he would like to tell me his reason for refusing to wear uniform at first he said no, then after about two hours in his cell he bang on his cell door asking to speak to me, telling me his horrific storey of why he wanted out of the army and his reason in refusing to go on soldiering. I contacted the regimental sergeant major and the piquet officer reference his storey of how he was being sexually abused by a person of senior rank that his own platoon officer refusing to believe, and that those who force their evil sexual practices upon him for their pleasure he said had repeatedly assaulted him.

Other than suicide he chose refusing to wear uniform as his only option to getting out of the nightmare in seeking the help and attention he wanted. The perpetrators were charged and dishonourably discharge and I had a thank you note from him on his leaving Germany and the army a few week later. As police sergeant you have the inside of what happen in a court martial when in progress and the security you as the court police sergeant responsible in charge must ensure is correct, i.e. the court lay out, no camera or recording instrument hidden, check all persons attending are present. I attended one court marshal and saw the person walk free when all knew the offender was guilty but the court's hands were both tied.

A young German girl only sixteen had been raped and her mother and father came along to give her their support, she was unable at the rape trial in front of an all-male judge panel, able to describe to the court what the accuse did to her. The accused soldier lawyer asked the young girl if she could describe again in her own words to the court what happen on the day the allege rape took place. She looked at him in the court and the horror of what happen to her was raw and vivid so much she was unable to say aloud anything. It was for her being rape again that she buckle, crumble, in shock, in a mess, the senior judge called for a half hour recess in the hope it would give her time to compose and carry on with her evidence. She refused to return to the court and face her rapist again who walk free noted by everyone present that somehow justice for the fragile girl was not served.

I felt sad for that young girl thinking how I would feel if such a thing happen to my daughter who was then only eleven years old, and I felt bad for the girl and her family who were broken inside. Looking back on my year as regimental police sergeant the early months as regimental police sergeant I felt went well and I believe I was doing a reasonable good job under the regimental sergeant major annoying demand that change day to day and his ringing the guardroom constantly wanted this done yesterday, and when I had no staff available to do his bidding due to gate cover, escorts duties, he would lose his rag and go into wild

Myself as regimental police sergeant greeting General Sir Michael Gow, General Officer Commanding British Army On the Rheine, who presented the Irish guards their shamrock on behalf of her majesty Queen Elizabeth the Queen mum on Patricks day Oxford Barracks Munster Germany 17th March 1982.

Germany 1984 wearing nuclear biological suit on a battalion exercise.

Germany 1985 Guardsman Oliver, L/Sgt John Fitzpatrick and myself standing as John Fitzpatrick practice his general address.

Germany 1985 Company Sergeant Major John Smith & myself having a tea break on Soltau–Luneburg heath training area.

tantrum that it became as a bad marriage that turn sour. I knew it was time for me to move on and ask for a military divorce for nothing I did for him was ever right he was always on mine and the police staff's back, that I felt if I don't leave this job I end up a gibbering wreck like himself who through taking the top job has become for all to see a true Dr Jeckle and Mr Hyde.

Before I left the job as regimental police sergeant I had put forward a recommendation that guardsman John Radley who prove himself a great access to the regimental police staff be put forward for the next corporal course and I was happy in my time left with the Micks to see that John Radley reach lance sergeant on my leaving the Micks was still climbing in the ranks that for all he been through showed you cannot keep a good Mick down.

I was rescue by the quartermaster Captain Ray Cowap who heard of my request for another job, and he offer me the position of ration sergeant it was to be my last and best role in the Micks. I had in my time as police sergeant got to know many young Micks through them being on barracks guard and my closing the Alexander club a night haunt that was the guardsmen own club be it their own mess in the same way the officers, sergeant, and corporal each had their own. The crack in the guardsmen club was a tough one to calm when as piquet sergeant you had to called time and see the club close at eleven. I myself having been a police sergeant knew most guardsmen by name that was a gift when it came to my turn as piquet sergeant to close the Alexander club named after our top colonel as to who might be the chancer in keeping the craic and the club going. A good piquet sergeant needs to close down without making the lads feel bad and help them leave and go on their merry way at closing time.

I saw out the remainder of my time in Germany and the Micks as the ration sergeant getting my teeth stuck into a job that gave me great satisfaction and one I saw the end result that made what I did worthwhile, and not being badgered as I was when regimental police sergeant question on every task as to why I did or didn't do it this way that really nagged me. It was my number one reason why I asked for a transfer that I no longer could handle the regimental sergeant major childish impetuousness over every little thing. I think in hindsight the Fish McLean was unhappy in his life and under great stress that he used the police staff as an easy target to expel his rage and energy on.

Now I'm appreciate and left to do my job as ration sergeant, and if I have a problem or a question I was free to ask the quartermaster without him shouting a load of obscenities. Capt. Ray Cowap was a gentleman in his dealing with everyone and in all the years I knew him in the Micks he was never a screamer but a listening gentleman that as orderly room clerk come chief clerk in the regiment was always available and helpful to all rank in his easy nature that made him stand out and very approachable.

The ration sergeant job was a grafter number with a staff of four myself, lance sergeant V Buckley guardsman Terry Mc Sherry, Hartles and L/Cpl Sammy Wilson, and Stanley who was butcher assistance to lance Sergeant Davy Dawson who threw the putt shot for the battalion on the athletic team.

Between the four of us we all muck in and loaded the ration from the ordnance depot and were hands on at every level of collection and storing. I had to learn quickly about the rotation of can and fresh and to keep a proper account of daily use as the ration stores was broken down into three different types of storage, meat and dairy, compo, dry and fresh which was issue to the master chef on his request form every day.

As to the daily requirement of rations, company quartermaster's sergeant of the five company sent in their breakdown numbers daily of who in their companies were on what duties weather they are married or single which applied to all rank, as the officers and sergeant mess stewards had to send in their numbers as to single or married sergeant or officer on their daily duty form. Ration to the three messes was tightly control by the quartermaster and supervise by the ration sergeant and deliver to the messes by the ration staff.

My working out the daily ration required against the status sent sheet to the ration office that told me how many single in all three messes require meals and how many married that were having meals due to being on duty as stated by their company quartermaster sergeant on the daily claim allowances.

The status of those on ration in Germany was important as Germany was class as a home posting so married were only fed while on actual duty or on exercises in the field. All soldier single married are added to all meals on battalion training on a major exercise when everyone is on the same ration.

Rations ordered and issues to the messes are audited daily to ensure no fraud or theft was being carried out in that the piquet officer of the day on behalf of the commanding officer check what is left in stores against the stores outgoing of the day and what remain correspond with the ration log books that he sign after checking all is correct, and if not he make the quartermaster aware of his finding and log it in the piquet officers report.

The issue of ration is laid down in the military manual of the allowance that can be claimed for a single soldier per day and a married unaccompanied. While married men on duty up the money by charging them as laid down due to them being paid extra allowance that single soldier do not received. The officer's mess was also suspect as the officer mess return did not state their true status that under the same scrutiny I charge married officers taking advantage of single men ration that I brought to the steward attention Sgt Jimmy Halford. It was thought I was a Scrooge in that I gave the barracks guard two tea bags per man and controlled the hotplate when meals were being serve in as much one sausage per man and not a free for all. Often I heard the remark you think it was coming out of his pocket little did they know I was looking after the single man's money.

In my years as ration sergeant I got to know every guardsman as they passed through for their meals and many volunteer their service to do pan diving and cookhouse fatigues be that it was the military way of making reparation for their army sins with military absolution.

In mid-1983 the Fish McLean said his goodbye and my old stores company quartermaster of headquarter company in 1975 at Buller barrack Rob Kelly a gentleman Mick by any standard took up his new role as regimental sergeant major beside the new commanding officers Lieutenant Colonel Shaun O' Dwyer, a little later and both brought an air of calm and a steady change that was notable after the Fish and swannee also known as the smiling assassin left as both were promoted on their new postings to the UK.

I was sad to see my good friend Major Ray Cowap MBE posted back to London after six months in ration stores but I was happy that the tech quartermaster Major Frank Groves was in the same vain and good to work for and as I have been a battalion person my whole career and I have known many of the quartermasters since my Chelsea days, from Major P Mercer, A Bell, V Sullivan, J Williams, P Duffy, R Cowap, and the new quartermaster Major Frank Groves and the new tech quartermaster captain Bill Mathews now join us that on my leaving the Mick would be my last quartermaster 18 March 1987 I then left the Micks on six months' garden leave.

I have to say my life on leaving the regimental police turn for the better as just an ordinary battalion sergeant getting on with my work in the ration stores and overseeing meals in the cookhouse. I remember being attach to the cookhouse years ago in Aden when I first understood the real worth of the battalion cooks and the heat and hours they worked under that today is carried out by chefs of the army catering corps and the master cook is now call master chef be that the guards regiment still refer to them with the old regimental name master cook. As a live in sergeant mess member and no longer the police sergeant I am able to once again relax and when not on exercises or duty free to be part of the Munster Garrison players that became a great outlet from soldiering and an opportunity to mixed with other outside of the military like the German civilian member who were part of the garrison Munster players for them also to have an opportunity to have good relation within the garrison and us the local community.

One event that stood out for me over my time as ration sergeant was a training fortnight in Soltau in Germany when over the middle weekend the battalion laid on transport for Hamburg which I thought was good for those that wanted to let their hair down and let a bit of steam off. The following morning a young Catholic guardsman ask me in the mess hall if there would be transport to go to church for mass as there was for Hamburg yesterday evening. I was quiet impress with that young Mick asking me that I assure him I would find out as I myself was deeply interested to the same and would find out. I contacted the piquet officer and asked that question who started scratching his head as no plan had been made for the battalion spiritual needs, and noting a can of worms was about to be open a decision at the top was made sharply either kidnap the garrison padre or send transport to which the latter was the answer and all ended well causing the battalion to start the next part of the exercise a few hours late.

In the summer of 1984 the battalion heading to France in the Sarnac region for a three week exercise with the French military, and I saw this as an opportunity for my children to join me as my son Francis has a good grip on his French language and a real opportunity for him to use and practise it as I could have him as my own personal interpreter. I asked my quartermaster Major Frank Groves if I could go early as it would give me the opportunity to see the lay of the land and the barrack where the battalion would be staying, and to find out about where I collect the ration and make ready my stores and have a meal prepare for the main party arrival on the following Friday.

I collected Francis and Margaret and was not able to bring Miriam due to her work commitment in Frimley Park Hospital. I brought the children to France and we camped in our trailer tent on a local campsite three miles from the French Army barracks as I had got permission to bring my children as my son spoke French and he would be my translator in helping me do my job. The exercise commanding officer was to be Major Sabastian Roberts who spoke French and would be arriving on the Tuesday to sign for the camp and all its inventories. I call in on the Monday just to get my bearing when I was introduced to a Lieutenant Pierre who insisted I start signing for this and that as the French Army he said do not work after four o' clock on Friday as they go home to their families for the weekends and with so much to sign for he just started. I tried explaining through my son that I'm here as the battalion ration sergeant and come to see where my stores will be and where it is I go to collect the daily ration and that the officer in charge will be here tomorrow who speak fluent French and he will sign for the camp. He would have none of it and told me I should start now taking over and when the officer arrived I can hand over to him what I sign for.

It transpired that the advance party did not make Tuesday, Wednesday or Thursday as they were detained by some attractions in Paris, and my checking and taking over was fortuitous in that I sign for the barracks/camp handing it over to the company quartermaster sergeant that first weekend. The exercise commanding officer Major Sabastian Roberts was very pleased that the battalion arrive to a hot meal and their accommodation ready that he asked Francis to be a battalion interpreter giving him a great experience as a fourteen year old boy that on completion of the battalion training exercise with the French forces, Francis was presented with a silver armour personnel carrier by Major Sabastian Roberts for his sterling work with the Micks a gift that he still treasure and take pride of place at home.

When we first arrive at our camp site in Sarnac we pitched our trailer tent with awing as we had no electric light but the usual Tilly lamp poor camper use. Francis on our first day setting up on the camp site heard the posh camper beside us talk to his dog in polish when Francis said hello in polish to him that he ask are you polish, Francis said no but I go to a polish private school in England run by the Marion fathers at Fawley Court in Oxfordshire and to that end I have learn a little polish. He then explained to my son that his family have no interest in his mother tongue and that is why he talk to his dog in polish as it keep him sane to hear his language be it his own voice and the fact that his dog understand is great for him.

That evening he sat with Francis and seeing we had no electric light connected a lead from his electric point and gave us a secondary light. It was great every morning taking my children into work and Francis was busy helping out who ever grab him while Margaret enjoyed reading and eating in the cookhouse and being spoiled by all the cookhouse staff. Margaret thought Pierre was fantastic in that he let us call mum back in Frimley from a military phone that he carried in a portable bag that no matter where he was he just connected to any telegraph pole line wire and it was up and running, this was years before personal mobile phone were dreamed off.

When the battalion training in France was over I drove the children home and had a spot of leave and a week holiday on the isle of white in a Butlin's type camp that were becoming popular for family cheap holiday. I left the children and their mum and return to Germany getting on with the world of rations. When I was not on duty or exercises I took the opportunity to get back to Frimley for long weekends and always on annual leave. I was a full-time member of the Munster Garrison players an outlet to soldiering and escapism that kept me sane as a live in mess member that anything was better than looking at the four walls in your bunk, and a rest from drinking and keeping the bar profit up. As a member of the Munster Garrison amateur players it was a good way of meeting and making German friend and other military people of all rank who enjoy amateur dramatic that in rehearsal we use first names and not rank that our German civilian players knew us as we did them on first name basic only without any rank being mentioned.

Chapter 15

Over my years in the garrison players I did many big musicals and at Christmas the Munster players became a choral choir in which the Christmas of eight four and eighty-five we performed at York barracks theatre headquarters for all in the Munster Garrison. I can say I made great German friends I kept in touch with but forty years on most have gone to their heavenly reward as I to have climb the age tree ladder myself and now seventy-six/army seven.

October 1984 the Dubliners played a few night at the Munster Halle that a few of us from the sergeant mess went on their first night and as we got through to the foyer and the bar for drinks, with the place packed out with lookalike German/Dubliner a German resembling the loud Luke Kelly cry out when he heard a member of the bar staff say there's no Guinness that he nearly caused a riot, when the German Luke Kelly shouted Vhat no Guinness' in his disbelief that it being an Irish show and what Dublin is famous for had him sounding very disappointed, and the way he said it had myself and bullets sergeant John Fitzpatrick's in tears of laughter. For the next few days after whenever we met in the sergeant mess bar bullets in his best put on German accent shouts Vhat no Guinness that again had all in the sergeant mess on their knees laughing.

September 1984 the commanding officer Lieutenant Colonel Shaun O Dwyer resurrected an old Mick tradition that each company should put in an act for the battalion end of year review with the officer and the sergeant messes making their own contribution. Many a night in the sergeant mess bar the craic is usually in full flow and memory of an Ireland left are never far as songs of home in a sing along fashion is the medicine needed and Bullets Fitzpatrick ammunition sergeant would usually kick off with his signature song Old Shep.

The Dubliners visiting Munster gave us our idea that we in the mess should put on a folk group and that how the Irish Guard's folk group Shillelagh was born. Auditions for the group were held in the mess bar and the talent found for the first group was myself, Burt Smith his wife Margaret, Tony Feeney, Larry Templeton, Ronnie Kirkland, Paddy Shields, late joiners John Stranix, and Sean Kelly.

The battalion revue of Christmas 1984 went down so well that our skit of a group Shillelagh capture the commanding officer attention, and he thought it a great idea for the folk group to go one step more and do a gig for Her Majesty the queen mum on her St Patricks visit in March 1985 at the general officer commanding residence in the Munster Garrison that senior Irish Guards officer would also be present with the queen mum in residence having dinner.

Shillelagh was a great success that we became the new boy on the folk scene after the Christmas revue it was decided we should go out on the folk scene which was quite big in Germany and we found ourselves in great demand, and although we were new and raw it may well have been that which what made our success that we were given a monthly slot at the Senden folk club in Munster and booked by other regiment on their folk and barn dances night.

This in some respect gave us another opportunity to practice for our royal gig that would forever be only recorded in Mick history and not for Joe public, X Factor, or BGT shows. Her majesty came and distributed her gift of shamrock to the Irish Guards and during her visit to Germany March 1985 we had the pleasure of being the after dinner entertainment for her in that we did a Irish set piece of about three song that Her Majesty enquired if we would sing something in Irish as it was St Patrick's feast day, I sang Hail Glorious St Patricks in Irish, and saw that our queen mum was well beside herself and love it that no doubt our royal success earned us a large Jameson from our commanding officer and a few brownie point in his new creation that forty years on new blood has kept the folk group Shillelagh alive and still performing and one of its original talent now a Major Paddy Shields has led the group for forty years as a serving member while member over the years have come and gone.

As ration sergeant since October 1982 I have seen life in the cookhouse change hands as no longer are guardsmen used to do cookhouse chore as in this new age of army cuts civilian staff do all the domestic work about the barrack as everything unmilitary is contracted out and the quartermaster nominate his second in command the RQMS to oversee the civilian work force. My good self was put in charge of the cookhouse civilian work force in filling out their duty roster and timekeeping. Regimental cook of the past was long gone and the kitchen is fully manned by the army catering corps who soul job is cooking and are not added to any of the battalion guard duties. The old days of the piquet officer seeing up the meals and taking complaint has all but vanish as the standard of cooking is more professionally laid out that the piquet officer role is more in being seen than hearing complaint. The choices are many that in my earlier years it was less than three meat choices where now there are anything up to ten or more, and with the Mick version of McDonald having been introduced by the quartermaster Major Frank Groves on weekends with a new meal he called brunch that is breakfast and lunch together. Personnel on duty can still have a standard breakfast from seven to eight while the remainder can have a proper weekend lie in with brunch running from ten to two pm. The introduction of water cooler, soft drinks and snack machine, with a selection of many different types of sauces and help yourself tea and coffee point was welcome by everyone. The quartermaster gave the profits from the drinks and snacks to the PRI that the soft drink/snack company filled and maintain. Over my years in the Micks I have seen big changes in that the army moving toward a softer approach in its professional outlook of younger men at the helm that twenty years before in 1964 some senior rank were in their mid-forties and serving out their last days having first sign up as conscript in the war that now in 1984 I see full sergeant and company sergeant major well under thirty years of age, while I with less than three to finish am rushing towards forty in three with my extra year added having join not at eighteen but seventeen years old, completing not twenty-two but twenty-three in the Irish Guards.

The four St Patrick's days 1983/1987 as battalion ration sergeant in charge of looking after the shamrock that the quartermaster received from Ireland is kept in cold store so it remain green and I pray it does not lose colour prior to Her Majesty the queen mum presenting her gift to the Irish Guards that it only after the St Patricks day parade can I or my staff relax and enjoy a well earn pint of Guinness. 1985 all round was another successful and hectic year with the battalion meeting all it commitment as for me looking back it would have to be the personal gig our folk group Shillelagh put on for Her Majesty the queen mum that stand out as a treasure moment in Mick time. As a Munster Garrison players I perform my last Christmas show at York barracks theatre a show put together by Colonel David Newton medical corps call Sir Singalot, and said to be his best that at the after party I knew it was my goodbye as our battalion is London bound in the new year and with an extra year to do that having slip under the age radar in 1964 I had to correct for pension that my contract of twenty-two finishing in 1986 became 1987.

After Christmas leave and the new year bell rang in 1986 the battalion knew it be back in London to good old Chelsea Barracks I moved over on the advance party late January as the battalion follow in February leaving one company that would stay on with the grenadier guards until July, while the battalion move forward into their ceremonial role in what the guards do best. By end of February 1986 the battalion had return and after a spot of annual leave were back on Chelsea Barrack Square doing what guardsmen do best getting ready for our first St Patricks day back in London after four years away in Munster Germany.

Life was back to normal and once again all in the battalion are kitted out with their home service clothing to restart royal duties as guardsmen. For no longer are we a mechanise battalion but back to the serious work of spring drills preparing for St Patrick's Day on our old stamping ground that many old comrade and family are expected to celebrate with the regiment return from Germany and again on the home turf Her Majesty the queen mum has consented to present the shamrock to the Irish Guards on St Patricks day along with her infectious smile that is her beautiful trademark.

March eighty-six saw great changes about to happen as the guarding of the royal palaces which was the sole preserves of the five regiment of foot the military high command tried to maintain as guardsman only territory. But because of government cut over the years they tried doubling queen guards duty from twenty-four to forty-eight hours, and still this was not enough to keep it as the foot-guards preserve, that they had to considered the military as a whole and its overseas commitment to N A T O, its troops numbers in west Germany, Cyprus, and the Falkland islands and its own home security that the army numbers to do everything are not there.

This changing of the guards saw the army top brass in the Ministry of Defence bow to the new thinking that other military unit of the three services would throw a new spin on the changing of the guards, while given Her Majesty other units the opportunity to be seen and shine in carrying out these duties at Her Majesty royal palaces including the Tower of London and Windsor Castle.

The regiment chosen to do the first changing of guards that would not be a guards regimented was the Ghurkha battalion station in the Aldershot army garrison. My quartermaster Major Frank Groves ask me to contact the Ghurkha quartermaster and find out what guard ration they require, as guard regiments just have standard ration their regimental cook orders, and being the London base resident unit at Chelsea Barracks and its ration sergeant it was down to us to order in all rations for the other unit on queen guards duties to order and supply.

With the Ghurkha it was thought by the quartermaster that they have a much different dietary food coming from Nepal and to that end I was asked to check with their quartermaster as to what ration they would like order.

The Ghurkha quartermaster told me they like fresh vegetables brown and white rice, and fresh chicken not frozen, pita bread, curry powder, sauces, tea, coffee, and fresh fruit.

The morning of their first mounting royal duties I issue the Ghurkha cooks the ration for their twenty hour guard but on receipt of his ration the cook said the chicken are alive, I inform him that their quartermaster said the Ghurkha like their chicken very fresh not frozen and to that end I ask are they not fresh enough, and he look at me to say yes fresh but next time dead fresh, and plucked, I left saying yes the next time dead fresh and plucked.

The mess room staff did all the domestic work and were predominantly from the Caribbean and exceptionally polite only acknowledging each other as Mr, when I first introduce myself to them as the ration sergeant that I also oversee the roster duty and timekeeping and holiday sheet, to which they ask is it not Mr Joseph and Mr George job who do that, and after having a chat with the quartermaster about the staff only wanting to know their work hours from their own civilian supervisor he agree that it has work so far so no change and to that end Mr Joseph, and George did a fantastic job and both were great gentlemen that on leaving a year later a few week after St Patrick day 1987 to go on six-month gardening leave the new quartermaster Major Bill Mathews carry it on without any changes.

Having done twenty-two years I knew I had come full circle having first started in Chelsea barrack in three company number two platoon in 1965 excited about living in London doing royal guards of which for me the Tower of London guards was the best for when not on stag you could go for walk about the Tower and hear the beefeater tell its history in their actor's type voices as they entertain the visiting crowds, and see the jewel house that today has been upgraded and under alarm and close circuit television, protected behind bullet proof glass, that in my hay day of the mid-sixties was physical security only guards and yeomanry staff of the Tower and no electronic gizmos of any sort. Had I my long service and good conduct medal on leaving the Irish Guards I would have asked to join the beefeater as I loved the Tower of London its history where time is unchanged and a place you know the ghost of the tower keep watch and their own secret.

Vince McEllin from county Mayo my last regimental sergeant major and one I knew very well over his years in the Micks was very fair in his dealing with everyone and was a strong family man that made him the good man he was. One encounter with Vince I like to tell at regimental dinner was the time he saw sergeant Tommy Meyler cross the battalion square without saluting the paymaster to which he reply when ask by RSM Vince, Sgt Meyler why you not salute the paymaster, as quick as a flash Tommy tell the RSM the paymaster had not paid me sir, his reply floored Vince, the RSM then told Sergeant Meyler next time salute.

My last guard in the Micks was Windsor Castle and the officer of the guard was Captain Lowther Pinkerton who had just return after being the queen mum equerry and who later join the SAS as an action man. He became a member of the two prince's protection team remaining by Prince William's side after his appointment as colonel of the Irish Guards for a while. When Prince William got married wearing his Irish Guards uniform to his girlfriend Catherine Middleton, Major Lowther Pinkerton son was chosen by Prince William to be a mini Mick page boy on so special occasion in the marriage of Her Majesty grandson that it showed a great friendship and trust had grown between them.

With gardening leave on the horizon and job offer coming in from regimental headquarters via our orderly room I was approach by the RSM Vince mc Ellin if I would be interested in a long service employment and the job on offer was to good not to take up and that was to be house Sgt i.e. the running of General Travers a Dublin born man who would take up his new post at Wellington house Aldershot as head of south east command. I was sent to Aldershot to do a six-week steward course in learning all the service of looking after a general household, and the course was fascinating in the details of little things as in folding napkins and the layout of cutlery, and the serving of food and drinks in a silver service know-how. The handing of the household expense and accountable of expenditure against the ongoing guest dinner and regimental nights and parties the general would have to host in order that he meet all officer senior and junior during his time as head of south east command.

I completed the course and my new job would start in a few week time but first I had to see the provost marshall of the Aldershot garrison as to be accepted for the job. The provost marshal welcome in and got straight to the point that I being Irish if I had any relative visiting from Ireland or friends they would have to be clear by his office before them visiting. You know that the job entails you and your wife as a team living in, to which I thought that my living in Frimley I could do the job commuting to and from my own house. He emphasise the need of my living in as each night no matter the hour when the general retires and you made secure the premises you must ring the provost office that all is secure and that the general has retire for the night and again at dawn on him getting up.

I was not a happy bunny leaving the provost office as I could see no way was Miriam going to give up her house and job to look after any general and as soon I was back in barrack I saw the RSM that the job was a living in number and that my wife would be part of the job if I took it. I knew nothing about living in and my wife as head house keeper before getting the full lowdown from the provost marshal office that I must say no before it too late. It did not go down well but I had two more offer one was from Lieutenant Colonel B F Holt that there was a school he knew in need of security supervisor and would I be interested, the job was in the Midlands a bit away from our house and again I must say sorry but no thank you sir. the third offer was in Northern Ireland and it would have been right up my street running Palace barrack ration stores, again I had to say no as my wife and children fear the troubles had not gone away and being southern Irish born I did not wish to temp faith and decline gracefully.

The families' office too take an interest in a person leaving much in the vain of have you a place to go on leaving especially if you have an army quarter that they will want back and don't want you as a demob soldier squatting for having no council house or family home to go to. Having bought our own house a few years now the only thing I was looking for was a nice handy job close to home. I was offered a demobbed course that many do but I had it already in my head to join the corps of commissionaires in London as I had visited their offices in Cowshot Street and enrolled myself onto their temporary employ list that would give me money and time to check out other avenues of employment. The day was approaching fast and with St Patrick's Day and my last Windsor Castle done I left at the end of March 1987. My whole service within the regiment bar six months gardening leave in the Micks were over and from now I would be class in my new role as a member of the Irish Guards Association.

Leaving the Micks and entering civilian life would no doubt be lonely and that feeling of being afraid facing the unknown with a family depended on me was a bit scary. I left the Micks with skills and knowledge that when I first started out all those years ago from Ireland not yet seventeen knowing nothing of the world but Paddy Maher escapades on the high seas that fired my teenage mind and imagination to want and see the world for myself. The Micks was everything Sgt Smylie said it was in 1964 of the Micks being a family was so true and it's the family I do belong to even now. Eddie who I started out with from that Liverpool recruiter office remain a good friends throughout our service be that Eddie left the Micks with fifteen years under his belt as a L/sergeant in number two company and his road in the Micks took a different paths to mine.

My regimental and farewell dinner night I will never forget and many who were there remember my last speech in which I told how I join the Irish Guards and the naiveties of my ignorance when just an Irish hobo of seventeen thinking I was joining the Garda Siochana the Irish police that had my drunken brothers Micks rolling on the ground of how an eejit like me came to be an Irish Guardsman that RQMS Ray Graham told me later at the bar that he attended many farewell and heard many after dinner speeches telling me that my storey in how I join the Micks will take some beaten. The quartermaster farewell was another good night and it too in those moment of real family farewell as tear fall knowing life without the Micks is a life wasted. I left as a sergeant and did fulfil my dreams in that I got to see the world for free thank you C/Sgt George Smylie. Being married now to a wonderful Maltese lady from Gozo Malta for over 55 years, we have two fantastic children Francis and Margaret, both with two children of their own and wonderful devoted and loving spouses Debbie and Gareth, in summery my life is complete. I go into my twilight years asking for nothing for no longer am I an orphan, I fulfilled my childhood dreams, and have two families I keep in my prayers each day that they will always be well and healthy, the Micks and the McDonnells.

Mounting my last queen guard Combermere barrack Windsor March 1987.

Officer mounting and inspecting my last Queen guards is Captain Jamie Lowther –Pinkerton march 1987.

The lad went overboard no one lost their name, and it was my last time as sergeant on Queen Guard.

PHILIP ANTHONY McDONNELL

May 1987 I'm in the Corps of commissionaire's as temporary employ, photo taken at Lord Scott of Antarctic Hampshire estate, that Mars chocolate sponsor this equestrian charity event.

www.ingramcontent.com/pod-product-compliance
Lightning Source LLC
Chambersburg PA
CBHW061244230426
43662CB00020B/2413